Hands-On Business Intelligence with Qlik Sense

Implement self-service data analytics with insights and guidance from Qlik Sense experts

Pablo Labbe
Clever Anjos
Kaushik Solanki
Jerry DiMaso

BIRMINGHAM - MUMBAI

Hands-On Business Intelligence with Qlik Sense

Commissioning Editor: Sunith Shetty
Acquisition Editor: Devika Battike
Content Development Editor: Rhea Henriques
Technical Editor: Sayli Nikalje
Copy Editor: Safis Editing
Language Support Editors: Storm Mann, Mary McGowan
Project Coordinator: Manthan Patel
Proofreader: Safis Editing
Indexer: Mariammal Chettiyar
Graphics: Jisha Chirayil
Production Coordinator: Nilesh Mohite

First published: February 2019

Production reference: 1280219

Published by Packt Publishing Ltd.
Livery Place
35 Livery Street
Birmingham
B3 2PB, UK.

ISBN 978-1-78980-094-4

www.packtpub.com

`mapt.io`

Mapt is an online digital library that gives you full access to over 5,000 books and videos, as well as industry leading tools to help you plan your personal development and advance your career. For more information, please visit our website.

Why subscribe?

- Spend less time learning and more time coding with practical eBooks and Videos from over 4,000 industry professionals

- Improve your learning with Skill Plans built especially for you

- Get a free eBook or video every month

- Mapt is fully searchable

- Copy and paste, print, and bookmark content

Packt.com

Did you know that Packt offers eBook versions of every book published, with PDF and ePub files available? You can upgrade to the eBook version at `www.packt.com` and as a print book customer, you are entitled to a discount on the eBook copy. Get in touch with us at `customercare@packtpub.com` for more details.

At `www.packt.com`, you can also read a collection of free technical articles, sign up for a range of free newsletters, and receive exclusive discounts and offers on Packt books and eBooks.

Contributors

About the authors

Pablo Labbe is a BI consultant with over 18 years of experience. In 2008, he was presented with QlikView, the former product by Qlik and the seed for Qlik Sense. Since then, he was focused on delivering BI solutions in a new way. Now, he is the principal of ANALITIKA Inteligencia, delivering BI projects and training that is focused on Qlik products and other technologies that embrace self-service BI. He is an active member of Qlik Community and other social media sites. You can follow him on Twitter @pablolabbe and find him on LinkedIn.

Clever Anjos is an experienced business discovery professional with several years of experience with Qlik, Microsoft, and other **business intelligence (BI)** technologies. He holds a bachelor's degree in computer science from Universidade Federal de Uberlândia (Minas Gerais State—Brazil). He works at Qlik as a solution architect, helping companies to use Qlik technologies to enable their professionals to be fully data literate. He has several Qlik certifications and awards (such as Qlik Luminary, Qlik MVP, and Presales Rookie of the Year—Americas 2018).

> *I would like to thank specially my wife, Emelinne, for supporting me in my decisions and giving me my wonderful kids (Olavo, Maitê, and Anita). I would like to thank my parents (José Natal and Ana Maria), who have always been a beacon inspiring me and showing me the right path to walk. And, of course, thanks to all the people who have shared moments with me at work and in life.*

Kaushik Solanki is a computer engineer by profession. He works at Predoole Analytics Pvt Ltd as a Qlik architect and delivery manager. He has nine years of experience working with Qlik technology. His passion is to educate everyone about data literacy and Qlik. He loves to spend time on Qlik Community helping Qlik developers learn and excel.

He has a great understanding of project delivery, right from business requirements to final implementation. His experience in various domains has helped businesses to take valuable business decisions.

First of all, I am thankful to my parents for supporting and educating me all throughout my life. Secondly, I am thankful to my wife and my daughter for their support and patience while I wrote this book. Lastly, I would like to thank everyone who has directly and indirectly helped me in my professional life.

Jerry DiMaso is an Analytics Advisory Consultant who has spent the past 10 years developing applications, advising on data and analytics strategies, and coaching organizations on how to build efficient analytics operating models. His work in more than 100 organizations in dozens of different industries has inspired him to take on the mission of improving the world's analytics capabilities through a series of practical frameworks and methodologies, most notably the Analytics Enablement and Axis Academy programs that he has created.

Thank you to my wife, Erika, whose encouragement and support inspire me to be all that I am.

About the reviewer

Nitesh Kumar Sethi has more than a decade of experience in the BI industry and has been widely recognized and accepted as an expert in the field. QlikTech has awarded him Qlik Luminary awards for two years running, in 2018 and 2019. With deep drive, great passion, and plenty of expertise, Nitesh champions the vision of turning data into insights that lead to transformative discoveries.

Nitesh held the first Qlik meet in India, which was even the first in the Asia-Pacific region. He is also an official Qlik captain, as recognized by QlikTech.

Packt is searching for authors like you

If you're interested in becoming an author for Packt, please visit authors.packtpub.com and apply today. We have worked with thousands of developers and tech professionals, just like you, to help them share their insight with the global tech community. You can make a general application, apply for a specific hot topic that we are recruiting an author for, or submit your own idea.

Table of Contents

Preface

Qlik Sense allows you to explore simple-to-complex data to reveal hidden insights and data relationships to make business-driven decisions. *Hands-On Business Intelligence with Qlik Sense* begins by helping you get to grips with underlying Qlik concepts and gives you an overview of all Qlik Sense's features. You will learn advanced modeling techniques and understand how to analyze the data loaded using a variety of visualization objects. You'll also be trained on how to share apps through Qlik Sense Enterprise and Qlik Sense Cloud and how to perform aggregation with AGGR. As you progress through the chapters, you'll explore the stories feature to create data-driven presentations and adopt a better way to update an existing story. This book will guide you in exploring the GeoAnalytics feature with the geo-mapping object and GeoAnalytics connector. Furthermore, you'll learn about self-service analytics features and perform data forecasting using advanced analytics. Lastly, you'll deploy Qlik Sense apps for mobile and tablets. By the end of this book, you will be well-equipped to run successful business intelligence projects using Qlik Sense's functionality, data modeling techniques, and visualization best practices.

Who this book is for

If you're a data analyst or interested in **business intelligence (BI)** and want to gain practical experience of working on Qlik Sense projects, this book is for you. You'll also find it useful if you want to explore Qlik Sense's next-generation applications for self-service BI.

What this book covers

Chapter 1, *Getting Started with Qlik Sense*, will focus on getting started with Qlik Sense with the Qlik Sense Desktop application and the Qlik Sense Cloud web-based application. We'll take a quick overview of the high-level features of Qlik Sense so it's clear how the Qlik Sense platform can be leveraged for individuals and enterprises, then we will jump right into using Qlik Sense.

Chapter 2, *Loading Data in Qlik Sense*, will cover a series of tasks to load data from several sources, such as text files and Excel spreadsheets. We will find data quality issues (such as null values in a field) with data profiling and create a data model, associating the data source using key fields to link tables.

Chapter 3, *Implementing Data Modeling Techniques*, will help you learn about various data modeling techniques along with the best data modeling practices for Qlik Sense. It will also cover topics such as joins, concatenation, filtering, and the use of **Qlikview Data (QVD)** files, which will help you to build the perfect data model. You will also learn how to handle dates using canonical date, how to handle accumulations and rolling averages in script using As-Of Table, and how to handle multiple fact tables in data models using link tables. Finally, we will focus on improving script performance using optimization techniques.

Chapter 4, *Working with Application Structure*, will explore the key concepts of a Qlik Sense application design. Along with this, we will look at the principles of building a Qlik Sense app using the **Dashboard, Analysis, Reporting (DAR)** methodology, learn how to use the visualization objects that are available to the user, and see how to create and use master items to reuse dimensions and metrics across visualizations. Finally, we will learn how to use the Qlik Sense user interface and look at the basics of calculation expressions.

Chapter 5, *Creating a Sales Analysis App Using Qlik Sense*, is where we will create a sales analysis application to explore and analyze the data model that we created in Chapter 2, *Loading Data in Qlik Sense*. During the development of the application, we will apply the use of the DAR methodology explained in Chapter 4, *Working with Application Structure*.

Chapter 6, *Interacting with Advanced Expressions*, will teach you about the power of the calculation engine. After reading this, you will know how to create a calculation with conditions, as well as how to use aggregation scope, inter-record functions, and advanced aggregation with AGGR. Finally, you will learn how to use set analysis to create a calculation with very specific data selection.

Chapter 7, *Creating Data Stories*, will look at an effective way to communicate insights using a Qlik Sense application called storytelling. The whole idea of storytelling in BI is to take an idea or an insight and turn it into an appealing story to show what we think about it. The story makes our insight more interesting. This also happens in everyday life; stories have always been the go-to method to grab someone's attraction.

Chapter 8, *Engaging On-Demand App Generation*, will explore how to create a summarized application, which is a regular Qlik Sense app where the fact table is aggregated. This application is capable of analyzing a database containing the data of a million bike trips without sacrificing too much RAM. By integrating a template, we give the user the capability to dig into detailed information. When the user needs to see detailed data in Qlik Sense, we will use the template to generate another application with the detailed data that the user has requested.

Chapter 9, *Creating Maps Using GeoAnalytics*, looks at GeoAnalytics, which is an add-on to Qlik Sense and Qlikview. This product has mapping capabilities that leverage Qlik Sense to analyze data that has geospatial naming conventions, exposing geographic relationships between data points. We are going to use those capabilities to analyze vehicular collisions that have occurred in New York City.

Chapter 10, *Working with Self-Service Analytics*, is where you will discover how to explore the self-service analytics features provided by Qlik Sense Enterprise and Qlik Sense Cloud Business. When using Qlik Sense Enterprise, you will learn how to build new sheets and create new visualizations using the master items library. You will also learn how to share insights with other users, creating community sheets and approving an analysis sheet to act as a baseline for developers. In Qlik Sense Cloud Business, you will learn how to co-create apps with other users in the same workspace.

Chapter 11, *Data Forecasting Using Advanced Analytics*, is where we will work together to enable Qlik Sense applications to predict how business **Key Performance Indicators (KPIs)** will perform in the future. This is not is about using technology to predict business behavior, but is instead a matter of using technologies from data science such as **machine learning (ML)**.

Chapter 12, *Deploying Qlik Sense Apps for Mobile/Tablets*, will show you how to deploy the sales analysis application we will have built for use in mobile devices and tablets. This enables us to freely access information wherever we are, even if we don't have a network connection. You will learn how to craft your dashboard so that it can be visualized on a small screen. We will discuss what we need in order to enable an application to be downloaded to a device and used offline. These activities are important for creating a great experience for users when they interact with the application from a small device.

To get the most out of this book

No prior experience of working with Qlik Sense is required.

Download the example code files

You can download the example code files for this book from your account at www.packt.com. If you purchased this book elsewhere, you can visit www.packt.com/support and register to have the files emailed directly to you.

You can download the code files by following these steps:

1. Log in or register at `www.packt.com`.
2. Select the **SUPPORT** tab.
3. Click on **Code Downloads & Errata**.
4. Enter the name of the book in the **Search** box and follow the onscreen instructions.

Once the file is downloaded, please make sure that you unzip or extract the folder using the latest version of:

- WinRAR/7-Zip for Windows
- Zipeg/iZip/UnRarX for Mac
- 7-Zip/PeaZip for Linux

The code bundle for the book is also hosted on GitHub at `https://github.com/PacktPublishing/Hands-On-Business-Intelligence-with-Qlik-Sense`. In case there's an update to the code, it will be updated on the existing GitHub repository.

We also have other code bundles from our rich catalog of books and videos available at `https://github.com/PacktPublishing/`. Check them out!

Download the color images

We also provide a PDF file that has color images of the screenshots/diagrams used in this book. You can download it here: `https://www.packtpub.com/sites/default/files/downloads/9781789800944_ColorImages.pdf`.

Conventions used

There are a number of text conventions used throughout this book.

`CodeInText`: Indicates code words in text, database table names, folder names, filenames, file extensions, pathnames, dummy URLs, user input, and Twitter handles. Here is an example: "Create a field called `Processing Time` that calculates the gap between `OrderDate` and `ShippedDate` using a function called `Interval` that formats the gap time."

A block of code is set as follows:

```
num (sum (Discount*SalesAmount)/sum (SalesAmount), '0.00%')
```

Any command-line input or output is written as follows:

```
install.packages("Rserve", lib = "C:\\R\\R-3.5.2\\library")
```

Bold: Indicates a new term, an important word, or words that you see onscreen. For example, words in menus or dialog boxes appear in the text like this. Here is an example: "Creating new sheets is a breeze: to start from an existing sheet, just right-click and duplicate, or click the **Create new** button to start from a fresh blank sheet."

 Warnings or important notes appear like this.

 Tips and tricks appear like this.

Get in touch

Feedback from our readers is always welcome.

General feedback: If you have questions about any aspect of this book, mention the book title in the subject of your message and email us at customercare@packtpub.com.

Errata: Although we have taken every care to ensure the accuracy of our content, mistakes do happen. If you have found a mistake in this book, we would be grateful if you would report this to us. Please visit www.packt.com/submit-errata, selecting your book, clicking on the Errata Submission Form link, and entering the details.

Piracy: If you come across any illegal copies of our works in any form on the Internet, we would be grateful if you would provide us with the location address or website name. Please contact us at copyright@packt.com with a link to the material.

If you are interested in becoming an author: If there is a topic that you have expertise in and you are interested in either writing or contributing to a book, please visit authors.packtpub.com.

Reviews

Please leave a review. Once you have read and used this book, why not leave a review on the site that you purchased it from? Potential readers can then see and use your unbiased opinion to make purchase decisions, we at Packt can understand what you think about our products, and our authors can see your feedback on their book. Thank you!

For more information about Packt, please visit `packt.com`.

Section 1: Qlik Sense and Business Intelligence

In this section, we shall introduce **business intelligence (BI)**, the modern concepts raised in the early days, and setting up Qlik Sense products for upcoming projects.

This section shall contain only one chapter:

- Chapter 1, *Getting started with Qlik Sense*

Getting Started with Qlik Sense

1

In today's consumer-driven world, with tremendous competition and rapidly-developing technologies, it is imperative for organizations to leverage data to drive decision-making across all aspects of business to lower costs, increase revenues, and mitigate risks. However, this is much easier said than done; there are hundreds of tools and technologies available in today's market that collect, process, and serve data, but choosing the right technologies is often a challenge. In this book, we discuss one particular technology that provides an enterprise solution for processing and serving analytics: Qlik Sense.

Qlik Sense is a data-discovery and analytics platform composed of an in-memory associative database, a data-extraction and transformation engine that connects to dozens of data sources natively, an intuitive self-service data-modeling and visualization tool, and a set of open APIs that allow for complex customizations of workflow and visualizations. Qlik is a nine-time leader in the Gartner Analytics and Business Intelligence Platform Magic Quadrant (https://www.qlik.com/us/gartner-magic-quadrant-business-intelligence) and competes in the **business intelligence (BI)** market as a complete solution for enterprise analytics. Today, Qlik Sense is being used actively in virtually every industry, in hospitals, banks, manufacturing plants, and everywhere in between, to serve up analytics to users so they can make better decisions that drive better outcomes.

Qlik Sense is a self-contained platform that facilitates all aspects of operating. It is an expanding analytics organization, and as such includes a wide variety of features and functionality, from advanced administrative capabilities to self-service visualization elements to **artificial intelligence (AI)** engines. This breadth of capabilities, combined with continuing acquisitions of complementary software, such as Podium Data for data cataloging and CrunchBot for **natural language processing (NLP)**, is what helps to differentiate Qlik in the analytics and BI space and provide a truly scalable analytics solution that can serve dozens or hundreds of thousands of users.

In this chapter, we will focus on getting started with Qlik Sense with the Qlik Sense Desktop application and the Qlik Sense Cloud web-based application. We'll provide a quick overview of the high-level features of Qlik Sense, so that it's clear how the Qlik Sense Platform can be leveraged for individuals and in the enterprise, then we will jump into using Qlik Sense.

We will cover the following topics:

- An overview of the Qlik Sense product
- The Associative Engine
- Setting up Qlik Sense Desktop
- Setting up Qlik Sense Cloud
- Self-service with Qlik Sense

An overview of the Qlik Sense product

This chapter will provide an overview of several of the major facets of the Qlik Sense software and what you need to understand to get started with Qlik Sense. We will not be covering the administration components or delving too deep into the advanced extensibility capabilities, but, by the end of this chapter, you will understand what Qlik Sense is and how you can use it.

The components of Qlik Sense

In the following sections, we will cover four major components of the Qlik Sense software:

- In-memory associative database
- The **Extract-Transform-Load** (ETL) engine:
    - Data manager
    - Script
    - Data model
- The visualization platform:
    - The hub
    - Applications
    - Sheets
    - Objects
- API and extensibility capabilities

In-memory associative database

Qlik's in-memory associative database is the proprietary technology that Qlik invented in 1993 in Lund, Sweden, which allows large amounts of data to be compressed, stored in the RAM, and rapidly traversed in the Qlik Sense client. In other words, this is what makes Qlik, Qlik.

This database houses all of the data we need inside the Qlik Engine and allows us to explore the datasets in a way that facilitates analytics in a much better manner. We'll get into how and why this approach is better in the next section, *The Associative Engine*.

ETL engine

Qlik Sense includes a built-in ETL engine that allows us to connect to many different sources, such as Excel, SQL, and Hadoop, to extract data into Qlik Sense. We can also use this ETL engine to transform the data, to manipulate the data, to clean up dirty data, or to create new data.

This is a very powerful component of the Qlik platform because we don't have to leave Qlik to do mappings, create buckets, or fix bad data; we can do everything we need right inside Qlik Sense, and there is even an intuitive user interface that guides users with no programming knowledge required.

Data manager

The Qlik Sense Data manager provides a way to pull data into Qlik Sense through an intuitive user interface. It contains a way to connect to your data sources, select the data you are looking to analyze, pull the data in, and link it to other data you have pulled in. Using Qlik's Cognitive Engine, and AI created by Qlik, the Qlik Sense Data manager automatically profiles your data and recommends how to connect different tables based on similar data keys. We'll go further into this profiling capability and how to transform data in the *Self-service with Qlik Sense* section at the end of this chapter.

Script

For more advanced users, the Qlik Sense script provides the capability to programmatically extract and transform data from data sources. It uses a scripting language similar to SQL and allows more granular control over how the data is extracted and transformed. Most users will use the Data manager, but it is important to note that this capability exists for users who need to transform data in more complex ways:

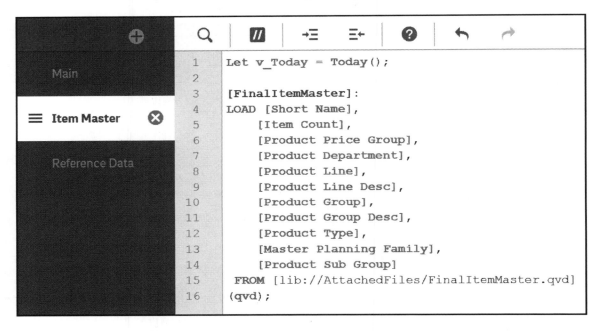

The preceding screenshot is of the Qlik Sense script setting a variable with the Today() function and loading a table from a QVD, which is a proprietary Qlik data file that is optimized for use in Qlik. Most users will not leverage QVDs directly, but there are many advanced use cases where they can and should be leveraged.

Data model

The Qlik Sense Data model viewer allows us to see all of the data we have pulled into Qlik Sense. This is similar to the Data manager view, but is intended more for understanding the relationships between the data than adding or transforming data. This view provides information on linkages between tables, including metadata about the tables and fields in our data model, and a preview of the data. This view is very useful for understanding the state of the data we've pulled into Qlik Sense and ensuring that everything is linked together in the way we want it to be linked:

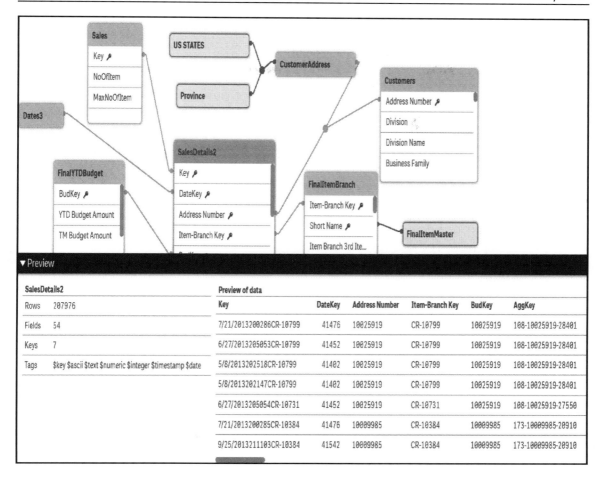

The preceding screenshot shows a sample Qlik Sense data model. The `SalesDetails2` table is selected, as can be seen by the dark orange highlight (dark gray), and tables that are directly linked to the `SalesDetails2` table are highlighted in light orange (light gray).

Visualization platform

The Qlik Sense client is what we, as users, interact with directly; this is the component that allows us to import and transform data, build charts, and perform analytics. Once data is loaded into the Qlik Sense application, we can use the Qlik Sense client to create visualizations on top of that data, such as line charts, bar charts, tables, and maps. Creating these visualizations is as simple as dragging a chart type onto the canvas and dropping in measures and dimensions. If you're looking to kickstart your vizzing, Qlik's Insight Engine creates visualizations for you at the click of a button. We will go through how to do that in the *Self-service with Qlik Sense* section.

Here are the components of the Qlik Sense client:

- The hub
- Application overview
- Sheets
- Objects

The hub

Here is a view of the hub, which houses applications. Note that the hub may look slightly different depending on whether you are using Qlik Sense Desktop, Qlik Sense Cloud, or Qlik Sense Enterprise. The hub is where you can search through and access all of your applications, create new applications, and find information about your Qlik Sense version:

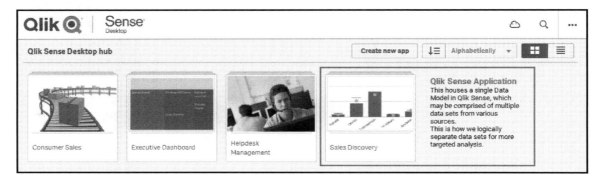

Application overview

A Qlik Sense application contains several components, most notably a single data model (see the *Data model* section for more information) and a collection of one or more sheets. Think of an application as a container for data and visualizations; it holds both the data and the visualizations to which we attach the data:

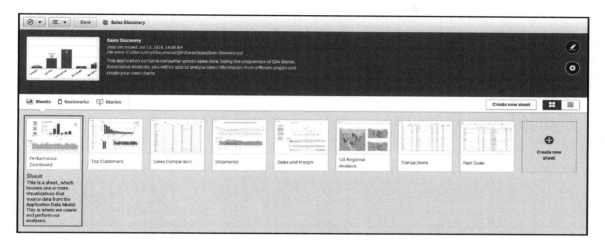

The preceding screenshot shows the application overview, which is the screen that shows us what the application contains, that is, **Sheets**, **Bookmarks**, and **Stories**. This view also allows us to edit the settings of the application, such as the name, description, or thumbnail image, as well as create new sheets and stories. Bookmarks and stories will be covered in a later chapter.

Sheets

Just as an application is a collection of sheets, a sheet is a collection of objects that can be customized and manipulated to facilitate analyzing the data. Each sheet may, and probably will, look different given that Qlik Sense provides a blank canvas on which to place objects:

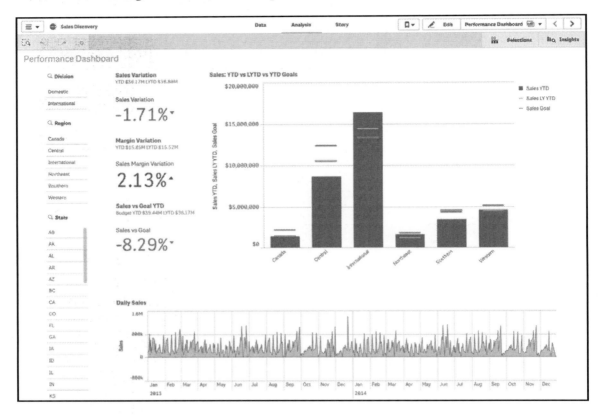

The preceding screenshot is a sheet contained in the Qlik Sense **Sales Discovery** demo application. This sheet has filter boxes down the left side, some **Key Performance Indicator (KPI)** objects oriented vertically in the center, a combo chart featuring three different sales metrics broken out by the **Region** field, and a line chart of **Sales** by day at the bottom.

Objects

Qlik Sense comes with a variety of different objects that can be used to visualize and analyze data. These objects range from filter boxes and simple bar charts to maps and scatter plots. Additionally, Qlik now ships with several extension objects that provide more complex visualizations and functionalities, such as Sankey and Radar charts, or buttons, and variable inputs. Objects allow us to create beautiful and insightful visualizations quickly and easily on the Qlik Sense canvas:

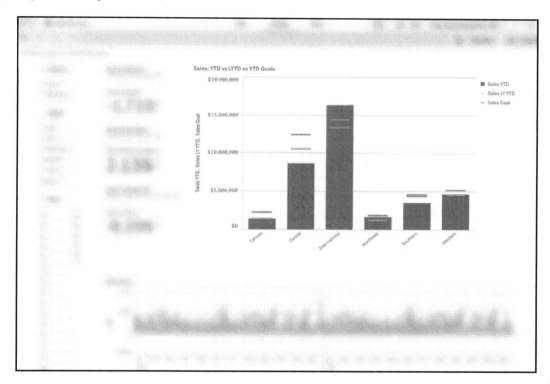

The preceding screenshot highlights a combo chart, which is a type of object that can accept multiple dimensions and measures as input. In this example, the dimension used is **Region** and the measures used are **Sales YTD**, which is represented by the blue bar, **Sales LY YTD**, which is represented by the yellow line, and **Sales Goal**, which is represented by the red line. This type of visualization allows us to compare multiple sales metrics across our six regions and see how close each one is to the prior year and goal.

Many other visualizations are available with the Qlik Sense client, and many more are available as extension objects. Check https://branch.qlik.com for hundreds of interesting extension objects that are created by others in the Qlik community.

Please note that not all extension objects are tested or supported, as many are open source. Qlik has created a certification program wherein they have certified several extension objects, but most remain uncertified, so use them at your own risk.

API and extensibility capabilities

We won't go too deep into the extensibility of the Qlik Sense platform here, but it's important to note that the capabilities of Qlik Sense far exceed what is available out of the box. Qlik comes with a comprehensive set of APIs that developers can use to create fully-customized web experiences using the ultra-fast in-memory Qlik Data model. These APIs significantly broaden what Qlik Sense can do from the perspectives of guided, operational, and predictive analytics:

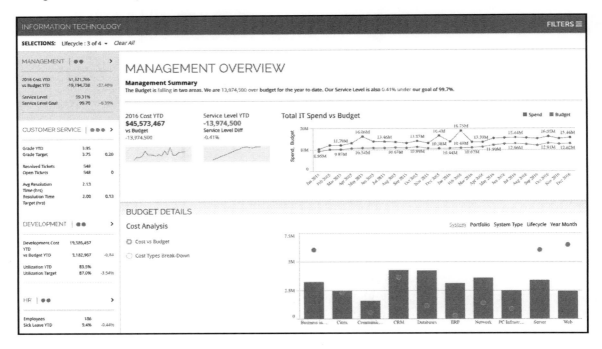

The preceding screenshot is an example of a customized mashup, created by Qlik, and illustrates the capability to extend Qlik Sense and create more guided applications with the look and feel of a website rather than a BI tool.

The Associative Engine

Qlik's Associative Engine is a remarkably fast and flexible in-memory database that enables users to leave the old world of query-based data pulls and enter the future of true data exploration through what Qlik terms the Associative Difference™. The power of the Associative Engine rests in the ability to start with the entire set of data and navigate the data not just linearly, which you may be used to in other tools, but also laterally, without having to define a path before you start your analysis. This mechanism facilitates analytics in the same way that our brains actually work; analytics is a creative process that evolves rapidly as we're performing the analysis. If you knew what answer you were looking for before you started, you wouldn't need a tool; you could just find that answer with a single query.

Consider how you find information about a restaurant: you go to your favorite search engine and type in the name of the restaurant. From there, you may explore some review sites, find the restaurant's website, take a look at the menu, and maybe you stumble on some related restaurants. One of the related restaurants catches your eye and you see they have availability through a reservation service. You then book that restaurant and go on to enjoy a fabulous meal. This is a simple use case, but it clearly illustrates how any analysis, no matter how small, is a journey and you don't necessarily know where the destination is when you start.

Qlik facilitates this creative analytics discovery process through a clever color scheme that highlights filter values throughout the application:

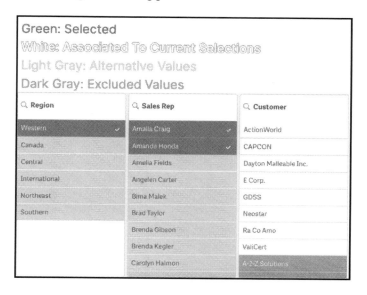

In the preceding screenshot, the selected field values are highlighted in green (dark gray); that is, **Western** in the **Region** filter box and **Amalia Craig** and **Amanda Honda** in the **Sales Rep** filter box.

The values highlighted in white are *associated with* or related to the selected values, that is, **ActionWorld**, **CAPCON**, and so on, in the **Customer** filter box.

The values highlighted in light gray are called **alternative values**. In other words, if I hadn't made any selections in the **Region** field, the remaining regions would be in white. The values highlighted in dark gray are called **excluded values**, which means that they are not associated with or related to selections made in other fields; in this case, the **Region** and **Sales Rep** fields.

The following screenshot illustrates this concept a little more clearly:

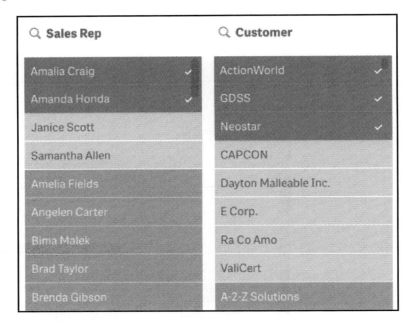

By selecting a few customers, I can see that **Janice Scott** and **Samantha Allen** are related to **ActionWorld**, **GDSS**, and **Neostar**, but are highlighted in light gray because I have made other selections in the **Sales Rep** field.

Conceptually, this may seem simple, but it allows us to see the whole universe of data all at once and helps our brains do what brains do best: identify patterns and irregularities. Let's say, for example, using the preceding filters, that Brad Taylor is also supposed to be covering ActionWorld. It sticks out immediately that Brad is not in the list of alternate Sales Reps. We recognize that irregularity and pivot our analysis on the fly, clicking Brad's name and digging around for why he's not selling anything to ActionWorld. In an alternative tool that doesn't have this capability, we miss this opportunity to discover, because we're only shown exactly what we've asked for:

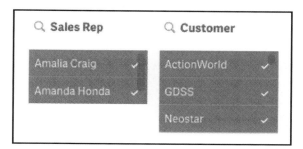

In addition to facilitating the creative analytics process through data highlighting, Qlik Sense also enables us to rapidly traverse data in a Wonkavator-like fashion; that is, navigating the data in every possible direction. The breadcrumb trail at the top of each application shows every selection we've made and allows us to change those selections in any order we want, not just navigating backward and forward. We can go down the path of **Region | Sales Rep | Customer**, but we're not bound to that path; for example, we can change the **Sales Rep** and leave the other selections intact, or clear **Region** and see how that affects the **Customer** and **Sales Rep** fields. We can also lock fields, select all values, select alternative values, or select excluded values, all right from the breadcrumb bar, which is always located at the top of the screen, as seen in the following screenshots:

The flexibility of Qlik's Associative Engine complements the naturally creative process of analytics and gets us to better decisions faster. So, let's get into Qlik Sense!

Setting up Qlik Sense Desktop

Qlik Sense Desktop requires a Windows 7 or later PC with at least 4 GB of RAM (keep in mind that Qlik Sense uses RAM to store data, so larger datasets will require more RAM). For non-Windows computers, your best option is Qlik Sense Cloud, which we will cover in the next section.

To download Qlik Sense Desktop (note that instructions may vary slightly depending on region), perform the following steps:

1. Navigate to the Qlik website: https://www.qlik.com
2. Click the **Try or Buy** button at the top right
3. Click **Try It Free** underneath **Qlik Sense Desktop**
4. Fill in your contact information or log in with your Qlik Account if you have one

> You will need to use these credentials to log into the Qlik Sense Desktop client later, so make sure you remember your username and password.

Alternatively, you can go to directly to https://www.qlik.com/us/try-or-buy/download-qlik-sense and then follow step 4. Once you submit the form, it should automatically start the Qlik Sense Desktop download.

To install the software, follow these instructions from the Qlik Help site https://help.qlik.com:

1. Double-click on Qlik_Sense_Desktop_setup.exe to start the installation. The welcome dialog is displayed.
2. Click **Custom Installation**. The License agreement dialog is displayed.
3. Read the License agreement, select the **I accept the license** agreement checkbox, and click **Next**.
4. Type or browse to the location where you want to install Qlik Sense Desktop and click **Next**.

5. Qlik Sense Desktop cannot be installed in locations where administrator rights are required, for example `C:\Program Files`.

6. Type or browse to the location where you want Qlik Sense Desktop to store app content, and click **Next**.

7. On the ready to install screen, select to create a desktop shortcut. Click **Install**.

8. In the extension bundles section of the *Ready to install* screen, select to create a desktop shortcut. Select which extension bundles you want to install from the list of those available for your Qlik Sense installation.

9. If you have chosen not to install the extension bundles, click **Install**. Otherwise, click **Next**.

10. If you are installing any of the extension bundles, accept the extension bundle license agreement. Then click **Install**.

11. When the installation has completed, the installation summary is displayed.

12. Click **Finish** to close the installation summary.

You can now open up Qlik Sense Desktop; you will have to log in with the credentials you used to create an account.

Once you open Qlik Sense Desktop, you can also navigate to it from a browser, such as Google Chrome, at the `http://localhost:4848/hub` web address. You must keep Qlik Sense Desktop open while using Qlik Sense from your browser.

 You can always access the Qlik `Help` directly from this screen by clicking the **Getting started...** button at the bottom, or going to `help.qlik.com`.

From this main screen, or the Qlik Sense Desktop hub, you can click on any of the thumbnails and explore a ready-made Qlik Sense application, courtesy of Qlik, to help jumpstart your orientation into Qlik Sense. We'll go into some more detail on using Qlik Sense in the *Self-service with Qlik Sense* section:

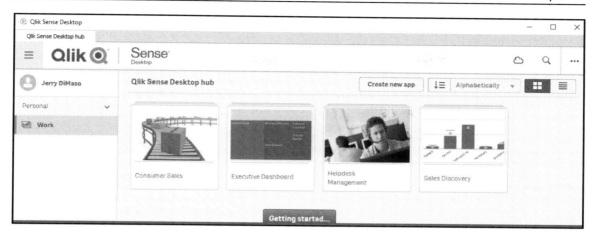

For the *Self-service with Qlik Sense* section, we'll be leveraging the **Sales Discovery** application, so if you'd like to follow along on your screen, click that thumbnail and you'll be taken into the sheet menu, then click on the first sheet. If you followed this section and don't wish to set up a Qlik Sense Cloud account, you can skip the next section.

Setting up Qlik Sense Cloud

For a more collaborative experience with Qlik Sense, or if you don't have a Windows PC on which you can install software, the Qlik Sense Cloud is a great option (and it usually gets the latest-and-greatest Qlik updates before they are available for download).

To create a Qlik Sense Cloud account (note that instructions may vary slightly depending on region and availability), perform the following steps:

1. Navigate to the Qlik Cloud website: https://www.qlikcloud.com/
2. Click the **Register** button at the top right
3. Click **Get A Free Account** underneath Qlik Sense Cloud
4. Fill in your contact information or log in with your Qlik Account if you have one

You will need to use these credentials to log into the Qlik Sense Cloud later, so make sure you remember your username and password.

If you've used Qlik Sense Desktop, the first thing you'll notice when you log into the Qlik Sense Cloud is that it looks a little bit different; there are additional menus down the left side, there are buttons to **Create a New app and Import data**, and it may have even pulled in a profile picture. These differences represent the collaborative nature of Qlik Sense Cloud: you can share applications and datasets that you create with others on the Qlik Sense Cloud platform. To follow along, navigate to the **Qlik Cloud resources** button at the left side menu, right-click on the **Sales Discovery** application, and click **Duplicate**. Now navigate to **My work** in the left-side menu and open the **Sales Discovery** application that you just created:

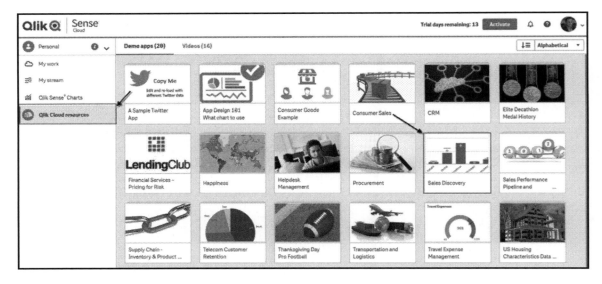

Right-click on the **Sales Discovery** application and click **Duplicate**:

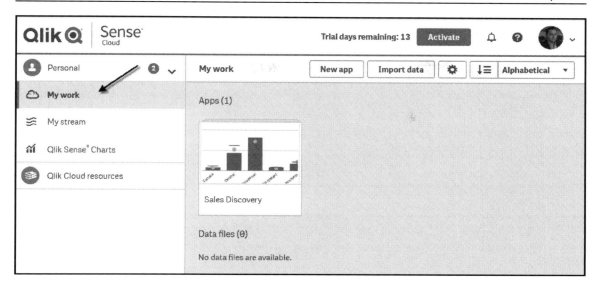

This is now what your **My work** should look like after duplicating the **Sales Discovery** application from the **Qlik Cloud resources** section.

The Qlik Sense Cloud is free to use for up to five users, while larger plans can be purchased for up to 50 users. There are some excellent video resources available in the *Qlik Cloud resources* section of the Qlik Cloud, as well as on YouTube.

Self-service with Qlik Sense

Finally, we are all set up with Qlik Sense and we're ready to jump into some analysis. This section will help you understand what self-service is in Qlik Sense and why you would want to use it. Later chapters will go deeper into how to pull in your own data and create visualizations. We will be using the Sales Discovery application available on the Qlik Sense Cloud or Qlik Sense Desktop, if you would like to follow along.

Qlik Sense self-service enables users to load their own datasets, create measures and dimensions, create visualizations, and create stories without another person or group, typically IT, having to intervene. This model has become exceedingly popular over the past few years, often to the chagrin of IT professionals who are looking to protect and lock down their infrastructures; it's a difficult challenge, especially in this age of constant cyber attacks and phishing scams, to allow users access to their data freely. Fortunately for business users and IT alike, Qlik Sense makes it much easier to employ governance practices *and* provide users with the access they need to make data-driven decisions.

We'll start with the data model piece, and remember we'll go much further into detail in the subsequent chapters on how to create your own data model. In the following screenshot, you can see that Qlik Sense has linked these various data sources together. There is a + button in the top-left corner that allows users to add more data to the data model. At the bottom (if you select a bubble), there is a mechanism to edit the table prior to loading it and perform various types of transformations:

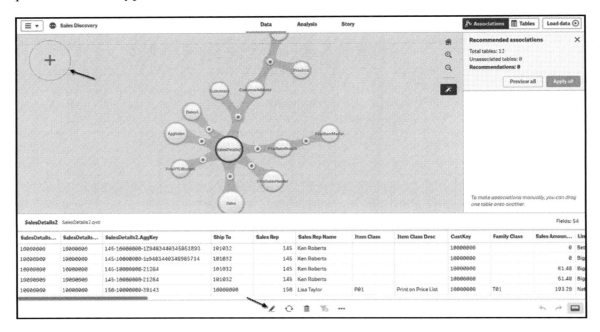

The data transformation interface in Qlik Sense is excellent for making basic changes to the data, such as mapping, bucketing, adjusting null values, and creating new calculated fields from data that already exists; for example, *Price * Quantity* to make a Sales field. Qlik Sense is also smart enough to recognize what the field types are and can make intelligent suggestions on how you may want to transform the data. In the following screenshot, you can see that Qlik Sense has identified the selected field as a numerical field, and is suggesting a bucketing function to create a meaningful dimension by which to perform some analysis. This view also provides analytics and metadata about the tables and fields you're exploring, and is a very useful tool for analyzing data integrity prior to creating visualizations:

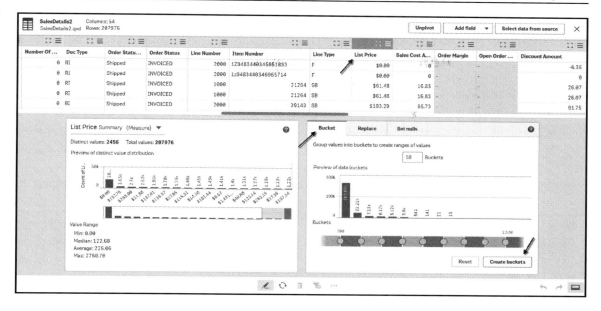

Once the data has been loaded, it populates the application with fields, which you can then use to create **Master items**, including measures, dimensions, and visualizations. For many users, these **Master items** will already be pre-populated by the developer who created the application, which allows for easier and faster creation of visualizations, since the user doesn't have to come up with the calculations. A later chapter will detail how to create expressions and calculations of your own in Qlik Sense.

This Master library helps maintain repeatability and governance of the application, but keep in mind that changing an item in the Master library changes it globally in the application.

It is now very easy to begin modifying and creating dashboards with the drag-and-drop functionality that Qlik Sense provides:

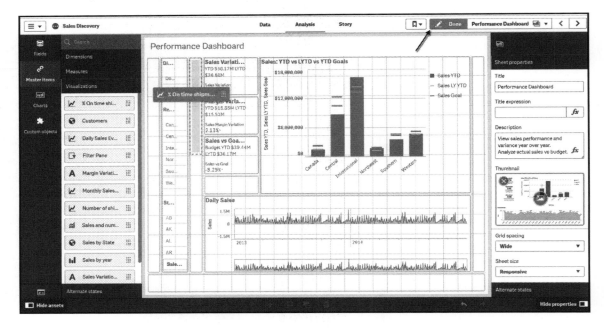

Creating new sheets is a breeze: to start from an existing sheet, just right-click and duplicate, or click the **Create new sheet** button to start from a fresh, blank sheet:

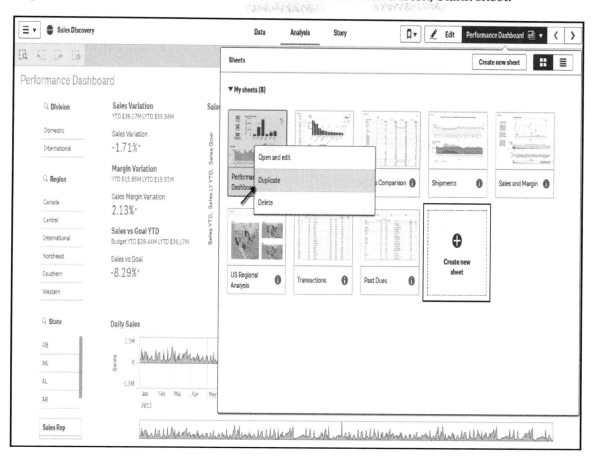

It's even easier with the Qlik Sense Insight Advisor: to create charts, you just need to drag some measures and dimensions onto the canvas and Qlik Sense will automatically identify the field types and create meaningful visualizations for you:

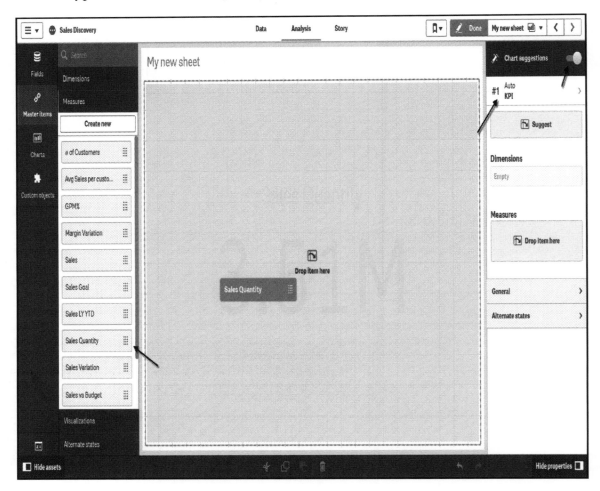

Or, there's always the EASY BUTTON™; just click on the **Insights** button in the top-right corner (outside of Edit mode) and click **Generate insights** for charts to automatically be generated. With NLP, you can type in fields that you care more about to get more specific results as well:

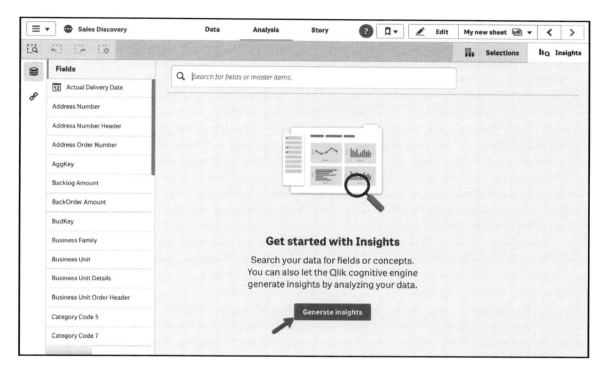

Self-service is extremely easy with Qlik Sense, and it's getting better with each release; however, it is important that we all make sure to create and share data ethically and safely. Self-service can easily get out of hand and open up risk for both IT and the business, so it is everyone's responsibility to remain educated on the tools and governance best practices available. Combining the right education program with appropriate governance practices, a concept known as **Governance Through Education**, will ensure that everyone operates in a safe and healthy environment for self-service.

Summary

In this chapter, we learned about the capabilities of Qlik Sense, including the various components that make Qlik Sense such a powerful analytics platform for many use cases. We also covered how to get started with Qlik Sense Desktop and Qlik Sense Cloud, both of which are free to download and use. We learned about self-service in Qlik Sense and how Qlik Sense helps to facilitate the analytics workflow through simple interfaces and **natural language processing (NLP)** capabilities so users can get to real insights faster.

In the next chapter, we'll cover how to load data into Qlik Sense and create a data model that we can use to start making visualizations.

Section 2: Data Loading and Modeling
2

Learn how to load and prepare data to visualize it in the Qlik Sense application, mashing data from several sources (SQL, flat files), create table associations, refine a data model, and shape the data to be better suited for analysis.

In this section, we shall go through the following chapters:

- Chapter 2, *Loading Data in Qlik Sense*
- Chapter 3, *Implementing Data Modeling Techniques*

2
Loading Data in Qlik Sense

In this chapter, we will cover a series of tasks to load data from several sources such as text files or Excel spreadsheets. We shall find data quality issues (such as *null* values in a field) with data profiling and create the data model associating the data source using key fields to link the tables.

The following topics will be covered in this chapter:

- Data loading process
- Loading data from data sources
- Table associations
- Data profiling

Technical requirements

The technologies that are used in this chapter are as follows:

- Qlik Sense Enterprise, Qlik Sense Desktop, or QlikCloud
- CSV files and Excel spreadsheets

 You can find the code for this chapter on GitHub at the following link: `https://github.com/PacktPublishing/Hands-On-Business-Intelligence-with-Qlik-Sense/tree/master/Chapter02`.

Data loading process

When using Qlik Sense (Cloud, Personal, or Enterprise) you can load data from several sources, including spreadsheets, text files, Microsoft Access bases, SQL databases, Big Data data lakes, REST APIs, and much more. We can load data without learning a script language, despite the fact that we can use a script to leverage our access to data, and improve our control over the process. We can apply transformations such as creating calculated fields based on pre-existing information or aggregate data. The final goal is to create a data model that can be used to create dashboards and provide information to the users to analyze information.

The data loading process (demonstrated in the following diagram) consists of gathering data from different sources, associating those sources (transformed in tables) by key fields, applying transformations (creating derived fields, clean data, aggregate data, and so on), and finally, creating a data model that consists of a consistent group of tables linked by keys that represent a business model:

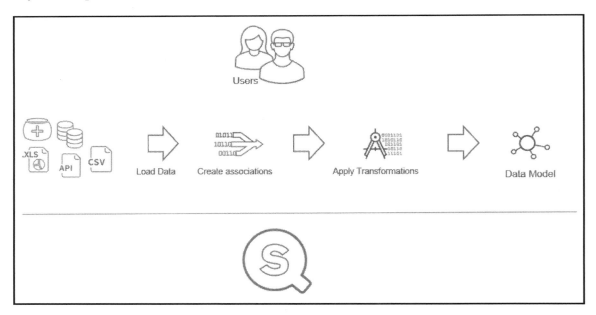

We can carry out this entire process on Qlik Sense itself, without any external tool to load or wrangle data.

Loading data from data sources

The first decision that we have to make when we create a Qlik Sense application is how we load our data. Once you press the **Create new app** button and name your application, a prompt like this appears:

As we can see, we have two different ways of loading data:

- **Add data from files and other sources**: This option will trigger Data manager, which is a wizard that will guide you during the whole process of data loading. Behind the scenes, the Data manager creates a script for every option or step you take during the usage of the wizard. This script can be edited later using the **Script editor** if you want or need to change something that can be done using the wizard.
- **Script editor**: This is a text editor where your script is written. This has access to all functions and other features for data loading.

You can choose which one you are more comfortable with using by keeping the following table in mind:

Data manager	Script editor
Easy to use, error-prone	Full access to all functionalities
Guided use, user-friendly	Full control over the sequence of commands being applied

Data connections

Before loading data, we need to explain one crucial Qlik Sense concept. Data connections are the entry points of data into Qlik Sense. It does not matter if you are loading text files, spreadsheets, database data, or big data. Data that will be loaded into Qlik needs to be referenced by a data connection—that way, Qlik Sense will know the data path. These are as follows:

- Reusable across your script and across all applications that you create.
- Consistent, meaning that it can be used in the same way, whether no matter what type of data is being retrieved and no matter if it is a SQL database or Big Data. Regardless, the final user has the same experience.
- In an enterprise environment, data connections can be governed, have a security policy, and be shared across users.

Data manager

Let's use the Data manager to load some files (please refer to the *Technical requirements* section to find the repository address). Download all files from that repository to a folder on your machine.

First, let's practice the easiest way of loading a data file—dragging it into your application.

 Depending on your Qlik Sense environment (Desktop, Enterprise, or Cloud), the screens will vary slightly.

Dragging a data file into your application

The following steps should help you drag and load the data onto the Qlik Sense application:

1. Start a new application with the help of the **Create new app** button and name your application. When prompted for the data loading method you want, just drag `Orders.xlsx` onto the screen:

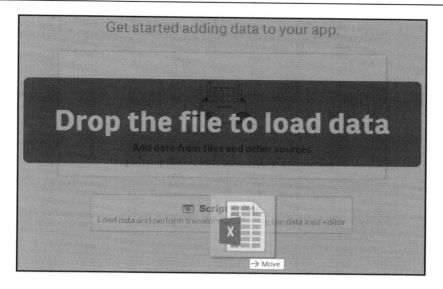

2. Once the file is dropped, it will be uploaded to the Qlik Sense environment and a wizard will open to assist you in importing the data to the application:

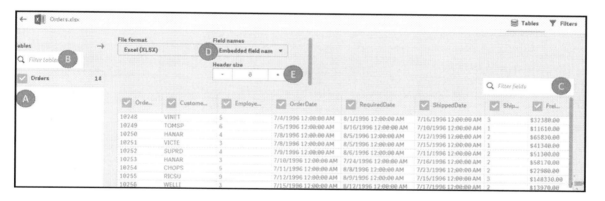

The following options are available on the wizard:

- We will load tables (**A** in the panel on the left) and then the **Orders** table is preselected. If your Excel has more sheets, every sheet will be represented as a different table. We can load as many tables as we want and we can use search box **B** on the top left panel that's marked to filter tables if you have a substantial table quantity.

- For each selected table, you can choose which columns should be loaded. You can do this by selecting/deselecting the checkbox on top of each column. You can use the search box **C** to filter columns if you have a substantial quantity.
- The **File format/Field names**, option **D**, should be correct, since Qlik Sense will identify it correctly. We will focus on this later in this section when loading text files.
- Use the **Header size**, option **E**, if your Excel sheet is structured with empty rows on top, so that Qlik Sense will skip them before loading the data.
- The Filters option can be used (located on the screen top-right corner of the screen) to apply filters for each table, or for the column you're loading. In the following example, we're filtering the **Orders** table for rows that have **USA** in the **ShipCountry** field only. You don't need to apply this filter at this moment—it is merely being used to understand the concept of applying filters. In the following example we are filtering only the records that have **ShipCountry = USA**:

TABLE	FIELD	CONDITION	VALUE
Orders	**ShipCountry**	=	USA ⊗
	⊕ *Add filter*		

3. Make sure that the **Orders** table is selected, all columns are checked, and no filters are applied, and then press **Add data** on the bottom-right corner:

4. After a few seconds, a screen like this will be displayed, indicating that the table from the Excel file was loaded successfully:

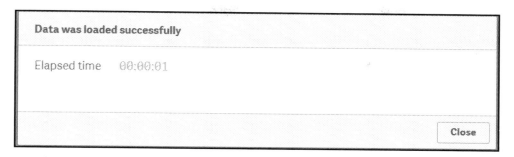

When you press the **Close** button, you're going to get an **Insights** screen. However, before we go there, let's load some more data using different modes.

Loading a data file from a folder (Qlik Sense Desktop)

Previously, we learned how to load data by dragging and dropping our files onto the Qlik Sense application. In this section, we are going to continue the exercise, as follows:

1. Press the **Data** button that lies at the top of the screen:

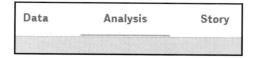

2. There is a big circle representing the **Orders** table, along with a big **+** at the upper-left corner. Here, press the circle:

3. The screen will now show all the connectors. Currently, we are interested in the option on the left-hand side, **FILE LOCATIONS**, which gives Qlik access to the folders on your machine:

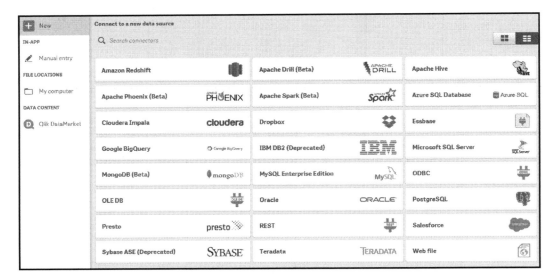

4. Using the **FILE LOCATIONS** option, navigate up to where you have downloaded your files and select the Customers.txt file. You will then be prompted with a screen like this:

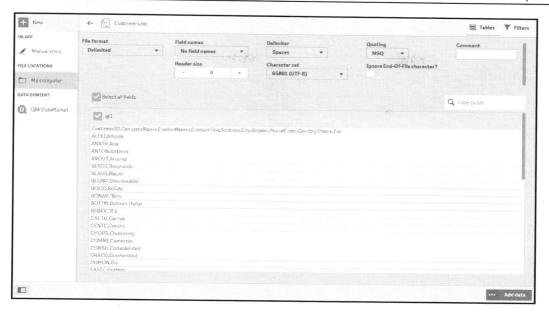

5. Qlik Sense automatically tries to identify how your data file is structured. Qlik Sense has inferred that the file has spaces as a field delimiter. We know that the delimiter is a comma, so we change the way Qlik Sense will split the lines by changing the **Delimiter** option to **Comma**, as we can see in the following screenshot, and instruct Qlik Sense to use the **Embedded field names** for **Field names** and check all columns:

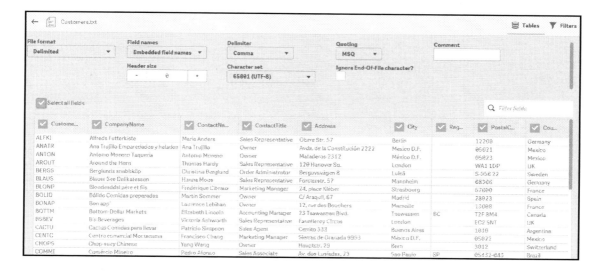

6. Now that we have a proper view of our data, press the **Add data** button. From here, we're going to see a screen just like this:

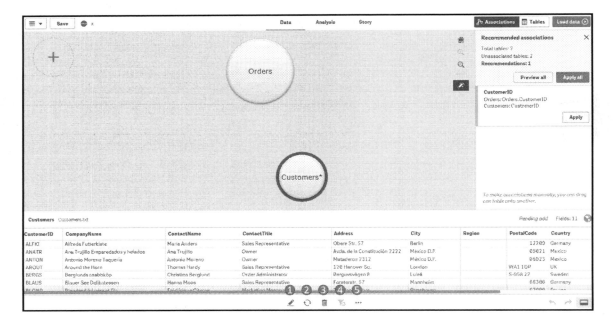

Now, we have two tables (represented by two circles). When you click on one of the circles, a preview of the table it represents is shown in the bottom panel. As you can see on the bottom menu, we have the following five options for each selected table:

- Edit the selected table.
- Reload the data from the selected table.
- Delete the selected table from our model.
- Clear filters (if you have applied any filter when loading your table). If you don't have any filters, this buttons is disabled.
- More options (concatenate tables and view details).

Loading a data file from data files (QlikCloud)

In the *Loading a data file from a folder (Qlik Sense Desktop)* section, we learned how to load data into the Qlik Sense Desktop application. QlikCloud has a special repository for the data files. In this section, we are going to continue with the exercise for QlikCloud:

1. The repository for data files can be accessed through the QlikCloud hub using the **Import data** option, as shown in the following screenshot:

2. The **Import data** button on QlikCloud will give you the option to upload one or more files by dragging them into the gray area, or selecting them using the **Choose file** option:

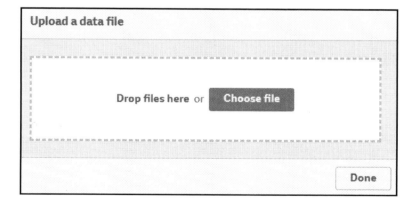

3. Upload your `Customers.txt` file and, then press the **Done** button:

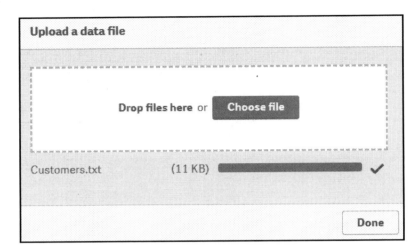

4. Go back to the application and press the **Data** button at the top of the screen:

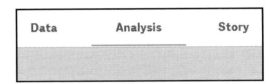

5. There is a big circle representing the **Orders** table, along with a big + on the upper-left corner. Press the circle, as follows:

6. The screen will now show all the connectors. Currently, we are interested in the option on the left-hand side called **Data files**, which gives Qlik access to the files that have been uploaded:

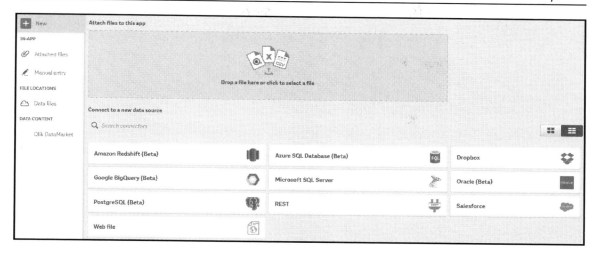

7. Select the `Customers.txt`. From there, then you will be prompted with a screen just like this:

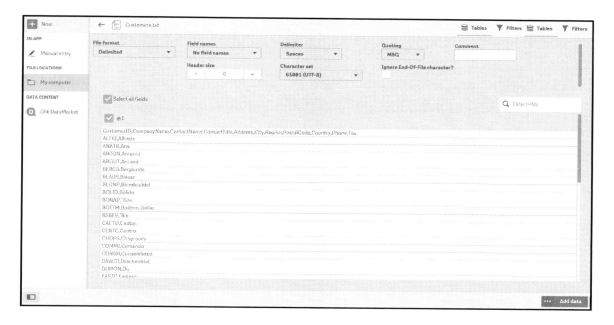

8. Qlik Sense automatically tries to identify how your data file is structured. Qlik Sense has inferred that the file has spaces as a field delimiter. We know that the delimiter is a comma, so we change the way Qlik Sense will split the lines by changing the **Delimiter** option to **Comma**, as we can see in the following screenshot, and instruct Qlik Sense to use the **Embedded field names** for **Field names** and check all columns:

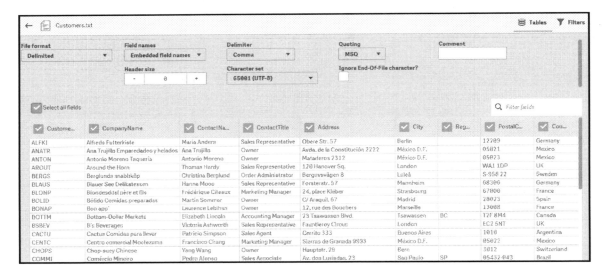

9. We now have a proper view of our data. After pressing the **Add data** button, we're going to see a screen just like this:

Now, we have two tables (represented by two circles). When you click on a circle, a preview of that table is shown, like in the previous screenshot. As you can see, we have five options for each selected table:

- Edit the selected table.
- Reload the data from the selected table.
- Delete the selected table from our model.
- Clear filters (if you have applied any filter when loading your table). If you don't have any filters, this buttons is disabled.
- More options (concatenate tables and view details).

Creating calculated fields

Calculated fields are new fields that exist only in the Qlik Sense data model. They are derived from the data that has been loaded.

Using the Data manager, you can edit your table and add another field, which means you can derive more information about your data by editing the table structure. To add these fields, do the following:

1. Go to the **Data** section and select your **Orders** table. After doing this, select the small pencil that signifies the edit button at the bottom:

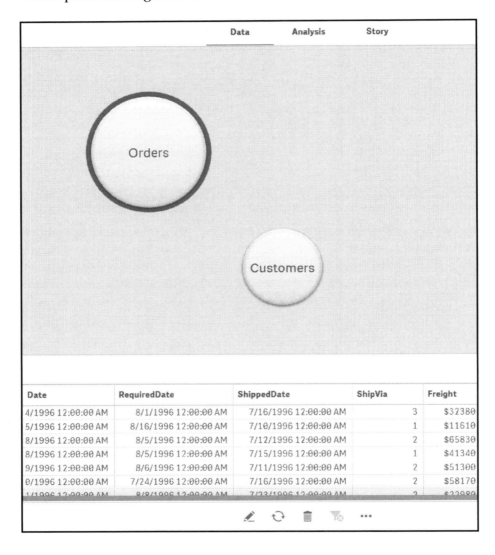

2. The following screen then appears:

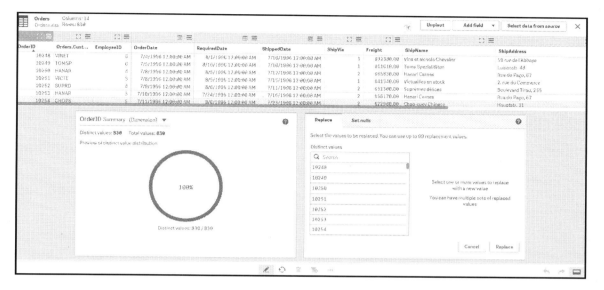

Let's discuss some options (please refer to *Further reading* section for a link to the entire documentation on table editing).

For each selected field, you can do the following:

- **Replace values**: By using this option, you can change values into new values, and fix data quality issues, like mistypes values. An example of this is shown in the following screenshot:

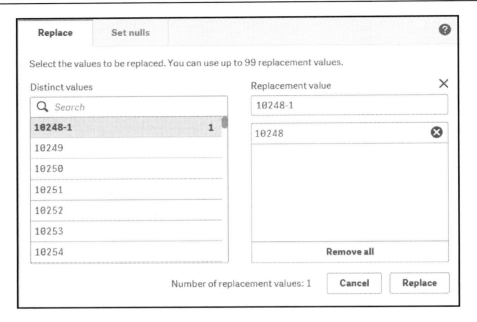

- **Set nulls**: By using this option, you can change values into nulls, which means the null values will not be shown on Qlik Sense. As we can see in the following screenshot, **10249** and **10248** will be replaced with null values:

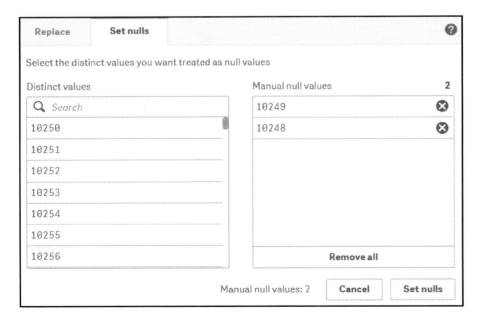

As we can see in the following screenshot, we have some options for each field:

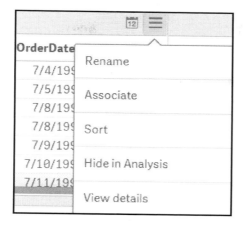

We have the following options:

- **Rename**: As the name states, this merely allows you to rename the field
- **Associate**: This allows you to associate this table with another table (we will focus on this later in this chapter, in the *Table associations* section)
- **Sort**: This option helps sort the field values based on values from that field
- **Hide in Analysis**: If this option is used, this field will not be displayed in Qlik Sense
- **View details**: This is a shortcut to a screen that shows if this field is calculated or not

All of these options are related to existing fields, but we can create calculated fields using the **Add field** button that lies on the upper-right side of the screen. To do this, follow these steps:

1. Press **Add field** and then select **Calculated field**:

	Unpivot	Add field ▼	Select data from source	✕

Calculated field

eight	ShipName	ShipAddress
$32380.00	Vins et alcools Chevalier	59 rue de l'Abbaye
$11610.00	Toms Spezialitäten	Luisenstr. 48
$65830.00	Hanari Carnes	Rua do Paço, 67
$41340.00	Victuailles en stock	2, rue du Commerce
$51300.00	Suprêmes délices	Boulevard Tirou, 255
$58170.00	Hanari Carnes	Rua do Paço, 67
$22980.00	Chop-suey Chinese	Hauptstr. 31

2. A popup containing a form will appear, as follows:

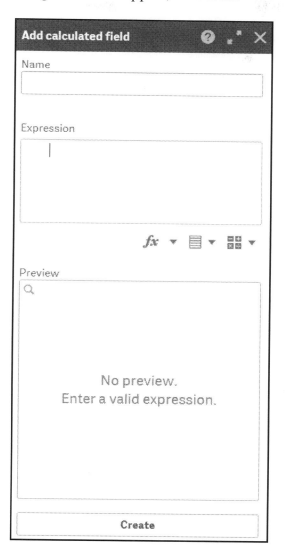

3. Create a field called `Processing Time` that calculates the gap between the `OrderDate` and `ShippedDate` using a function called `Interval` that formats the gap time:

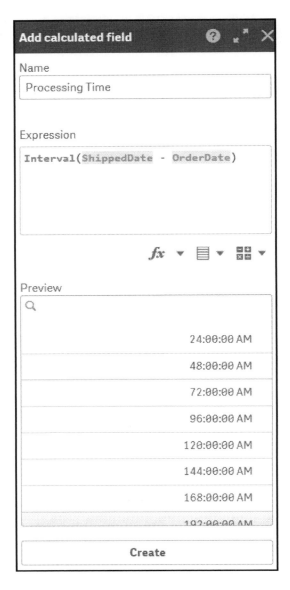

4. To consolidate our new field, please press **Load data** on the upper-right of the screen. Our application will be refreshed and the field will be created in the data model:

Now, we have created a field that can be used in our application like any other that came from our original data file.

Data load editor

Another approach to loading data into Qlik Sense is by using the **Data load editor**. When you add data tables, fields, or associations in the Data manager, a data load script code is automatically generated, and this script can be edited later using the **Data load editor**. You can access the **Data load editor** using the main menu from the upper-left corner and selecting it, as shown in the following screenshot:

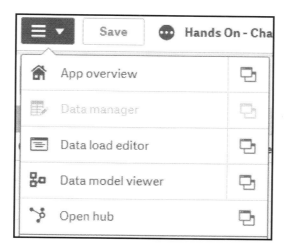

This option will enable a text editor, so an experienced Qlik professional can edit a script that will be responsible for loading data, applying transformations, aggregating data, and addressing any needs from a data modeling perspective.

In this section, we will describe how to use this editor to create or edit the script from our application.

The interface of the **Data load editor** is divided into some sections, as we can see in the following screenshot:

Let's understand each of these sections:

- **A section**: You can split your code into several sections to organize your code. Press the + button to add another section.
- **B (Text editor)**: Here, you can edit the script code. Each line is numbered and color coded by syntax. There is an IntelliSense feature that auto completes the code while you edit. Here is where you can type in your code, thus adding more tables, creating derived fields, and whatever else is needed to clean or modify the data.
- **C (Data connections)**: As discussed in the *Data connections* section, data connections are the entry points for data, so you can create one data connection using the **Create new connection** button that fires the wizard to assist you in creating that connection. If you want to load data from a data connection, you can do that by pressing the **Select data** button, as follows:

- **D (Debug and Load data buttons)**: Use these buttons when you want to debug (verify your code step by step) or reload your data by running your script.
- **E (Toolbar)**: Contains commands for search and replace, Ident/Unindent, Help, and Undo/Redo. The script already contains some predefined regional variable settings, for example, **SET ThousandSep=**. You should not touch these lines unless you're familiar with how Qlik Sense handles numbers and date formats.

The full understanding of Qlik scripts is beyond the scope of this book; if you want to have a deeper understanding, please refer to the *Further reading* section to access the links to the documentation about scripting.

Table associations

The power of Qlik Sense Associative resides in how your tables are associated. Unlike SQL tools, you don't have to worry about Many-To-One and One-To-Many relationships and predefine the exploration path between your data. You can load your data, set which fields (usually called **key fields**) are the links between the tables, and Qlik Sense Associative takes care of the rest.

Now, let's see how we can create the associations between the two tables we have loaded:

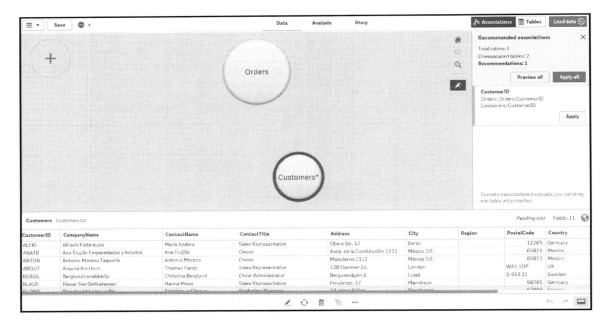

On the right-hand side of the screen, you can see a section called **Recommended associations.** While loading your data, Qlik Sense analyzed your tables and proposed how to associate your tables based on a complex algorithm that considers distinct values of each field, column names, and the frequency of each value for each table.

Press the **Preview all** button to check how Qlik Sense is proposing to associate our tables. It should look something like this:

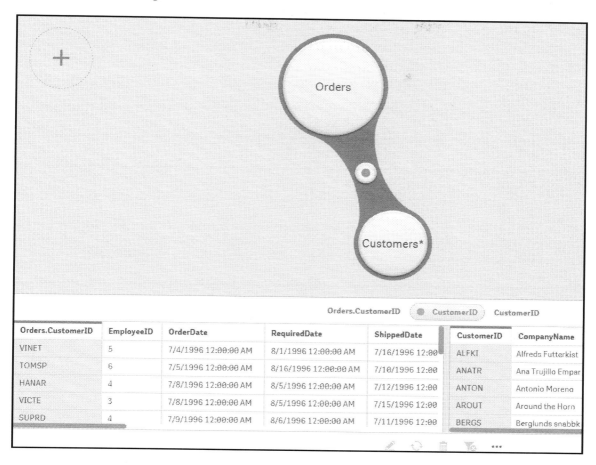

As you can see, Qlik Sense will draw a blue association between the two tables and highlight the columns in green that it is using as link keys between the two tables. In our case, Qlik Sense chooses **CustomerID** for both tables as fields that are eligible to link our tables. As an example, **VINET** values from **Orders** will match with **VINET** values from customers. Now, press the **Apply all** button; you're going to see that the blue connection becomes a dark gray one, indicating that the association was created:

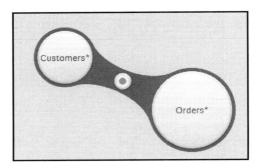

Now, we have to load all tables using the **Load data** button, and then create all the associations:

If you go to **Data model viewer**, you will see your tables linked:

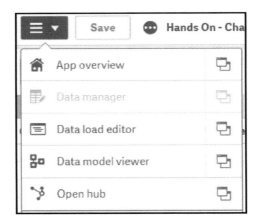

In the following screenshot, we can see our two tables and how they are associated:

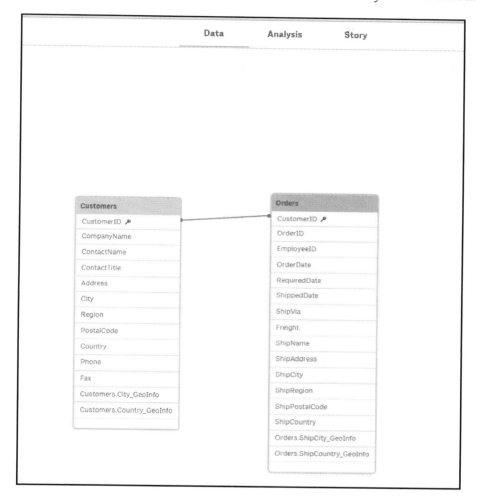

Data profiling

When loading data and creating your data model, you can examine the data available from your data source, and collect statistics or summaries from your data model. The purpose of these statistics may be to do the following:

- Find out whether the data tends to a particular standard of quality
- Add metadata using tags or descriptions

- Discover the frequency and analyze if the data should be cleansed or transformed

You can profile your data model using the Data manager or the Data model viewer.

Profiling using the Data manager

You can access information about every field and table of your model with this step:

1. Go to **Data manager**, select the **Orders** table, and click the small pencil that lies at the bottom, entering the table editor mode that shows a preview of your data, which shows some information about the table:

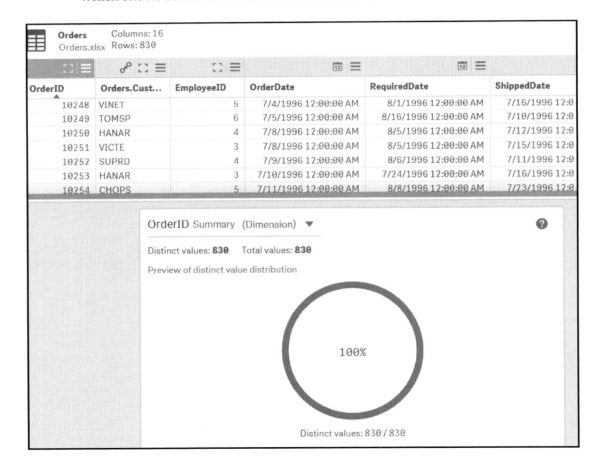

In the preceding example, we can see that the **Orders** table is selected and that the **OrderID** field is highlighted. Here, Qlik Sense will display information about that field. We can see the following information:

- The **Orders** table has **16** fields and **830** rows
- The data comes from an Excel file (`Orders.xlsx`)
- There are **830** distinct values and **830** total values, so we can deduce that there are no duplicate values in the table
- This field will be considered as a **Dimension**, so Qlik will not propose aggregations (count, sum, average, max, min, or others) for that field

If we select the **EmployeeID** , we will see the following:

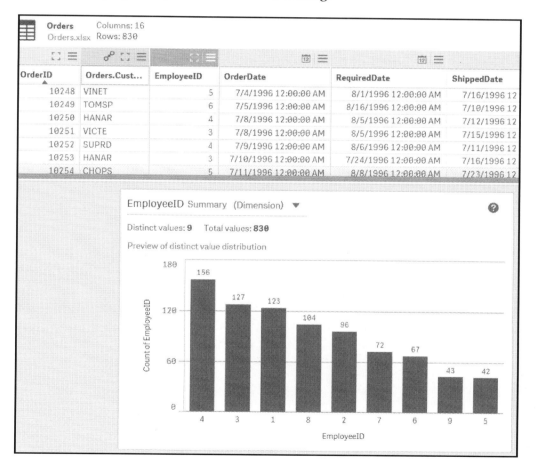

For this field, we can see that there are some duplicate values, since we have only nine distinct values. Qlik generates a histogram for each value, showing how many values there are for each combination, so that we can check that value distribution makes sense and does not indicate data quality issues.

If we select the **Freight** field, we are going to see that this field will be considered as a **Measure,** so Qlik Sense will propose aggregations (count, sum, average, max, min, or others) over this field and Qlik also provides some statistics about it (minimum, median, average, and maximum values):

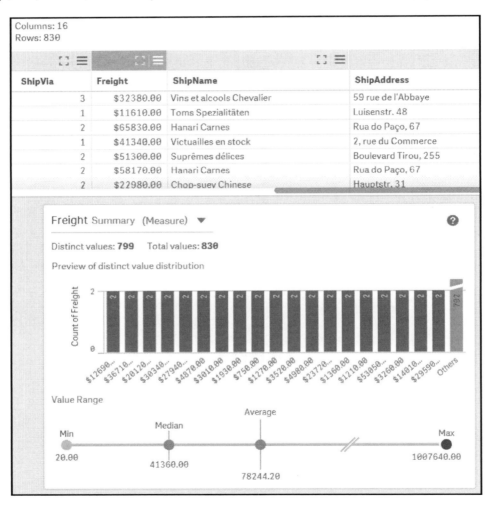

We will now move on to understanding how to profile with a Data model viewer.

Profiling using the Data model viewer

Another way to profile data is by using the Data model viewer. Follow these steps to do so:

1. The **Data model viewer** can be accessed using the top-left menu, as follows:

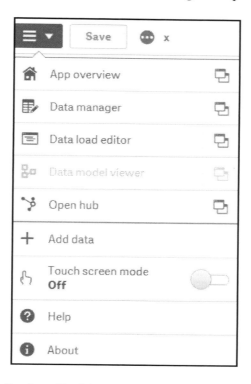

   This option will display all tables from your data model as rectangles that show every field that was loaded.

2. At the bottom-right of the screen, you can see a **Preview** button that, once clicked, shows the details for each selected table of the field. Let's do this by discussing an example of when you select the **Orders** table:

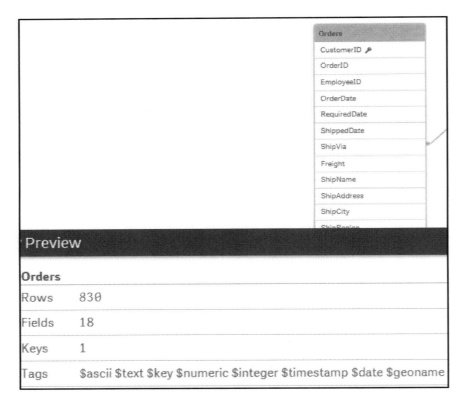

 The Data model viewer will highlight the selected table in orange.

As we can see from the preceding screenshot, our table has been loaded with 830 rows, 18 fields and 1 keys (indicating that this table is associated with another).

3. A preview with the first few rows of your table is also displayed. When you click on any field, you can retrieve more information about it:

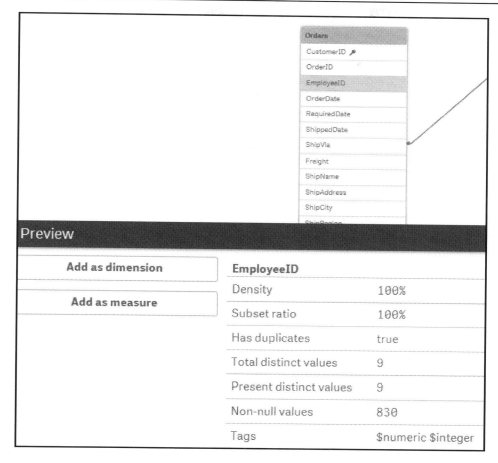

In the preceding example, we can see that the **EmployeeID** field has the following:

- A **100% Density,** meaning that for every row, there is a value stored in the table. In other words, there are no null values in that field.
- A **100% Subset ratio.** The subset ratio is the percentage of distinct values in the table for this field versus all values from this field in all tables (there will only be a subset ratio of 100% when you are profiling a key field, because if the field is referenced only in one table, all the values will be stored).
- **Has duplicates** as **true,** meaning that some values are duplicated across the table.
- **Total distinct values,** which shows how many distinct values were found in this table.

- **Present distinct values**, which shows how many distinct values were found in all tables (this value will always be the same as **Total distinct values** from non-key fields).
- **Non-null values**, which shows how many non-null values were found for this field.
- **Tags**, which shows metadata associated with this field.

Now, let's take a closer look at a key field (**CustomerID**) by selecting the **Orders** table and then the **CustomerID** field. As you can see in the following screenshot, both tables were selected and the keys fields are highlighted:

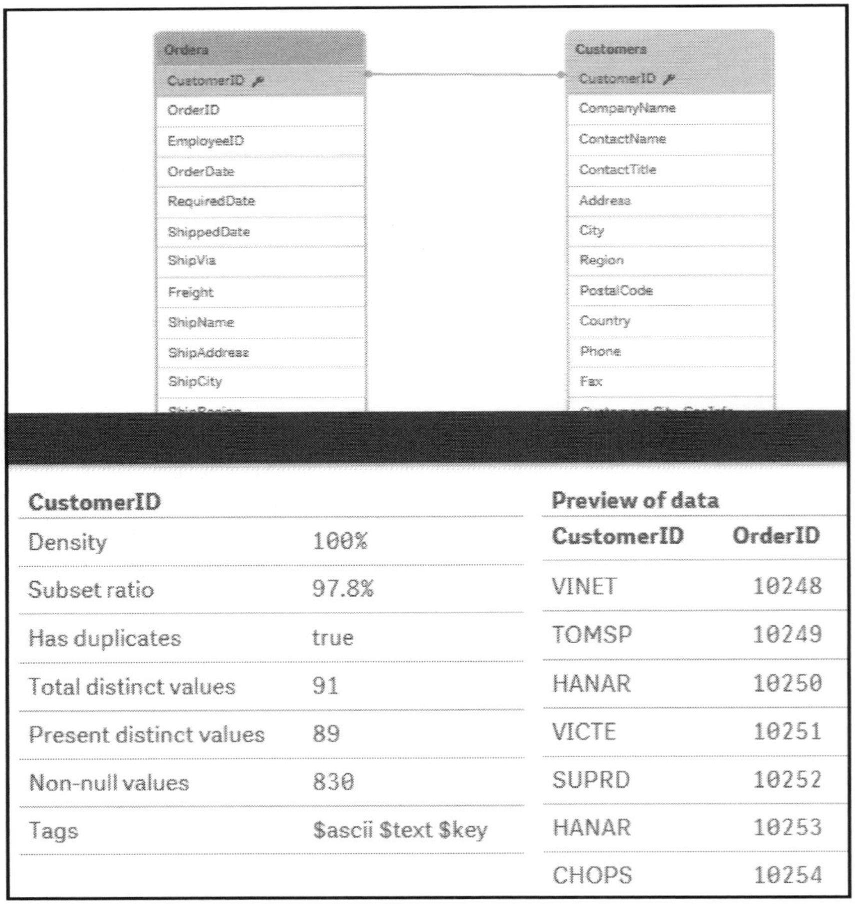

Orders	Customers
CustomerID 🔑	CustomerID 🔑
OrderID	CompanyName
EmployeeID	ContactName
OrderDate	ContactTitle
RequiredDate	Address
ShippedDate	City
ShipVia	Region
Freight	PostalCode
ShipName	Country
ShipAddress	Phone
ShipCity	Fax

CustomerID

Density	100%
Subset ratio	97.8%
Has duplicates	true
Total distinct values	91
Present distinct values	89
Non-null values	830
Tags	$ascii $text $key

Preview of data

CustomerID	OrderID
VINET	10248
TOMSP	10249
HANAR	10250
VICTE	10251
SUPRD	10252
HANAR	10253
CHOPS	10254

As we can see, the description for this field is as follows:

- A **100% Density**, meaning that for every row, there is a value stored in the table. In other words, there are no null values in that field.
- A **97.8% Subset ratio**, which means that for the **Orders** table, we have **97.8%** of all possible (all tables included) values from that table. In other words, there are **CustomerID** values that are not reflected.
- **Has duplicates** is **true**, meaning that some values are duplicated across the table.
- **Total distinct values**, which shows how many distinct values were found in this table.
- **Present distinct values**, which shows how many distinct values were found in all tables. As we can see, this table has **89** distinct values from a total of **91** distinct values.
- **Non-null values**, which shows how many non-null values were found for this field.
- **Tags**, which shows the metadata associated with this field.

Now let's take a closer look into a key field (**CustomerID**) by selecting the **Customers** table and then the **CustomerID** field:

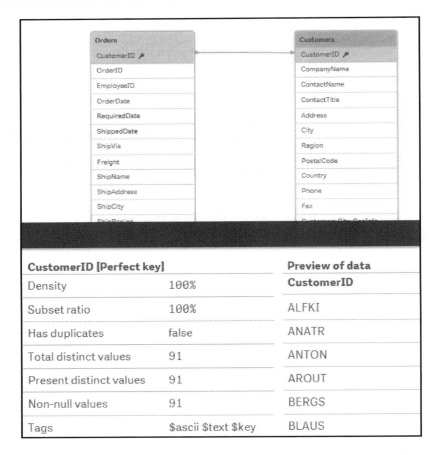

CustomerID [Perfect key]		Preview of data
Density	100%	**CustomerID**
Subset ratio	100%	ALFKI
Has duplicates	false	ANATR
Total distinct values	91	ANTON
Present distinct values	91	AROUT
Non-null values	91	BERGS
Tags	$ascii $text $key	BLAUS

Now, as we can see in this table, **Customers** have a subset ratio of **100%**, which means that all values from **CustomerID** are stored in our **Customers** table. Comparing the subset ratio from the **Customers** (100%) table against **Orders** (97.8%), we can conclude that all customers are represented in the **Customers** table, but there are customers that don't have orders (2.2% of them) since they are not represented here.

If for some reason you find a situation in which there are two or more tables that share a key field, and none of them have a **100% Subset ratio**, this may conclude that we have a data quality problem. For example, we may have orders that have no customer associated with them.

Summary

In this chapter, we have been through the process of loading data into a Qlik application. We have looked at how this process works, as well as the concept of Data connections, exploring how they can be created and reused. We also loaded data from different sources (an Excel file and a text file), adding a new field using the Data manager, and discussing that there is a script that is generated when you use the Data manager; this can be edited using the Data load editor. We also learned how to associate two or more tables to create a data model, and to check your data quality, view some metadata from the data you have loaded.

In the next chapter, we are going to discuss some basic data modeling concepts, as well as look at data modeling techniques that will improve our data model.

Further reading

- **Qlik Associative Difference**: https://www.qlik.com/us/products/associative-difference
- **Qlik Help**: https://help.qlik.com/en-US/sense/November2018/Subsystems/Hub/Content/Sense_Hub/LoadData/managing-data.htm
- **Qlik Help—Data load editor**:
  https://help.qlik.com/en-US/sense/November2018/Subsystems/Hub/Content/Sense_Hub/LoadData/use-data-load-editor.htm

3
Implementing Data Modeling Techniques

In this chapter, we are going to focus on the basic concept of data modeling. We will look at the various types of the data modeling techniques and learn which technique is best suited for the Qlik Sense dashboards. We will also learn about the methods for linking data with each other using joins and concatenation. We will throw some light on how to we filter unwanted data while loading the data.

We will learn about the Qlik Data format, **QlikView Data (QVD)**, and why it should be used in the data modeling. We will also look at how to link multiple tables with different granularity (granularity being the level of data that is stored in the tables) of data using the link table.

We will see how to handle the situation in which multiple dates are involved in the data model and situations when you want to calculate the accumulated values and rolling averages. Finally, we will look at the script optimization techniques to improve the script loading time.

This chapter will cover the following are the topics:

- An overview of data modeling
- Joining
- Concatenation
- Filtering
- Use of QVDs
- Link table
- Canonical dates
- As-Of Table
- Script optimization

Technical requirements

For this chapter, we will use the app already created in `Chapter 3`, *Implementing Data Modeling Techniques*, as a starting point with a loaded data model.

You can also download the initial and final version of the application from the book repository on GitHub at `https://github.com/PacktPublishing/Hands-On-Business-Intelligence-with-Qlik-Sense/tree/master/Chapter03`.

After downloading the initial version of the application, perform the following steps:

- If you are using Qlik Sense Desktop, place the app in the `Qlik\Sense\Apps` folder under your `Documents` personal folder
- If you are using Qlik Sense Cloud, upload the app to your personal workspace

An overview of data modeling

Data modeling is a conceptual process, representing the associations between the data in a manner in which it caters to specific business requirements. In this process, the various data tables are linked as per the business rules to achieve business needs.

Let's understand data modeling using a real-life example. Assume that we want to understand the buying pattern of a customer in the retail industry. For this analysis, we would require the following details:

- **Customer details**: This detail is stored in the `Customer` table
- **Sales transactions**: This detail could be stored in multiple tables, but let's assume that this data is available in the `Sales` table
- **Product details**: This detail is available in the `Product` table

If we wish to find what products are bought by a customer, we need to link all the preceding tables with each other to get the required information. The mechanism of linking tables with each other entails the process of building the data model.

In our example, once we link the required tables with each other, we get following data model:

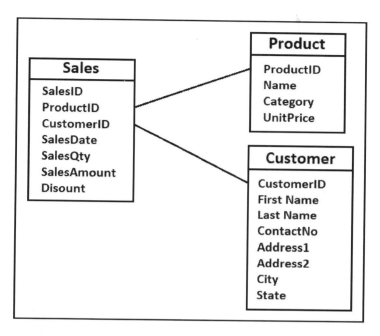

Data modeling helps a business in many ways. Let's look at some of the advantages of data modeling:

- **High speed retrieval**: Data modeling helps to get the required information much faster than expected. This is because the data is interlinked between the different tables using the relationship.
- **Provides ease of accessing data**: Data modeling eases the process of giving the right access of the data to the end users. With the simple data query language, you can get the required data easily.
- **Helps in handling multiple relations**: Various datasets have various kinds of relationship between the other data. For example, there could be *one-to-one*, or *one-to-many*, or *many-to-many* relationships. Data modeling helps in handling this kind of relationship easily.
- **Stability**: Data modeling provides stability to the system.

Data modeling techniques

There are various techniques in which data models can be built, each technique has its own advantages and disadvantages. They are created with the intention of catering to some specific use cases. So, not all techniques are used for all kinds of requirements. The following are two widely-used data modeling techniques.

Entity relationship modeling

The **entity relationship modeling (ER modeling)** technique uses the entity and relationships to create the logical data model. The ER modeling technique was developed by Peter Chen in 1976. This technique is best suited for the **Online Transaction Processing (OLTP)** systems.

An entity in this model refers to the any thing or object in the real world that has distinguishable characteristics. Each entity has some properties and the corresponding values of these properties. Consider, for example, Customer, Employee, Product, and so on. Each of these entities has some specific properties.

For example, the Customer entity has a name, address, contact number, city, state, and so on. These are called the **properties**, and each property has a value associated with it.

A relationship in this model is the relationship between the two or more entities. There are three basic types of relationship that can exist:

- **One-to-one**: This relation means each value from one entity has a single relation with a value from the other entity. For example, one customer is handled by one sales representative:

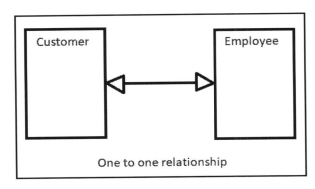

- **One-to-many**: This relation means each value from one entity has multiple relations with values from other entities. For example, one sales representative handles multiple customers:

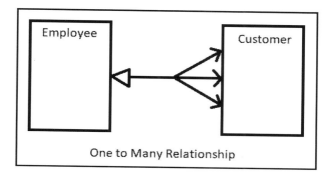

One to Many Relationship

- **Many-to-many**: This relation means all values from both entities have multiple relations with each other. For example, one book can have many authors and each author can have multiple books:

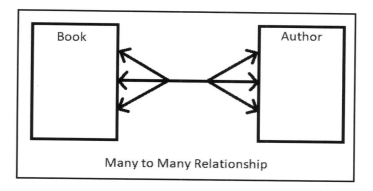

Many to Many Relationship

An example of the sample ER diagram is shown as follows:

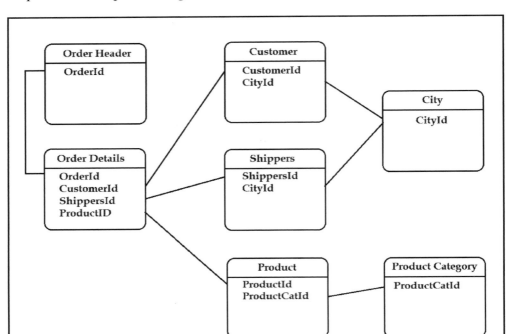

Dimensional modeling

The **dimensional modeling** technique uses facts and dimensions to build the data model. This modeling technique was developed by Ralf Kimball. Unlike ER modeling, which uses normalization to build the model, this technique uses the denormalization of data to build the model.

Facts, in this context, are tables that store the most granular transactional details. They mainly store the performance measurement metrics, which are the outcome of the business process. Fact tables are huge in size, because they store the transactional records.

For example, let's say that sales data is captured at a retail store. The fact table for such data would look like the following:

```
┌─────────────────────┐
│     Sales Fact      │
├─────────────────────┤
│ SalesNumber         │
│ Date                │
│ ProductID           │
│ CustomerID          │
│ SchemeID            │
│ SalesmanID          │
│ Sales Qty           │
│ Sales Amount        │
└─────────────────────┘
```

A fact table has the following characteristics:

- It contains the measures, which are mostly numeric in nature
- It stores the foreign key, which refers to the dimension tables
- It stores large numbers of records
- Mostly, it does not contain descriptive data

The dimension table stores the descriptive data, describing the who, what, which, when, how, where, and why associated with the transaction. It has the maximum number of columns, but the records are generally fewer than fact tables. Dimension tables are also referred to as companions of the fact table. They store textual, and sometimes numerical, values. For example, a PIN code is numeric in nature, but they are not the measures and thus they get stored in the dimension table.

In the previous sales example that we discussed, the customer, product, time, and salesperson are the dimension tables. The following diagram shows a sample dimension table:

```
┌─────────────────────┐
│    DimCustomer      │
├─────────────────────┤
│ CustomerID          │
│ First Name          │
│ Last Name           │
│ EmailID             │
│ MobileNo            │
│ OfficeNo            │
│ Address1            │
│ Address2            │
│ City                │
│ State               │
│ Pincode             │
│ Category            │
└─────────────────────┘
```

The following are the characteristics of the dimension table:

- It stores descriptive data, which describes the attributes of the transaction
- It contains many columns and fewer records compared to the fact table
- It also contains numeric data, which is descriptive in nature

There are two types of dimensional modeling techniques that are widely used:

- **Star schema**: This schema model has one fact table that is linked with multiple dimension tables. The name *star* is given because once the model is ready, it looks like a star.

  The advantages of the star schema model include the following:

  - Better query performance
  - Simple to understand

  The following diagram shows an example of the star schema model:

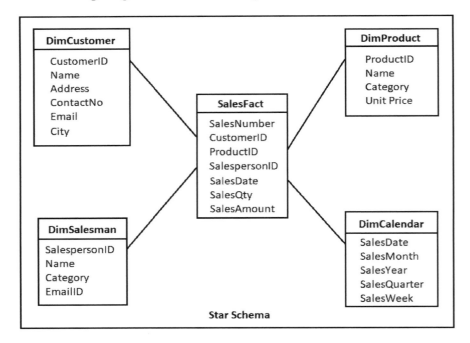

- **Snowflake schema**: This schema model is similar to the star schema, but in this model, the dimensional tables are normalized further.

The advantages of the snowflake schema model include the following:

- It provides better referential integrity
- It requires less space as data is normalized

The following diagram shows an example of the snowflake schema model:

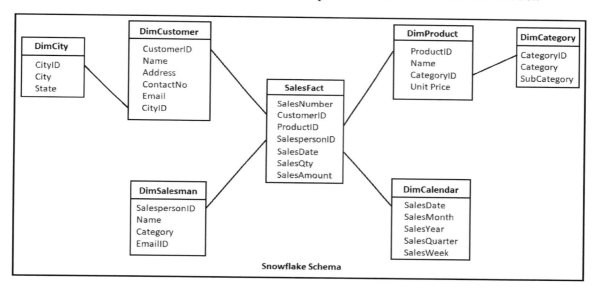

Snowflake Schema

When it comes to data modeling in Qlik Sense, the best option is to use the star schema model for better performance. Qlik Sense works very well when the data is loaded in a denormalized form, thus the star schema is suitable for Qlik Sense development. The following diagram shows the performance impact of different data models on Qlik Sense:

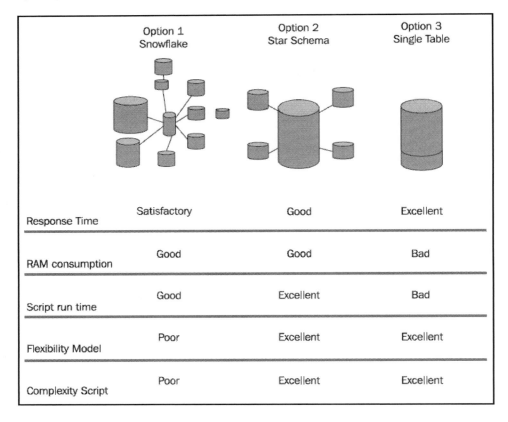

Now that we know what data modeling is and which technique is most appropriate for Qlik Sense data modeling, let's look at some other fundamentals of handling data.

Joining

While working on data model building, we often encounter a situation where we want to have some fields added from one table into another to do some sort of calculations. In such situations, we use the option of joining those tables based on the common fields between them.

Let's understand how we can use joins between tables with a simple example.

Assume you want to calculate the selling price of a product. The information you have is **SalesQty** in **Sales Table** and **UnitPrice** of product in **Product Table**. The calculation for getting the sales price is *UnitPrice * SalesQty*. Now, let's see what output we get when we apply a join on these tables:

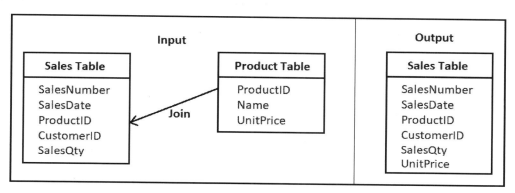

Types of joins

There are various kinds of joins available but let's take a look at the various types of joins supported by Qlik Sense.

Let's consider the following tables to understand each type better:

- **Order table**: This table stores the order-related data:

OrderNumber	Product	CustomerID	OrderValue
100	Fruits	1	100
101	Fruits	2	80
102	Fruits	3	120
103	Vegetables	6	200

- **Customer table**: This table stores the customer details, which include the `CustomerID` and `Name`:

CustomerID	Name
1	Alex
2	Linda
3	Sam
4	Michael
5	Sara

Join/outer join

When you want to get the data from both the tables you use the `Join` keyword. When you just use only `Join` between two tables, it is always a full outer join. The `Outer` keyword is optional. The following diagram shows the Venn diagram for the outer join:

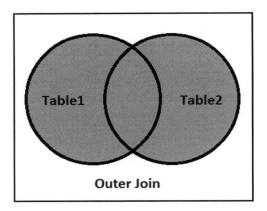

Now, let's see how we script this joining condition in Qlik Sense:

1. Create a new Qlik Sense application. Give it a name of your choice.
2. Jump to **Script editor**, create a new tab, and rename it as `Outer Join`, as shown in following screenshot. Write the script shown in the following screenshot:

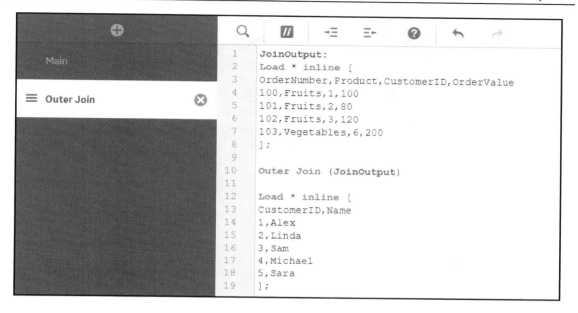

3. Once you write the script, click on **Load Data** to run the script and load the data.
4. Once the data is loaded, create a new sheet and add the **Table** object to see the joined table data, as shown in the following screenshot:

As output of **Outer Join**, we got five fields, as shown in the preceding screenshot. You can also observe that the last two rows have null values for the fields, which come from the **Order** table, where the customers **4** and **5** are not present.

Left join

When you want to extract all the records from the left table and matching records from the right table, then you use the `Left Join` keyword to join those two tables. The following diagram shows the Venn diagram for **left join**:

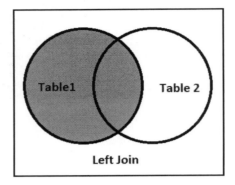

Let's see the script for left join:

1. In the previous application created, delete the `Outer Join` tab.
2. Create a new tab and rename it as `Left Join`, as shown in following screenshot. Write the script shown in the following screenshot:

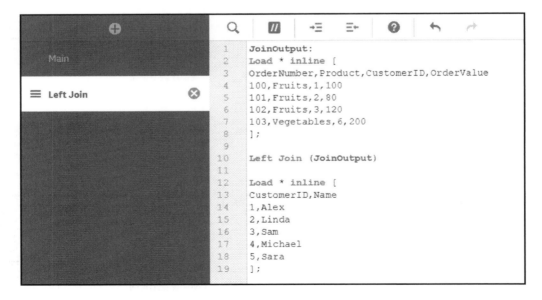

3. Once you the script is written, click on **Load Data** to run the script and load the data.

4. Once the script is finished, create a new sheet and add the **Table** object to see the joined table data, as shown in the following screenshot:

Left Join Output

OrderNumber	Product	CustomerID	Name	OrderValue
100	Fruits	1	Alex	100
101	Fruits	2	Linda	80
102	Fruits	3	Sam	120
103	Vegetables	6	-	200

Right join

When you want to extract all the records from the right table and the matching records from the left table, then you use the `right join` keyword to join those two tables. The following diagram shows the Venn diagram for **right join**:

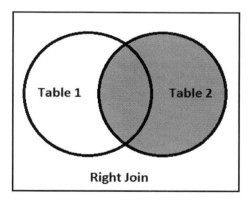

Let's see the script for **right join**:

1. In the previous application created, comment the existing script.
2. Create a new tab and rename it as `Right Join`, as shown in the following screenshot. Write the script, as shown in the following screenshot:

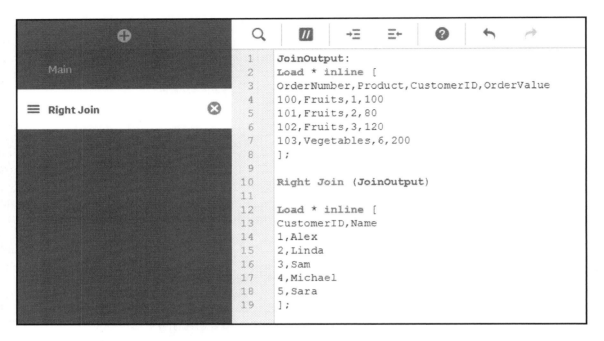

3. Once you the script is written, click on **Load Data** to run the script and load the data.
4. Once the script is finished, create a new sheet and add the **Table** object to see the joined table data, as shown in the following screenshot:

Right Join Output

OrderNumber	Product	CustomerID	Name	OrderValue
100	Fruits	1	Alex	100
101	Fruits	2	Linda	80
102	Fruits	3	Sam	120
-	-	4	Michael	-
-	-	5	Sara	-

Inner join

When you want to extract matching records from both the tables, then you use the `Inner Join` keyword to join those two tables. The following diagram shows the Venn diagram for **inner join**:

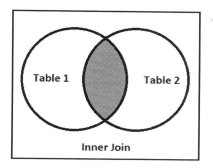

Let's see the script for **inner join**:

1. In the previous application created, comment the existing script.
2. Create a new tab and rename it as `Inner Join`, as shown in the following screenshot. Write the script shown in following screenshot:

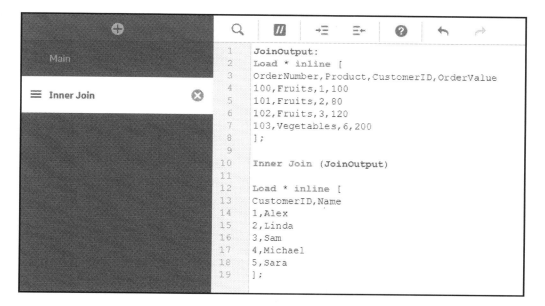

3. Once you the script is written, click on **Load Data** to run the script and load the data.

4. Once the script is finished, create a new sheet and add the **Table** object to see the joined table data, as shown in the following screenshot:

Inner Join Output				
OrderNumber	Product	CustomerID	Name	OrderValue
100	Fruits	1	Alex	100
101	Fruits	2	Linda	80
102	Fruits	3	Sam	120

Pitfalls of using joins

Joins are simple to understand and use, but there is one hidden pitfall that can create lots of issues in your output data. Until now, we have seen simple data that had a one-to-one relationship between the values of the joining field, but in some scenarios, you may encounter multiple relationships between data. In such a case, your output data may get duplicated and the overall result may turn out wrong.

Let's understand this using the same example we used in the preceding sections. The only change will be that we add the last record in the Customer table:

CustomerID	Name
1	Alex
2	Linda
3	Sam
4	Michael
5	Sara
3	Vinay

You can see in the preceding table that we added a new record, which makes a duplicate entry for the primary key; that is, CustomerID, with a value of 3.

When we use this table along with any join condition, it will create two records in the resulting table, because the record 3 has a duplicate value. Let's assume that we use left join the Customer table to the Order table. The resulting output would look like the following screenshot:

Left Join Output

OrderNumber	Product	CustomerID	Name	OrderValue
100	Fruits	1	Alex	100
101	Fruits	2	Linda	80
102	Fruits	3	Sam	120
102	Fruits	3	Vinay	120
103	Vegetables	6	-	200

You can see in the preceding screenshot that order number **102** has appeared twice, one with the customer name as **Sam** and the other as **Vinay**. You can also observe that **OrderValue** also got duplicated due to this new record. So, when you calculate on **OrderValue** from this resulting table, you will get the wrong value.

Thus, whenever you use any joins in Qlik Sense, you must make sure that the joining table has distinct records to get the correct values after joining.

One good way to check, which I also follow, is that the resulting table record count should be equal to the first table, because if there is a one-to-one relationship among the values, then the record count should be same. If they are not the same, then you should look for the duplicate values for the joining key in the joining table.

Concatenation

Sometimes you come across a situation while building the data model where you may have to append one table below another. In such situations, you can use the concatenate function. Concatenating, as the name suggest, helps to add the records of one table below another. Concatenate is different from joins. Unlike joins, concatenate does not merge the matching records of both the tables in a single row.

Automatic concatenation

In Qlik Sense, when the numbers of columns in two tables are same and the naming of those columns are same, Qlik Sense, by default, concatenates those tables without any explicit command. This is called the **automatic concatenation**.

For example, you may get the customer information from two different sources, but with the same columns names. In such a case, automatic concatenation will be done by Qlik, as is shown in the following screenshot:

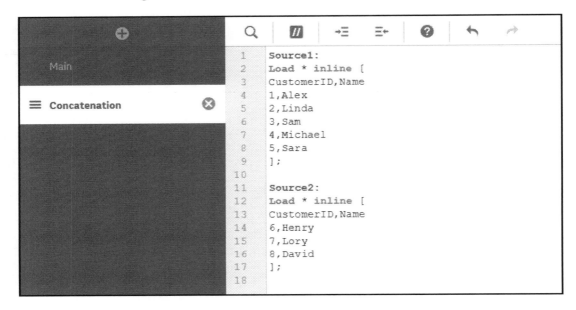

You can see in the preceding screenshot that both the **Source1** and **Source2** tables have two columns and the names of both the columns are the same (note that names in Qlik Sense are case-sensitive). Thus, they are auto concatenated. One more thing to note here is that, in such a situation, Qlik Sense ignores the name given to the second table and stores all the data under the name given to the first table.

The output table after concatenation is shown in the following screenshot:

Auto Concatenation	
CustomerID	Name
1	Alex
2	Linda
3	Sam
4	Michael
5	Sara
6	Henry
7	Lory
8	David

Forced concatenation

There will be some cases in which you would like to concatenate two tables irrespective of the number of columns and name. In such a case, you should use the keyword Concatenate between two Load statements to concatenate those two tables. This is called the **forced concatenation**.

For example, if you have sales and budget data at similar granularity and you want to concatenate them, then you should use the Concatenate keyword to forcefully concatenate both tables, as shown in the following screenshot:

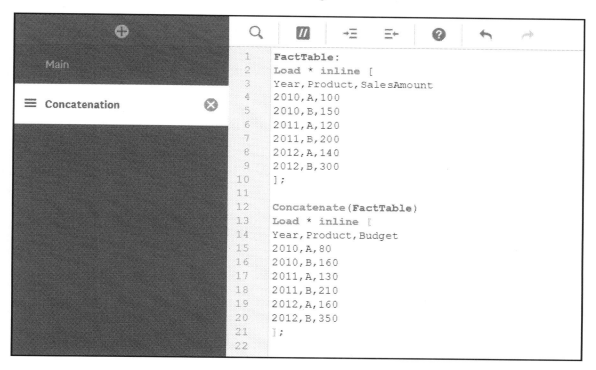

The output table after loading this script will have data for common columns, one below the other. For the columns that are not same, there will be null values in those columns for the table in which they didn't exist. This is shown in the following output:

Forced Concatenation			
Year	Product	Sales...	Budget
2010	A	100	-
2010	B	150	-
2011	A	120	-
2011	B	200	-
2012	A	140	-
2012	B	300	-
2010	A	-	80
2010	B	-	160
2011	A	-	130
2011	B	-	210
2012	A	-	160

You can see in preceding screenshot that the **SalesAmount** is null for the budget data, and **Budget** is null for the sales data.

Forced concatenation results in many null values, and thus you must handle nulls when you use forced concatenation.

The NoConcatenate

In some situations when even though the columns and their name from the two tables are the same, you may want to treat them differently and don't want to concatenate them. So Qlik Sense provides the NoConcatenate keyword, which helps to prevent automatic concatenation.

Let's see how to write the script for `NoConcatenate`:

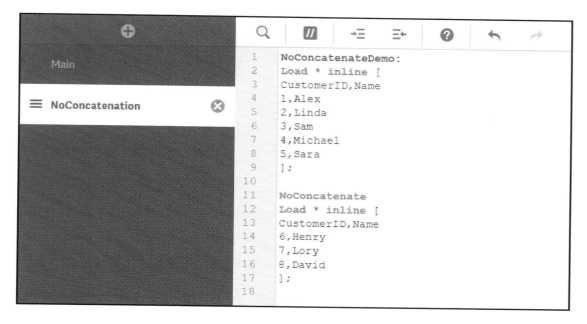

You should handle the tables properly; otherwise, the output of `NoConcatenate` may create a synthetic table.

Filtering

In this section, we will learn how to filter the data while loading in Qlik Sense. As you know, there are two ways in which we can load the data in Qlik Sense: either by using the Data manager or the script editor. Let's see how to filter data with each of these options.

Filtering data using the Data manager

When you load data using the Data manager, you get an option named **Filters** at the top-right corner of the window, as shown in the following screenshot:

This filter option enables us to set the filtering condition, which loads only the data that satisfies the condition given. The filter option allows the following conditions:

- =
- >
- >=
- <
- <=

Using the preceding conditions, you can filter the text or numeric values of a field. For example, you can set a condition such as `Date >= '01/01/2012'` or `ProductID = 80`.

The following screenshot shows such conditions applied in the Data load editor:

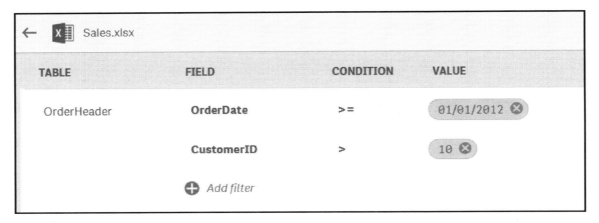

Filtering data in the script editor

If you are familiar with the `Load` statement or the SQL `Select` statement, it will be easy for you to filter the data while loading it. In the script editor, the best way to restrict the data is to include the `Where` clause at the end of the `Load` or `Select` statement; for example, `Where Date >= '01/01/2012'`.

When you use the `Where` clause with the `Load` statement, you can use the following conditions:

- =
- >
- >=
- <
- <=

When you write the `Where` clause with the SQL `Select` statement, you can use following conditions:

- =
- >
- >=
- <
- <=
- In
- Between
- Like
- Is Null
- Is Not Null

The following screenshot shows an example of both the statements:

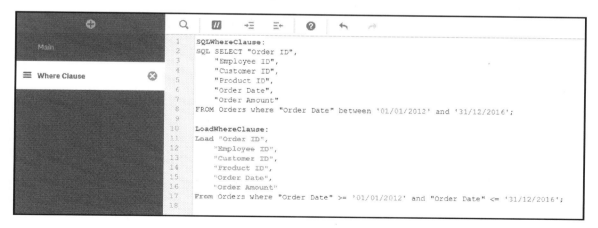

QVDs

Unlike other data sources, Qlik also provides its own data format in which data can be stored. There are multiple advantages over loading data from the Qlik format, instead of loading data directly from the data source. QVDs are created from the Qlik Sense script using the `Store` command. It stores only single table data.

The Qlik data format is called **QVD**. Qlik uses the XML technique to store data into QVD. QVD contains three parts:

- **The XML header**: This describes the fields in the table and some metadata
- **The symbol table**: This stores the relationship between the data
- **The actual table**: This stores the actual values of the field

Why use QVDs?

Let's understand why we should use the QVDs:

- **Decreasing load on the source system**: Most **business intelligence (BI)** tools fire a query on the data source when any selection or filtration of data is done. This causes heavy load on the data sources. When the data source is a transactional system, heavy load can crash the system. The QVD helps to avoid this, because it stores the same data in a compressed format. So, the Qlik Dashboard uses data from the QVD instead of direct data sources.
- **Increasing the load speed**: The QVD stores the data using a similar technique that is used by the Qlik Sense Engine to store data in memory. This enables Qlik Sense to load data faster from the QVD than loading it from the source system.
- **Allows incremental load**: The incremental load helps in decreasing the load on the source system and improving the load time. This is because in the incremental load, we fetch only the new records from the source system. The QVD helps in implementing the incremental load, because it holds the historical data and allows you to identify the last record of it, so that new data can be fetched from the source system.

- **Allows single source of truth for data**: Quite often, there are multiple copies of the same data available in multiple formats. The QVD helps to maintain the single source for all the analysis happening in various departments. For example, sales QVDs can be used by the sales team and the marketing team for their analysis.
- **Helps in creating scalable solutions**: When data grows, it becomes difficult to scale, but dashboards built with QVDs can be easily scaled-up. QVDs can be broken into multiple smaller QVDs that can be then used to scale up.

The syntax for creating the QVD is as follows:

```
Store [fieldlist from] TableName into QVDName;
```

Examples include the following:

```
Store Sales into Sales.qvd;

Store * from Sales into Sales.qvd;

Store SalesDate, Salesamount from Sales into
[Lib:\\Connectionname\Sales.qvd];
```

The following screenshot shows a script example:

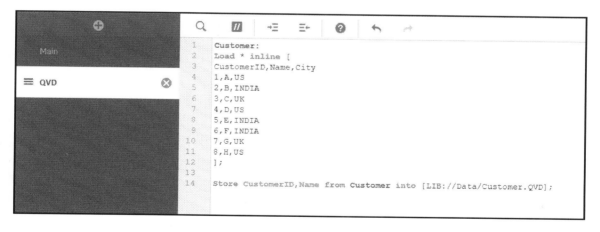

The following screenshot shows the data load from the same QVD, along with the output:

Link table

In the preceding section, *Data modeling*, we learned about the star schema, which includes one fact table and multiple dimension tables. But in the real word, there are situations when we need multiple fact tables in the data model. In such a situation, we can use two options to link them together. One is by using concatenation, and the other is by using the link table. If the granularity of the fact table is similar, we can use the option of concatenation, but if the granularity is not the same, we should use the link table option.

The link table concept requires three things:

- You need to create a composite key in each fact table
- You need to create a link table (which has common fields from both the fact table and composite key)
- If you have created the link table using resident load, you should delete the fields from the resident table that you have loaded in the link table

Let's understand the link table concept using an example.

Consider that the following are the tables that you want to load in the Qlik data model:

- **Sales**: This table contains the Country, Period, SalesPerson, ProductGroupID, and SalesAmount fields
- **Budget**: This table contains the Period, SalesPerson, ProductGroupID, and BudgetAmount fields
- **Product**: This table contains the ProductGroupID and Name fields

You can see that **Sales** and **Budget** are the fact tables and **Product** is a dimension table. When you load all three tables without changing the name of any fields, Qlik will generate the synthetic table, as shown in the following diagram:

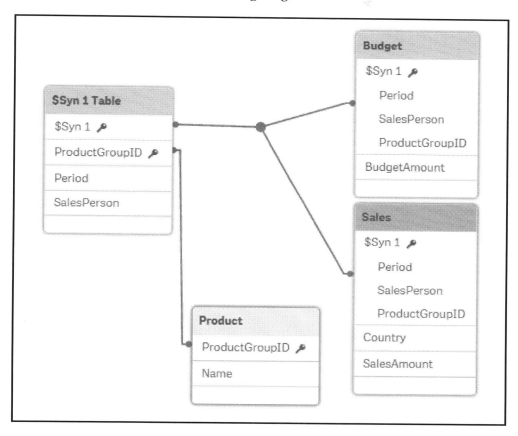

As shown in the preceding diagram, Qlik has generated the synthetic table (**$Syn1**), which is just a logical table that shows that there are common fields between two or more tables. In our example, the fields such as **ProductGroupID**, **Period**, and **SalesPerson** are common in the **Sales** and **Budget** tables and thus the synthetic table has been created.

The link table also helps in removing the synthetic table and building a proper data model to get correct values.

Now, let's see how to create a link table. The following screenshot shows the script to create a link table:

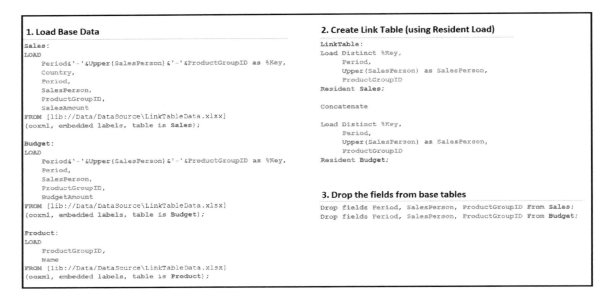

Once the preceding script is loaded, the following screenshot shows the created data model:

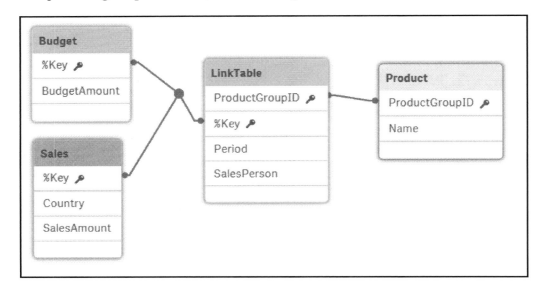

You can observe in the preceding data model that, this time, Qlik Sense did not create the synthetic table.

Canonical dates

Dates are the integral part of any data analysis. They help in analyzing the impact of something over a period of time. Thus, it becomes important to handle dates effectively to get actionable business insights. When there is only one date field in the data model, you don't need to worry, because a single master calendar can serve the requirement, but when there are multiple dates involved in data model, depending on business requirements, you can use one of the following two options:

1. **Create a separate master calendar for each date**: When the business requirement doesn't want to have a common calendar for multiple dates, you should use the separate master calendar for each of the dates. Because you do not have a common master calendar, users may get confused between the master calendars of different dates. Consider the following case:

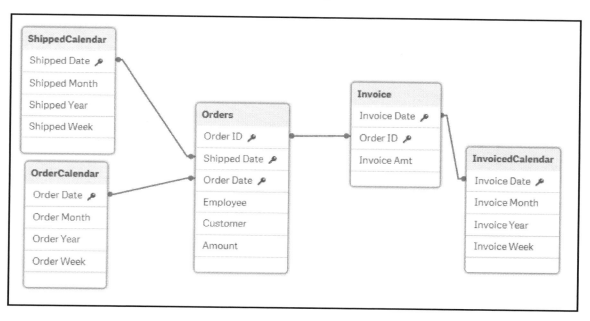

You can see in the preceding diagram that the **Orders** table has **Order Date** and **Shipped Date**, whereas the **Invoice** table has **Invoice Date**. Each of these date fields have their own calendars linked to them. This can help you answer such questions as, *can you show me the invoice month of the orders placed in January 2006?* Let's see the script in the following screenshot:

Seperate Master Calendar	Load base Data
``` Let vMin = Num(Makedate(2006)); Let vMax = num(MakeDate(2006,07)); Temp: Load Date($(vMin) + RowNo() -1) as Date AutoGenerate 1 While Date($(vMin) + RowNo() -1) < Date($(vMax)); OrderCalendar: Load Date as "Order Date", MonthName(Date) as "Order Month", Year(Date) as "Order Year", Week(Date) as "Order Week" Resident Temp; ShippedCalendar: Load Date as "Shipped Date", MonthName(Date) as "Shipped Month", Year(Date) as "Shipped Year", Week(Date) as "Shipped Week" Resident Temp; InvoicedCalendar: Load Date as "Invoice Date", MonthName(Date) as "Invoice Month", Year(Date) as "Invoice Year", Week(Date) as "Invoice Week" Resident Temp; Drop table Temp; ```	``` Orders: LOAD "Order ID", Employee, Customer, "Order Date", "Shipped Date", Amount FROM [lib://Data/Canonical Date.xlsx] (ooxml, embedded labels, table is Orders); Invoice: LOAD "Order ID", Floor("Invoice Date") as "Invoice Date", "Invoice Amt" FROM [lib://Data/Canonical Date.xlsx] (ooxml, embedded labels, table is Invoice); ```

The following screenshot shows the answer of the question we asked:

🔍 Order Month	🔍 Shipped Month	🔍 Invoice Month
Jan 2006 ✓	Jan 2006	Mar 2006
Feb 2006	Feb 2006	Jan 2006
Mar 2006	Mar 2006	Feb 2006
Apr 2006	Apr 2006	Apr 2006
May 2006	May 2006	May 2006
Jun 2006	Jun 2006	Jun 2006
Jul 2006	Jul 2006	Jul 2006

2. **Create a link table that can connect one date to multiple**: The previous method fails when you want to see the trend of order amount versus the invoice amount in a single chart. This is because both the tables have different calendars. To solve this, you need to create a link table that links all the dates together and creates a common calendar.

You need to follow these steps to create a canonical calendar:

1. Identify the table that has a fine granularity and can easily identify all the dates. This means each record should have only one value of each date (OrderId in the following example).
2. Create a link table using the common key and date from each table (the link table in the following example).
3. Add an identifier to know which date we are referring to the (the DateSource field in the following example).

Let's see the script for the same data source we used:

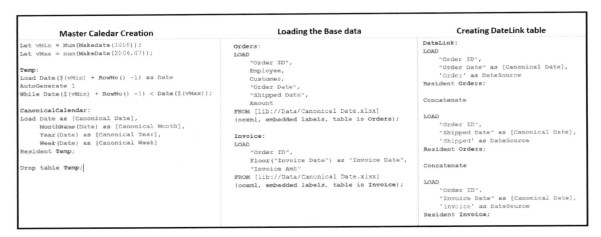

Master Caledar Creation	Loading the Base data	Creating DateLink table

```
Let vMin = Num(Makedate(2006));
Let vMax = num(MakeDate(2006,07));

Temp:
Load Date($(vMin) + RowNo() -1) as Date
AutoGenerate 1
While Date($(vMin) + RowNo() -1) < Date($(vMax));

CanonicalCalendar:
Load Date as [Canonical Date],
    MonthName(Date) as [Canonical Month],
    Year(Date) as [Canonical Year],
    Week(Date) as [Canonical Week]
Resident Temp;

Drop table Temp;
```

```
Orders:
LOAD
    "Order ID",
    Employee,
    Customer,
    "Order Date",
    "Shipped Date",
    Amount
FROM [lib://Data/Canonical Date.xlsx]
(ooxml, embedded labels, table is Orders);

Invoice:
LOAD
    "Order ID",
    Floor("Invoice Date") as "Invoice Date",
    "Invoice Amt"
FROM [lib://Data/Canonical Date.xlsx]
(ooxml, embedded labels, table is Invoice);
```

```
DateLink:
LOAD
    "Order ID",
    "Order Date" as [Canonical Date],
    'Order' as DateSource
Resident Orders;

Concatenate

LOAD
    "Order ID",
    "Shipped Date" as [Canonical Date],
    'Shipped' as DateSource
Resident Orders;

Concatenate

LOAD
    "Order ID",
    "Invoice Date" as [Canonical Date],
    'Invoice' as DateSource
Resident Invoice;
```

The following screenshot shows the model view after reloading the preceding script:

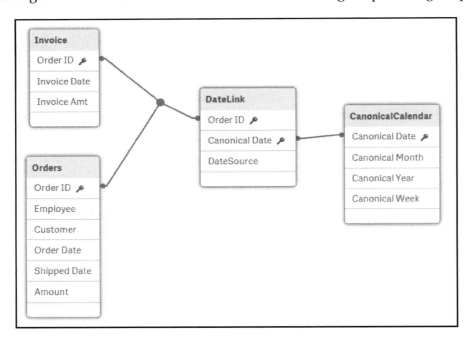

Let's see if we can plot the trends of **Order Amount** and **Invoice Amount** in a single chart with a common time dimension. The following screenshot shows the trends:

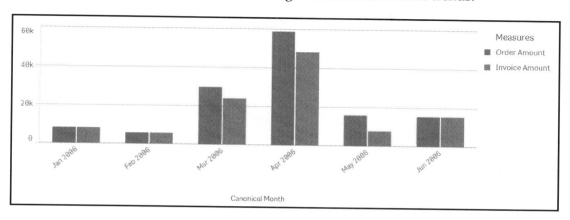

As-Of Table

We often get the requirement of calculating rolling averages and accumulations of values over a period of time. And we mostly think of calculating these on the frontend (in chart expressions) using the Above() function. This works fine when we have a small amount of data, but when the data grows, the chart that calculates the accumulations or rolling averages starts affecting performance. In such a situation, it is recommended to move the calculation somehow in the script. The **As-Of Table** helps to achieve rolling averages and accumulations in the script.

Before we start learning about the As-Of Table, let's understand what accumulations are.

An **accumulation** is the summation of the data from previous x dimension values, and mostly, it is calculated over a time dimension. For example, the following screenshot shows the full accumulation:

Month 🔍	Sales	Accumulation
Jan	40,363	40,363
Feb	43,065	83,428
Mar	40,276	123,704
Apr	29,280	152,984
May	26,783	179,768
Jun	28,768	208,535
Jul	27,690	236,225
Aug	22,196	258,421
Sep	21,813	280,235
Oct	25,155	305,389
Nov	19,962	325,352
Dec	29,989	355,341

You can see in the preceding screenshot that the accumulation value of **Feb** is the sales value of **Jan** + **Feb**. Similarly, for March it is **Jan** + **Feb** + **March** sales.

Now, let's see how we achieve same thing using an As-Of Table.

The As-Of Table is an intermediate table that contains the AsOfMonth field and Month field, which is further connected to the actual months. The As-Of Table is created using the **Cartesian join**. The following screenshot shows the script for the As-Of Table:

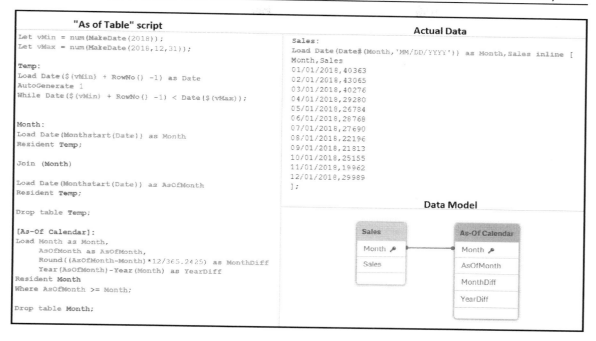

If you observe the preceding screenshot, you will see that we have created dates using the sample script, and then created a month from those dates. Then, that Month table is joined with a new field name, AsOfMonth. This way, we created a Cartesian table.

In a Cartesian table (Month), each value of AsOfMonth will have 12 values for the Month field. But the AsOfMonth value is relevant only when the Month value is lower than that; thus, we added a Where condition to filter unwanted values (0).

Now, when we create a table with `AsOfMonth` as a dimension and `Sum(Sales)` as an expression, we get the full accumulation, which we got by using the `Above()` function in the chart expression. The following screenshot shows the output:

AsOfMonth 🔍	Sum(Sales)
1/1/2018	40,363
2/1/2018	83,428
3/1/2018	123,704
4/1/2018	152,984
5/1/2018	179,768
6/1/2018	208,536
7/1/2018	236,226
8/1/2018	258,422
9/1/2018	280,235
10/1/2018	305,390
11/1/2018	325,352
12/1/2018	355,341

In the script, you will also see that two more fields are created. One is `MonthDiff` and the other is `YearDiff`. The `MonthDiff` field helps to set the accumulation month. So, if you want the accumulation only for the last three months, instead of all the months, you should use the following expression:

```
Sum({<MonthDiff = {"<3"}>}Sales)
```

The following screenshot shows an example:

AsOfMonth 🔍	Sum({<MonthDiff = {"<3"}>}Sales)
1/1/2018	40,363
2/1/2018	83,428
3/1/2018	123,704
4/1/2018	112,621
5/1/2018	96,340
6/1/2018	84,832
7/1/2018	83,242
8/1/2018	78,654
9/1/2018	71,699
10/1/2018	69,164
11/1/2018	66,930
12/1/2018	75,106

If you want to get the actual values of the sales per month, you should use the following expression:

```
Sum({<MonthDiff = {"0"}>}Sales)
```

The following screenshot shows an example:

AsOfMonth 🔍	Sum({<MonthDiff = {"0"}>}Sales)
1/1/2018	40,363
2/1/2018	43,065
3/1/2018	40,276
4/1/2018	29,280
5/1/2018	26,784
6/1/2018	28,768
7/1/2018	27,690
8/1/2018	22,196
9/1/2018	21,813
10/1/2018	25,155
11/1/2018	19,962
12/1/2018	29,989

Similarly, the `YearDiff` field is used to get the accumulation for the year. The expression for that would be `Sum({<YearDiff={"0"}>} Sales)`.

If you want to create the rolling 3 months average, you should use following expression:

```
Sum({<MonthDiff = {"<3"}>}Sales) / Count(Distinct {<MonthDiff = {"
    <3"}>}Month)
```

Script optimization

So far, we have seen various techniques that can be used while creating the data model, which can help to cater for complex business requirements. While handling complex requirements in the script, we often forget to keep the script optimized for better performance.

In this section, we are going to learn some important practices that should be followed to get better performance from the script and increase reload time.

Using Applymap instead of joins

We learned in the preceding section about joins and their use cases. When it comes to using joins in Qlik Sense, it has been seen that a join on larger tables slows down the data loading and, if not used properly, may consume higher resources. Also, we have seen the pitfalls of using joins, as they tend to increase the number of records.

When you want to perform the join to get a single field value, the best way is to use an alternative method: Applymap().

Applymap()

This function uses the earlier loaded mapping table data to replace a field value where it is used. It should be used with the Load statement:

The syntax for using Applymap is Applymap ('Map Table Name', Mapping FieldName or Expression, [Default Mapping]).

The following are the arguments passed in the function:

- Map Table Name: This is the name of the table that has been created earlier using the Mapping prefix. You must enclose the name of the table in single quotes.
- Mapping FieldName or Expression: This is the field or the expression for which the value should be mapped.
- Default Mapping: This is an optional parameter that is used when mapping is not found.

For example, imagine you have data with the name of the United States written in a number of different forms, such as USA, U.S., and so on. You want to replace the different values (as shown in following screenshot) to a single value of US. The following screenshot shows the script:

```
CountryMap:
Mapping Load * inline [
OldName, NewName
U.S.,US
USA,US
US,US
U.S,US
];

Data:
Load *,
Applymap('CountryMap',Country,'Unknown') as MappedCountry
inline [
Year,Country,Sales
2018,U.S.,1000
2018,INDIA,2000
2017,USA, 900
2017,UK, 800
2016,U.S,700
2016,INDIA,800
];
```

You can see in the preceding screenshot that we have created a mapping table before using the Applymap function. This mapping table has two columns, one for the old value and one for the new value. The old value is the field that contains the value that needs to be replaced, and the new value is the field that contains the value that it needs to be replaced with.

The output of the script is as follows:

Year	Country	MappedCountry	Sales
2016	INDIA	Unknown	800
2016	U.S	US	700
2017	UK	Unknown	800
2017	USA	US	900
2018	INDIA	Unknown	2000
2018	U.S.	US	1000

Reducing the size of data as much as possible

We all know that Qlik Sense loads all the data loaded using the script in RAM. The more the data you have, the more RAM is required, along with more time to transfer the data to the RAM. So, as a script optimization process, you should look at possible ways to reduce the size of the data.

Some ways to reduce the size of the data are explained in the following list:

- **Remove unwanted fields**: Often, it is seen that the developer loads all the fields available in the table in the Qlik Sense data model. This is fine when the data is small, and the numbers of columns are few, but when the data is huge, and the columns are many, the developer should remove or comment the unwanted fields from the data model. This helps to quicken the data loading process.
- **Reduce distinct values**: Qlik Sense stores only the distinct values in the RAM, so when you have more distinct values in data, your data size is more. Thus, you should try to decrease distinct data. For example, your source system may have a timestamp field, but for your analysis, you do not require the time. In such cases, you can remove the time from the timestamp field, which will reduce the size of the data.
- **Use the** `AutoNumber` **function**: While implementing the link table in the data model, we saw that we need to create the composite key, which is the concatenation of multiple fields. These composite keys are distinct in nature and contain text values, but they are needed only to link two or more tables with each other. In such cases, we can convert the text value of the composite key with the number using the `AutoNumber()` function.

The `AutoNumber()` function allocates each unique distinct value to the unique value of the text field. This way, you can reduce the data size, because the text value requires more space then numeric values.

Optimized QVD load

In a preceding section, we learned about QVDs and how to use them. One of the advantages of a QVD is that it improves the data load time, but there is the possibility to further optimize it to give better performance. The QVD load performance can be improved by using the optimized QVD load. First, let's look at the non-optimized QVD load.

Non-optimized load

When you use the following operations while loading data from the QVD, it is called **non-optimized load**:

- Adding a new field
- Use of any expression/calculation in a field
- Retrieving fields twice
- Joins using QVD

The non-optimized load doesn't improve load time at all; instead, it may increase the data load time.

The following script shows an example of the non-optimized load:

Example 1	Example 2
``Sales:
LOAD
"Order ID",
Employee,
Customer,
"Order Date",
MonthName("Order Date") as "Order Month",
"Shipped Date",
Amount
FROM [lib://Data/Sales.qvd]
(qvd);```	```Sales:
LOAD
"Order ID",
Employee,
Customer,
"Order Date",
"Shipped Date",
Amount
FROM [lib://Data/Sales.qvd]
(qvd) Where Amount > 1000;```

Optimized load

The optimized load is 100 times faster than the non-optimized load. This is because you do not perform any operations while loading the data. So, when there are no operations, Qlik can directly move the QVD data to the RAM, which makes it faster. There are a few operations that, when used on QVD, will be considered as the optimized load:

- Renaming of the field
- Use of existing functions with only one parameter

The following screenshot shows the optimized LOAD script:

Example 1:

```
Sales:
LOAD
    "Order ID",
    Employee,
    Customer,
    "Order Date",
    "Order Date" as "Calendar Date",
    "Shipped Date",
    Amount
FROM [lib://Data/Sales.qvd]
(qvd);
```

```
Started loading data

Sales << Sales
(QVD (row-based) optimized)
Lines fetched: 48
Creating search index
Search index creation completed successfully

App saved

Finished successfully

0 forced error(s)

0 synthetic key(s)
```

And the following is a second example:

```
DontLoadThisID:
Load * inline [
Order ID
32
38
45
51
62
68
72
];


Sales:
LOAD
    "Order ID",
    Employee,
    Customer,
    "Order Date",
    "Order Date" as "Calendar Date",
    "Shipped Date",
    Amount
FROM [lib://Data/Sales.qvd]
(qvd) where not Exists("Order ID");
```

```
Started loading data

DontLoadThisID << da555997-6049-4741-bda7-fa549ffb3fcc
Lines fetched: 7
Sales << Sales
(QVD (row-based) optimized)
Lines fetched: 41
Creating search index
Search index creation completed successfully

App saved

Finished successfully

0 forced error(s)

0 synthetic key(s)
```

If you want to know if the QVD load is optimized or not, you should look at the Qlik script logs or you can check the script progress window (just like seen in the preceding both examples). In the preceding both examples, you can see the highlighted text from the progress window. It shows that the load is the optimized load.

Dropping unwanted tables immediately after use

Quite often, we create temporary tables to do some calculations and, after using them, we drop them. Many developers consolidate such drop statements from all the tabs of the script and place them at the end of the script.

When they do this, they forget that the data used by the temporary tables remains in the RAM until the script reaches the drop statement for those tables. This increases the load time and the RAM required to load the data. This creates performance issues when the temporary tables hold a large amount of data.

For example, you may use the transactional table for some calculation and, after calculation, you may store it with a different name. Now, if you do not drop the table immediately, the script holds the data of both tables in the RAM, which unnecessarily increases RAM usage. The RAM will be released only when the drop statement for that table is executed.

Therefore, the suggested best optimization practice is to drop the unwanted tables immediately after use.

Summary

In this chapter, we learned about the data modeling techniques. We started with learning about the basics of data modeling. We looked at two types of data modeling: entity relationship modeling and dimensional modeling. We looked at dimensional modeling in detail and learned about the two widely-used data modeling schema: the *star schema* and the *snowflake schema*. We learned about which schema works best with Qlik Sense and why.

Moving ahead in chapter, we learned about different types of joins. We learned about what type of join is used for what purpose and what kind of output they generate. Then we looked at the pitfalls of using joins. It is important to keep thses in mind while using joins. Then, we learned about concatenation and the scenarios in which we should use the concatenation option. We also looked at automatic concatenation, forced concatenation, and NoConcatenation.

Further, we learned about the ways in which data can be filtered while loading in Qlik Sense. We also learned about QVD. We understood why we should use data loading from QVD, and not from direct data source.

Then we learned about the link table, which is used when you want to link multiple fact tables with different granularities of data. We learned about the way in which multiple dates can be handled in Qlik Sense using the concept of canonical dates. We saw that the best option is to create the accumulations and rolling averages in the script using the As-Of Table. Lastly, we learned about the various options to keep our Qlik Sense scripts as optimized as possible to get better performance.

Sample questions

1. What are two types of data modeling technique?
2. Which technique is most suitable for Qlik Sense and why?
3. Which joining condition should we use to get all data from the left table?
4. What precaution should we take while using joins?
5. What is NoConcatenation? When should we use it?
6. What is the link table? Can the link table help in removing the synthetic table? If yes, how?
7. In what scenario would we use canonical dates?
8. Why should we use the As-Of Table?
9. How do we optimize the script?

Further reading

Refer to the following links for more information on the topics covered here:

- *As-Of Table* (https://community.qlik.com/t5/Qlik-Design-Blog/The-As-Of-Table/ba-p/1466130)
- *Canonical Date* (https://community.qlik.com/t5/Qlik-Design-Blog/Canonical-Date/ba-p/1463578)
- *Join and Concatenate* (https://qlikviewcookbook.com/2009/11/understanding-join-and-concatenate/)

Section 3: Building an Analytical Application

You will learn how to analyze the data loaded using several visualization objects in the Qlik Sense app and share the app through Qlik Sense Enterprise or Qlik Sense Cloud.

The following chapters will be covered in this section:

4
Working with Application Structure

In this chapter, we will explore the key concepts of a Qlik Sense application design. Along with this, we shall look at the principles of building a Qlik Sense app using the **Dashboard, Analysis, Reporting (DAR)** methodology, learn how to use the visualization objects that are available to the user, and how to create and use Master items to reuse dimensions and measures across visualizations. Finally, we will understand how to use the Qlik Sense user interface and the basics of calculation expressions.

In this chapter, we will cover the following topics:

- Application overview
- Understanding the DAR methodology
- Creating visualization objects
- Creating Master items
- Calculation expressions

Technical requirements

For this chapter, we will use the application created in Chapter 3, *Implementing Data Modeling Techniques*, as a starting point with a preloaded data model.

You can also download the initial version of the `.qvf` file for this application, named `CH4_start.qvd`, from the book repository on GitHub at `https://github.com/PacktPublishing/Hands-On-Qlik-Sense/tree/master/Chapter04`.

After downloading the application, you should carry out the following steps:

- If you are using Qlik Sense Desktop, place the application in the `Qlik\Sense\Apps` folder, which is located underneath the `Documents` folder.
- If you are using Qlik Sense Cloud, upload the application to your personal workspace.

Application overview

A Qlik Sense application combines data in the form of a structured data model, visualizations, sheets, and stories. Dimensions, measures, and visualizations can be created as data items that can be reused between several visualizations (charts) and sheets (visualizations).

Let's take a look at each of these application components in brief. The components of an application are as follows:

- **Data model**: A data model contains all the data that is loaded by the load script as well as several tables, each connected by unique fields. Every time we change the data load script, we reload the application to update the data model.
- **Measures**: Measures contain expressions that we can implement in visualizations. These expressions have one or several field aggregate functions, such as sum, avg, min, and max. Changes in the measure expressions affect all related visualizations. Measures are stored in the **Master items** library.
- **Dimensions**: Dimensions define how to group data in a visualization. We can create a dimension with one field, or we can create a hierarchical dimension with two or more fields. Changes in the dimension field affect all related visualizations. Dimensions are stored in the **Master items** library.
- **Visualizations**: Visualizations are charts and tables that are created in a sheet. Visualizations can use dimensions and measures stored as **Master items**. A visualization can also be created as a Master item to be reused across sheets.

- **Sheets**: Sheets contains visualizations for a single analysis. We can create several sheets, each one with a different analytical purpose.
- **Bookmarks**: Bookmarks allow us to save the current selection on a sheet. We can open an app and directly select a bookmark to go back to the saved selection and sheet. We can also use this as our initial selection when opening the app.
- **Stories**: We can create a presentation using snapshots of visualizations with specific selections combining several visualizations on each slide. We can also use the entire sheet as a slide. Stories can be exported to PDF or PPTX format for further modification.

When opening an application, we can see the overview interface. From there, we have direct access to the sheets, bookmarks, and stories that have already been created.

When working with Qlik Sense Desktop, or a non-published application in Qlik Sense Enterprise or Qlik Cloud, we are free to add new sheets to the application. These are called **base sheets**.

When working with a published application on Qlik Sense Enterprise, if we have the permission to create new sheets, we can also create a private sheet. This sheet can be published and explored by the other users. In the Qlik Cloud, we can only navigate the sheets on a published application.

Toolbars

At the top of our screen, we see the main toolbar. Each button opens a menu that helps us access various tools, as shown in the following screenshot:

- **Navigation menu**: The first button opens the navigation menu. This gives us easy access to the data tools, such as Data manager, Data load editor, and Data model viewer. It also gives us a shortcut to access the hub to open another app.
- **Information menu**: The second button is the information menu. This allows us to access online help and information about the product.

- **Save button**: The third button is the Save button. This is only available on the Qlik Sense Desktop. For Qlik Cloud and Qlik Sense Enterprise, the changes in the application interface are saved automatically.
- **Toggle button**: The application title is a toggle button. Clicking on the title helps us hide or display application information. We can edit the application information (name and description), and there are also options to style the app.

The second toolbar can be used to manage sheets, bookmarks, and stories. The following screenshot depicts the various buttons on the second row:

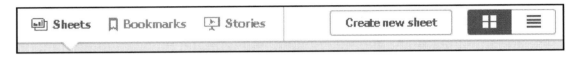

- **Sheets**: This shows the sheets available for exploration and also gives the option to create a new sheet
- **Bookmarks**: This shows the bookmarks available for direct and easy access to selections and sheets
- **Stories**: This displays the stories available for presentation and also helps to create stories

We can change the display by switching from grid view to list view using the buttons at the right-hand side of the toolbar.

Understanding the DAR methodology

DAR stands for Dashboard, Analysis, Reporting, as mentioned in the introduction to this chapter. In this section, we will learn about the DAR methodology that we will apply to our apps.

To keep it simple, we will begin by creating a Dashboard sheet, followed by several Analysis sheets, and finally a Reporting sheet. A Dashboard sheet shows business information at a high-level for quick overview. The Analysis sheets gives more detailed information showing interactive visualizations with various perspectives, such as customers, sales representatives, or products. The Reporting sheet displays the same information in a more granular form.

Let's look at these sheets more closely, as follows:

- **Dashboard**: The Dashboard sheet is one of the most important sheets of your app. This contains the most user relevant information. At a glance, this makes it easy for a user to understand whether the key performance indicator is getting better or worse. Let's look at the following screenshot, which gives us a quick overview of the business:

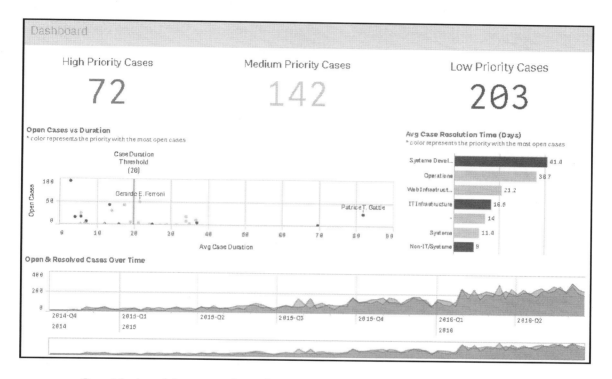

Considering this screenshot, if a user is curious about the **High Priority Cases** and wants more information about them, they can dig in deeper using a specific sheet created for Analysis.

- **Analysis**: While the `Dashboard` sheet shows information pertaining to several topics for a quick overview, analysis focuses on a single topic for data exploration. It does this with the help of more interaction using several sets of charts. This type of sheet allows the user to slice the data and delve deeper in order to achieve some insight. The following screenshot depicts an example of an `Analysis` sheet to review the performance of each **CaseOwner**:

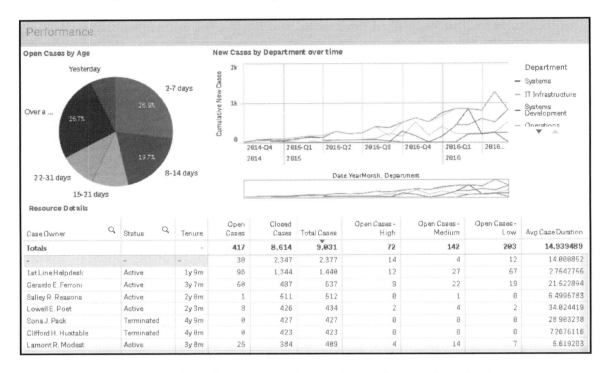

Case Owner	Status	Tenure	Open Cases	Closed Cases	Total Cases	Open Cases - High	Open Cases - Medium	Open Cases - Low	Avg Case Duration
Totals		-	417	8,614	9,031	72	142	203	14.939489
-	-	-	30	2,347	2,377	14	4	12	14.008852
1st Line Helpdesk	Active	1y 9m	96	1,344	1,440	12	27	57	2.7642756
Gerardo E. Ferroni	Active	3y 7m	50	487	537	9	22	19	21.522894
Salley R. Reasons	Active	2y 8m	1	511	512	0	1	0	5.4996783
Lowell E. Poet	Active	2y 3m	8	426	434	2	4	2	34.024419
Sona J. Pack	Terminated	4y 9m	0	427	427	0	0	0	28.983238
Clifford H. Huxtable	Terminated	4y 8m	0	423	423	0	0	0	7.2676116
Lamont R. Modest	Active	3y 8m	26	384	409	4	14	7	5.619283

A user selects a **CaseOwner** to understand how they perform individually or can select on.

- **Reporting**: Reporting sheets allow the user to see a more granular form of data. This mostly comes in the form of a tabular object. This type of sheet provides information that allows the user to take action at an operational level. The following screenshot gives an example of a Reporting sheet showing a detailed table:

The user can check the detailed information and export the selected data to the **CaseOwner** as well as checking why it takes so long to close some cases.

Creating visualization objects

Qlik Sense provides several visualization objects to explore and analyze the data that is loaded into the application. The visualizations can show information in the form of charts with bars, lines, gauges, pies, and so on. Tables and textboxes are also available to show text-based information. Maps are available to show geospatial information.

In this section, we will learn how to create charts using the existing data loaded into the application.

Getting started

The following steps will help us to create and use a new sheet, as follows:

1. Open the app and click on **Create new sheet**, as demonstrated in the following screenshot:

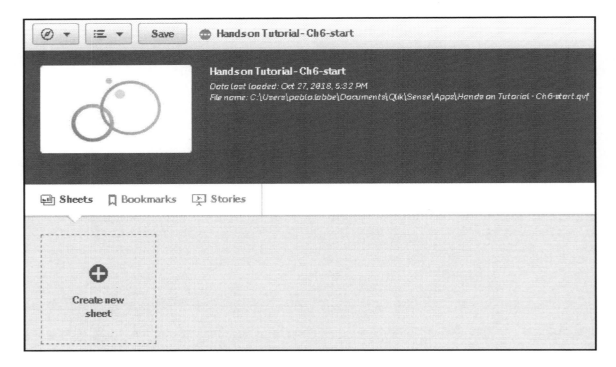

2. Set the title of the sheet to My first charts, as follows:

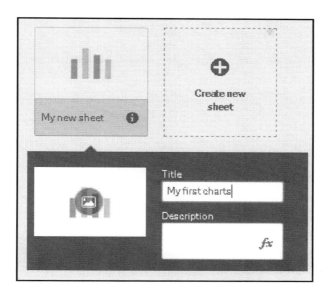

3. Click on the sheet icon to save the title and open the sheet to start creating visualizations, as follows:

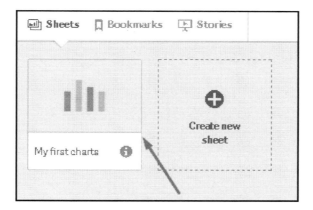

4. At this point, we can see an empty sheet. We now have two options that are highlighted in the following screenshot:

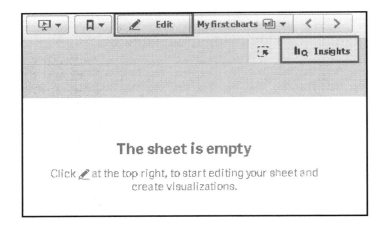

These options include the following:

- **Insights Advisor**: By clicking on the **Insights Advisor** button, we let Qlik Sense scan the data automatically and suggest some interesting visualizations.
- **Edit**: The **Edit** button will help us enter the sheet in edit mode. We can then start creating visualizations ourselves.

Generating visualizations using Insights Advisor

The Insights Advisor will let us explore our data. It does not care whether we have any previous knowledge about the information that is being presented to us. Instead, it uses the power of the new Qlik Cognitive Engine to create visualizations for us. We can generate visualizations that scan all of the data of our application, or we can select a field or a Master item and let Insights Advisor suggest some charts based on the data.

The following steps will help us to use Insights Advisor to the fullest:

1. Click on the **Insights** button and then click on the **Generate Insights** button, as shown in the following screenshot:

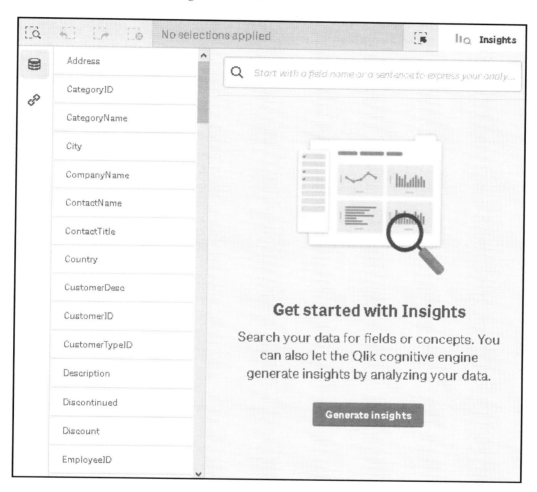

2. After a short amount of time, several visualizations will be generated and displayed on the screen.

3. Scroll down to review the suggested visualizations. We can add the one we find most interesting or informative to the sheet using the **Add to sheet** button. For this exercise, let's choose the first visualization and click on the **Add to sheet** button, and then select the **My first charts** sheet:

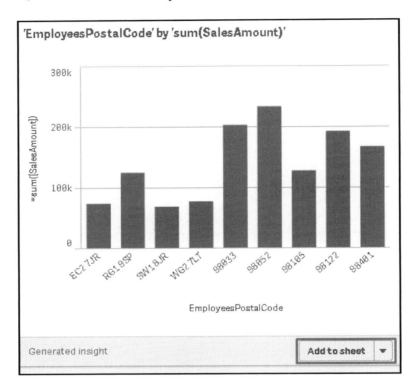

4. The **Add to sheet** message will be displayed at the bottom of the screen. This is just to confirm that the suggested chart has been added to the sheet. Optionally, we can click on the shortcut at the bottom-right of our screen in order to proceed to the sheet, as demonstrated in the following screenshot:

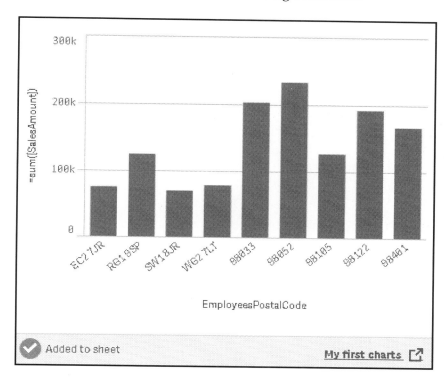

Generating visualizations using Insights Advisor for selected fields

In the following example, we will learn how to generate visualizations for selected fields:

1. We can select the fields we want on our sheet using the panel in the right-hand side of the screen. Alternatively, we can also type the field name or a sentence in the Insight search field, as follows:

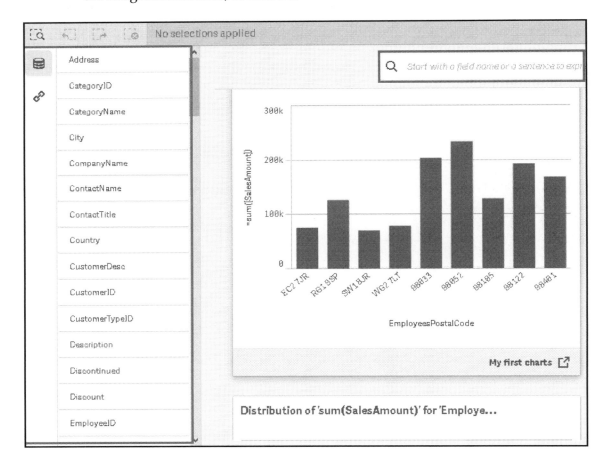

2. Here, we select the **CompanyName** button to see several visualizations related to any particular company name. We can see that the selected field name is added to our search box in the following screenshot:

3. Now, we type `Country` into the Insights search field. As we do this, we see a list of fields matching the criteria. Select **Country** from this list, as shown in the following screenshot:

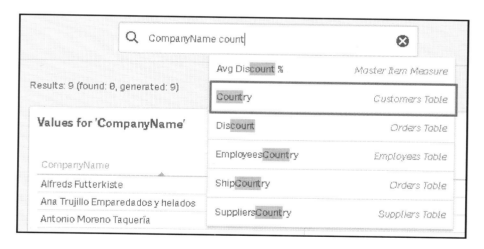

Several visualizations with a combination of `CompanyName` and `Country`, along with other fields, are created. Visualizations that only have the two fields are also created.

4. Let's scroll down and add two more visualizations. Add each one to the **My first charts** sheet using the **Add to sheet** button:

- The `'Country'` by `'countdistinct(CompanyName)'` visualization is as follows:

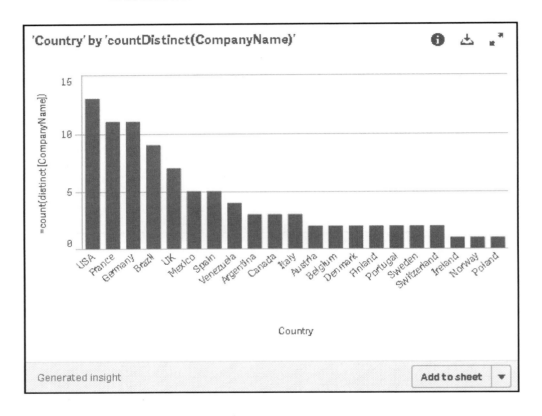

- The `Distribution of 'sum(SalesAmount)' for 'Country'` visualization is as follows:

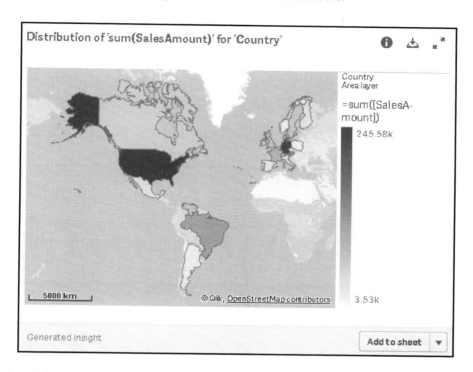

The Insights Advisor suggests some interesting visualizations, combining fields that we would never think could be combined.

We can select fields and **Master items** if we are working in an unpublished application on Qlik Sense Enterprise or Qlik Sense Desktop. We can only select **Master items** if we are using a published application on a stream.

We can also interact with the insight visualizations before adding them to the sheet. When we select a visualization, it expands and allows us to interact with it. Selections on the selected chart will carry over to other insight visualizations on the page, as well as visualizations that are already added to the sheet.

Creating visualizations using chart suggestions

Qlik Sense provides a wide range of visualizations, such as charts, tables, and maps. Selecting one of them could be a challenge, especially if the user is now using a data visualization tool. With the assistance of the cognitive engine, Qlik Sense suggests a visualization when we add a field to the sheet. Adding new fields in the visualization, changes it to show the best visualization for the selected dimensions and measures.

The following example will show us how to work with the chart suggestions:

1. Click on the **Insight** button to close it and go to the sheet. The sheet will look as follows:

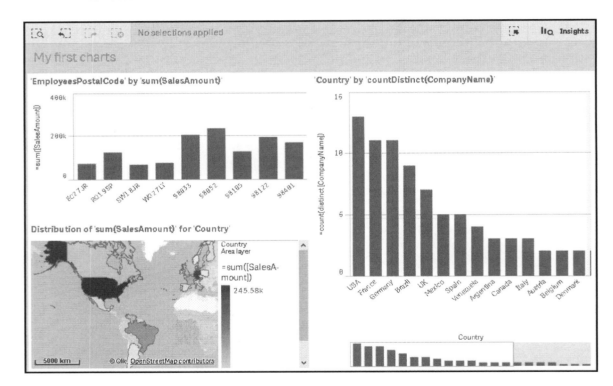

2. Use the **Edit** button to enter the edit mode on the sheet. Reduce the height of the bar chart on the right to add space for a new chart. Use the handlers at the border to change the size, and match the chart with the same height as the bar chart on the left, as demonstrated in the following screenshot:

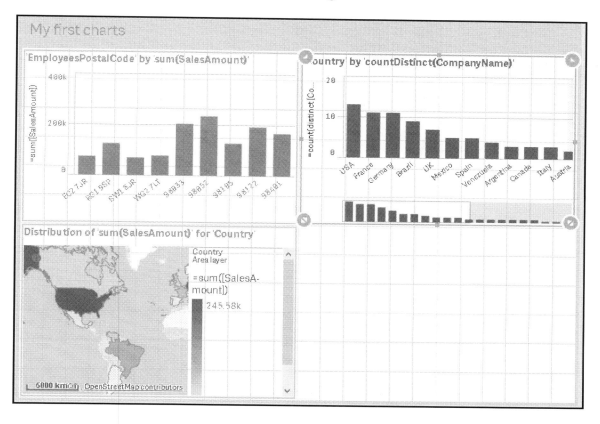

3. Now, click on the **Fields** button on the asset panel, which is on the left-hand side of the screen and search for the SalesAmount field. We can go through the entire list until we find this or type the name of field into the search box, as follows:

4. Click on the **SalesAmount** field and drag and drop it into the empty space on the sheet, as demonstrated in the following screenshot:

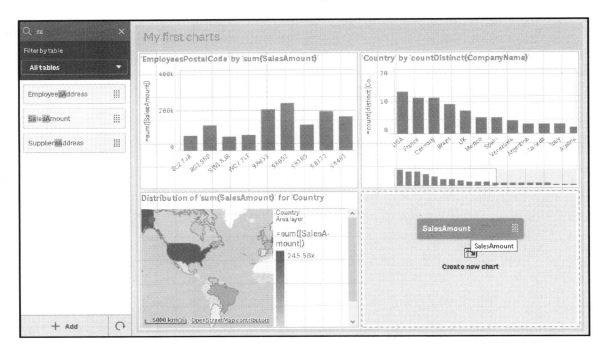

5. Qlik Sense creates a new visualization of the **Key Performance Indicator (KPI)** type because we have selected a field with numeric data, as follows:

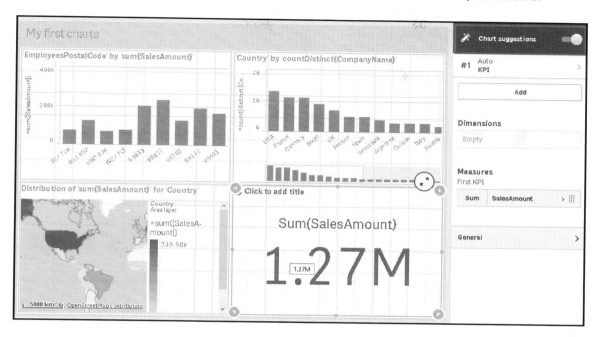

 Note that the **Chart suggestions** option lies at the top-right corner of the property panel.

6. Next, go to the field list on the right, clear the search box, and move the **Country** field, laying it on top of the new chart, as follows:

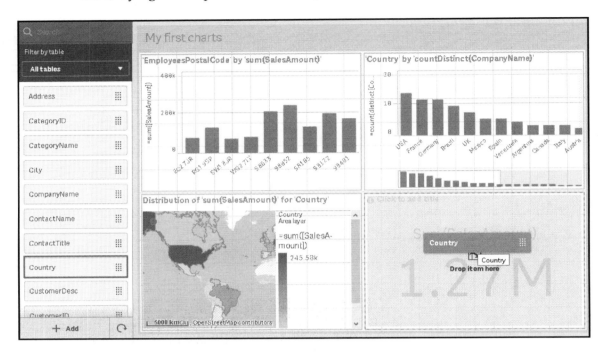

7. The chart suggestion then detects that the **Country** field provides location information, and this can be shown as a map as follows:

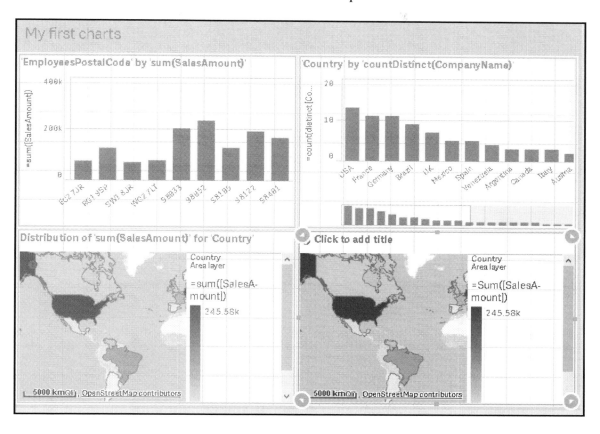

8. It is observed that the new chart is the same as the previous chart generated by the Insight Advisor. So, we already have a map with the same information. The question here is: can we show this information with a different chart? The answer to this is *yes*, and the **Chart suggestions** feature also allows us to view other recommendations. Click on the button highlighted in the following screenshot to open the recommendation panel:

9. The chart recommendation panel depicts several charts available for the selected fields, as follows:

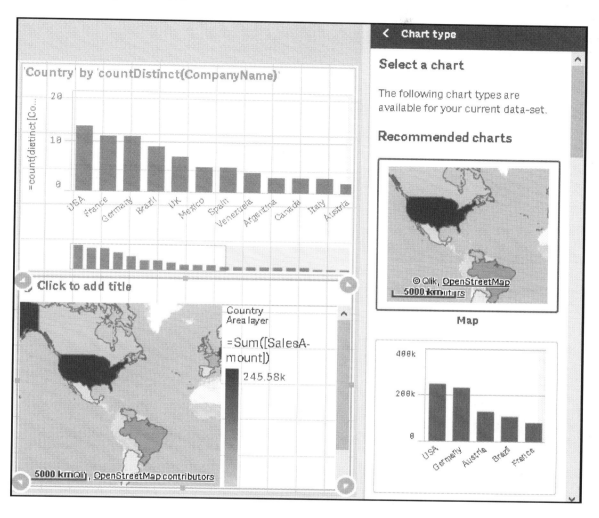

10. Click on the bar chart to change the visualization in the sheet, as follows:

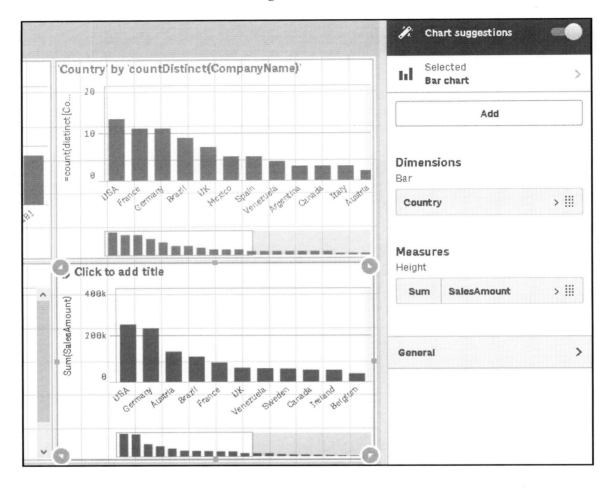

11. To add a title to the chart, we can click on the title placeholder inside the chart and type `Sales by Country`. We can also open the general section panel and set the **Title, Subtitle**, and **Footnote** buttons for the chart, as follows:

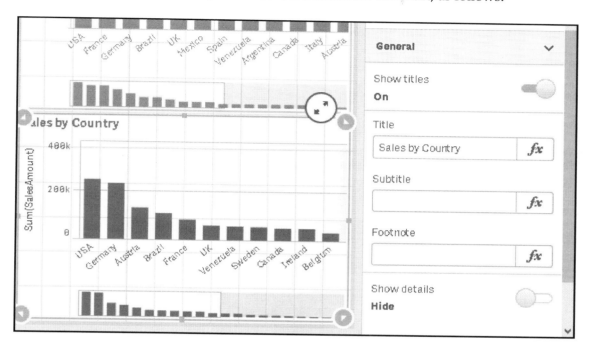

12. When we create a chart with a chart suggestion, we have limited options for customization. To fully customize any chart, we need to switch off the **Chart suggestions** button. Once this is done, the full property panel is available for chart customization of **Data** (dimensions and measures), **Sorting, Add-ons**, and **Appearance**, as follows:

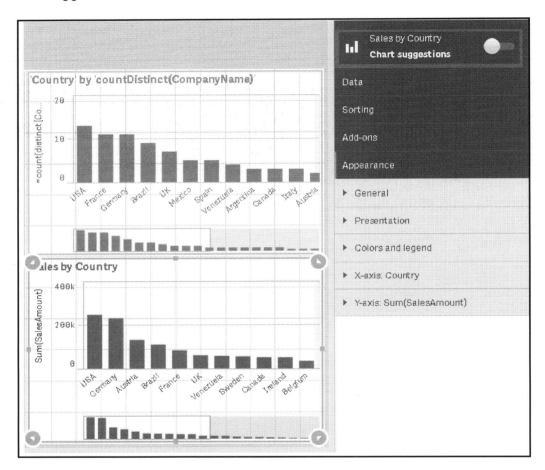

Creating visualizations manually

Once a user is familiar with the charts and their customization in Qlik Sense, they may prefer to create a chart manually. The following example shows how to create a chart manually, as well as how to apply some appearance customization:

We need to make room for the new chart. We do this by deleting one of the charts present on the sheet.

1. Select the first bar chart in the following screenshot with the title **'EmployeesPostalCode' by 'sum(SalesAmount)'**:

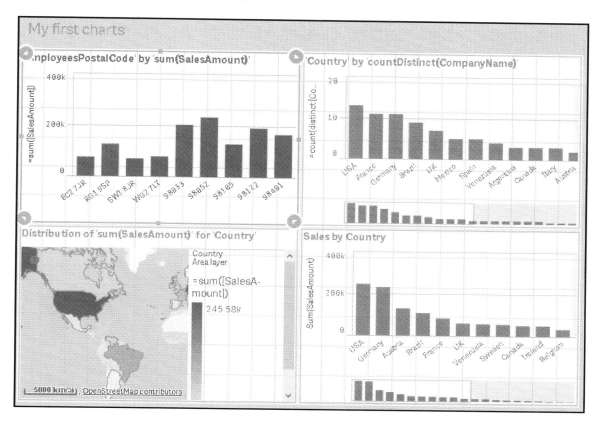

To delete the chart, select it by right-clicking the mouse and selecting **Delete from the menu**. You can also use the *Delete* key on the keyboard, or click on the **Trash** button on the panel at the bottom of the screen.

2. After deleting the chart, click on the **Charts** button in the asset panel and drag the **Pie chart** to the blank space on the sheet, as demonstrated in the following screenshot:

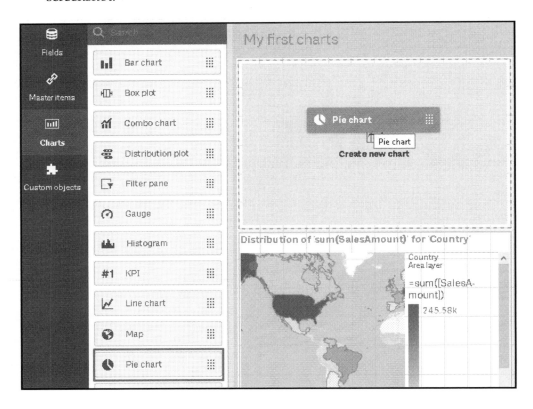

3. Click on the **Add dimension** button and select **CategoryName** from the **Fields** list, as follows:

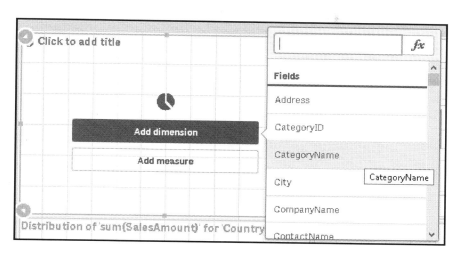

4. Click on the **Add measure** button and select **SalesAmount** from the **Fields** list, as follows:

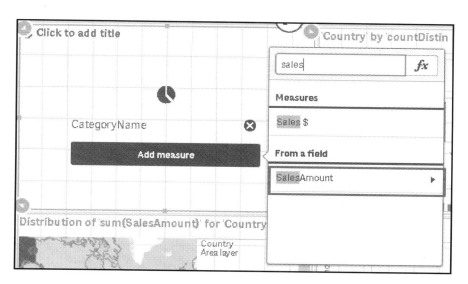

5. When selecting a measure from a field, we need to select the **Aggregation** button for the field. In this example, we select **Sum(SalesAmount)**:

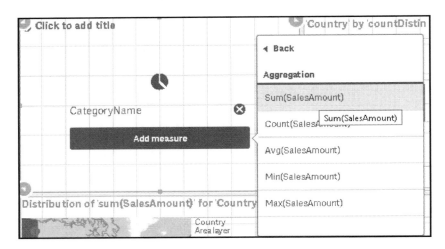

6. The chart will look like the following screenshot:

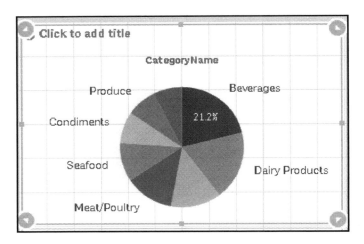

7. To help us to select and explore the data shown in the visualization at any specific point of time, we can also add a filter panel to the sheet.

8. Make some room at the top of the sheet by reducing the height of the charts and leaving a blank row.

9. Drag the **Filter panel** item onto the area of free space to create the chart, as follows:

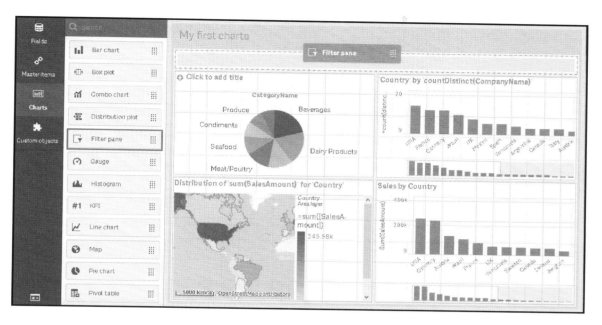

10. After the chart is created, in the right panel, click on the **Add dimension** button, as follows:

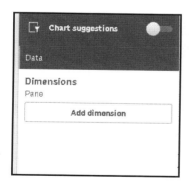

11. Add the following fields: **OrderYear**, **OrderMonth**, and **OrderDate**. These fields will be shown in the **Dimensions Pane**, as well as in the sheet, as follows:

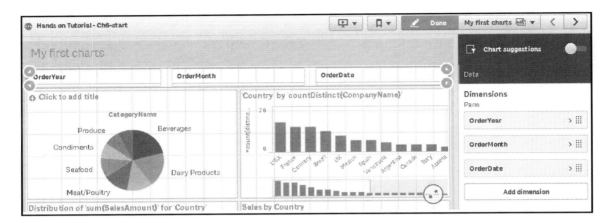

12. Click **Done** to enter view mode. Now, we can freely explore the visualization we've created so far, as follows:

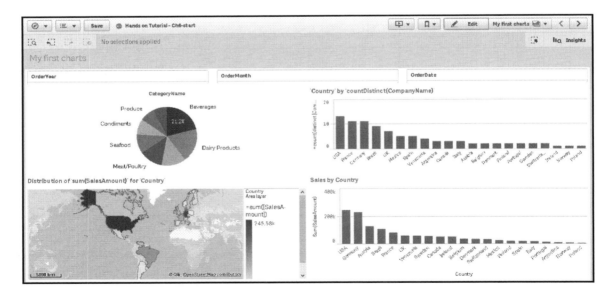

Creating Master items

When we create a chart, we select fields as the source for the dimensions and measures within the chart. For measures, we need to select the aggregation function. This process is repeated for each chart that we create in the sheet. Changing a measure in one chart doesn't affect the measures defined in other charts, even if they are related to the same field. Let's consider the **SalesAmount** example. Similar to when we change a field in a dimension, changing a dimension field in one chart doesn't affect the dimension defined in other charts.

It could become difficult to set the same business rule each time we create a new chart. It's also difficult to review and update all of the charts in an app when a measure expression changes. The best practice to overcome this situation is to create **Master items**.

Master items allow us to define a set of dimensions and measures that can be reused across various charts. This is a key function that enables the self-service creation of visualizations by business users. Changes in a dimension or measure in the Master item library carry over to the charts that are using it.

Visualizations can be added to the Master item library and converted to a linked visualization. A linked visualization can be added to multiple sheets. Changes in the linked visualization carry over to all sheets that it has been added to.

In this section, we will learn the basics of how to create master dimensions, measures, and visualizations.

Creating master dimensions

A dimension is used to define how data is grouped in a visualization. In the charts that we have created so far, under the `My first charts` sheet, we have the following fields used as chart dimension: `CategoryName` and `Country`.

The following steps depict how to create a master dimension:

1. If we are in view mode, click on the **Edit** button to enter the edit mode.
2. Click on the **Master items** button to open the Master item pane.
3. Click on the **Dimension** pane to expand it.
4. Click on the **Create new** button in the Dimension pane to create a new dimension.
5. In the Dimension editor panel, select **Country** from the field list. Keep the name the same as the field name.

6. To define a default color for the dimension, use the color combo box to open the color picker and select the color yellow, which has the hex code #ffcf02.

7. Click outside the color picker to close it and return to the Dimension editor panel, as shown in the following screenshot:

8. Next, click on the **Add dimension** button to create the dimension in the Master library.

9. Select the **CategoryName** field and repeat the same steps but define the following properties:
    - Name as 'Category'
    - Dimension color as dark blue with the hex code #4477aa

Now, there are two dimensions created in the Master library, as follows:

The master dimensions created here will be used in `Chapter 7`, *Creating Data Stories*.

Creating master measures

A measure is used to define an expression to aggregate data in the visualization. In the charts we have created so far, under the `My first charts` sheet, we have the following `SalesAmount` field defined as the chart measure.

The following steps depict how to create a master measure:

1. If we are in view mode, switch to edit mode using the **Edit** button.
2. Click on the **Master items** button to open the Master item pane.
3. Click on the **Measure** pane to expand it.
4. Click on the **Create new** button in the **Measure** pane to create a new measure.
5. In the Measure editor panel, click on the **fx** icon to expand the expression editor.
6. Write the expression and `sum (SalesAmount)` into the editor.
7. Click on the **Apply** button to close the expression editor.
8. Write `Sales $` in the **Name** field.
9. To define a default color for the measure, use the color combo box to open the color picker and select the dark green color, which has the hex code #276e27.

10. Click outside the color picker to close and return to the measure editor panel, as shown in the following screenshot:

11. The **Create** button at the bottom of the screen can be used to create the measure in the Master library.

12. Repeat the aforementioned steps to create the following measure. Each expression is defined in the code block as follows:

- **Measure name**: Avg Discount %

```
num (sum (Discount*SalesAmount)/sum (SalesAmount), '0.00%')
```

- **Measure name**: Order #

```
count (distinct OrderID)
```

- **Measure name**: Quantity #

```
sum (Quantity)
```

For each measure, the other properties will be set to their defaults.

The master measures created here will be used in `Chapter 7`, *Creating Data Stories*.

Creating master visualizations

If we create a visualization object and want to use it on multiple sheets, we can add it to the **Master items** and bring it to a new sheet. Visualizations added from the Master item are linked. Any change in the master visualizations are reflected on the linked copy.

The following steps demonstrate how to create a master visualization for the filter panel:

1. Use the right-hand clicker on the mouse to find a floating menu for the **Filter Panel** object.
2. Select the **Add to master items** option.
3. Set the name of the Master item to `Default Filters`.
4. Click on the **Add** button to create the master visualization:

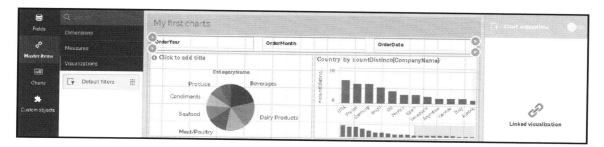

5. The new item is visible in the visualizations pane of the **Master items**. We can also see the message that states that the object is now a linked visualization.

6. If we need to edit the visualization, we should click on the **Edit** button found on the right-side of the panel.

The master visualization created here will be used in Chapter 7, *Creating Data Stories*.

Calculation expressions

In the previous section of this chapter, we created some master measures by writing calculation expressions for each one. Expressions combine functions, fields, and math operators to calculate a desired value. These can be applied not only to measures, but also to titles, subtitles, footnotes, labels, and descriptions on **Master items**, chart colors, dimension limits, calculation conditions, and various other tools and places.

Here are some guidelines for writing expressions, as follows:

- An expression used on a measure will always have an aggregation function. The most common aggregation functions are sum(), max(), min(), and avg(). Aggregation functions require at least a field name as a parameter. Let's look at some examples:
    - The sum(SalesAmount) calculates the summary of the SalesAmount field.
    - The count (distinct OrderID) counts the distinct values found in the OrderID field. The distinct clause removes duplicate values found in the field, counting only the first occurrence.
- The num (sum (Discount*SalesAmount)/sum (SalesAmount), '0.00%') is more complex in nature, as it calculates the discount percentage weighted by SalesAmount. The resulting calculation is formatted by num(calculation, format), which is more commonly known as the num function. The first parameter is the calculation expression, and the second parameter is the '0.00%' presentation format. The final values will be presented as a percentage.

The expression inside the `Discount*SalesAmount` aggregation function is calculated for each row before aggregation and the division operation between the aggregations is calculated after the aggregation of each `sum()` for each item in the dimension of the chart. It's important to know whether an expression needs to be calculated inside or outside of an aggregation function, as both will generate different results. When using expressions on labels and titles, if the result is numerical, use the `num()` function to format the result.

When using expressions in a dimension, this needs to be done with care. This is because they are resource-intensive. For performance reasons, it's always better to create calculations in the script editor. Sometimes, we need a dimension to be calculated dynamically in the form of range values, or in a Pareto analysis; for example, we need to find the products that represent the A category falling in the top 20% range.

Calculated dimensions are useful for changing the content of existing fields or creating new ones, especially if we don't have access to the script editor. The following example shows how to create an expression that can be used in the employee name dimension that can concatenate two fields: `EmployeesFirstName & ' '& EmployeesLastName`

Summary

In this chapter, we have learned how to design visualizations in a Qlik Sense app. We have also looked at the DAR methodology to build an application, focusing on how we can use this to help the user explore and analyze an application's information.

We also learned about using Insight Advisor, and how it helps us to select the correct visualization for analysis. We also created **Master items** to leverage the self-service creation of new visualizations and sheets. Lastly, we looked at how to create calculation expressions and how to avoid performance issues.

In the next chapter, we shall see how to create a sales analysis app and apply the DAR methodology.

Questions

- Why is the DAR methodology important when building a Qlik Sense App?
- What is a data model?
- Does the Insights Advisor create new charts? How does it do this?
- What is a dimension?
- What is a measure?
- How do we create a master item?
- How do we avoid performance issues in calculations?

Further reading

In Chapter 5, *Creating a Sales Analysis App Using Qlik Sense,* we will explore the concepts and the data with new visualizations and sheets.

5
Creating a Sales Analysis App Using Qlik Sense

In this chapter, we will create a sales analysis application to explore and analyze the data model that we created in Chapter 2, *Loading Data in Qlik Sense*.

While developing the application, we will apply the **Dashboard, Analysis, Reporting (DAR)** methodology that we explained in Chapter 4, *Working with Application Structures*.

We will create create four sheets, each with a very specific purpose, as follows:

- The dashboard sheet will give us a quick overview of the key performance indicators of sales amounts, average discount percentages, and the number of orders. It will also show us the sales share by category, the sales by top 10 customers, and a map showing the sales statistics for each country.
- The customer analysis sheet will help our users to understand how the sales are performing based on the customer, and which customers are the best ones, creating a combination chart for Pareto analysis (80/20).
- The product analysis sheet will help our users to understand how sales are performing by product, and to point out the products that are currently the best by using a scatter plot chart.
- The reporting sheet will help us to see the data in a more granular form. Using a table visualization, we will be able to see the detailed data by order transaction.

The chapter is organized as:

- Creating the dashboard sheet
- Creating the analysis sheet
- Creating the report sheet

Technical requirements

In this chapter, we will use the application that we created in Chapter 4, *Working with Application Structure*, as a starting point, with a loaded data model to eliminate the process of loading and modeling the data all over again.

You can also download the initial and final versions of the application from the book repository on GitHub, at https://github.com/PacktPublishing/Hands-On-Business-Intelligence-with-Qlik-Sense.

After downloading the initial version of the application, follow these steps:

- If you are using Qlik Sense Desktop, place the QVF application file in the QlikSense\Apps folder, under your document's personal folder.
- If you are using Qlik Sense Cloud, upload the application to your personal workspace.

Creating the dashboard sheet

Before we begin creating the dashboard, we need to review the information that is required by the business. The case study that we will address is as follows.

Suppose that the company is a worldwide wholesale seller of food and beverages. This means that they need to review information about the sales in several countries. They need to know their performance in each of them, and they require this information to be detailed by the customer name, category name, and product name. They also need to know the average percentage of discounts, how many orders they have issued, and the total sales amount. Each of these key indicators should be dictated by the month and year.

That explains the basis for this case. We need to find the perfect solution by accessing the right dashboard and displaying all of the data in the most consolidated fashion. Let's highlight some keywords that will drive our development:

- **Italic**: Visualizations that we need to provide
- **Bold**: Dimensions that we need to create and use on visualizations
- **Underline**: Metrics that we need to create and use on visualizations

This information is valuable as a starting point for our work, but it's not exhaustive. During the development of a dashboard, it's very common to create extra visualizations or metrics that are also valuable to the user when it comes to understanding the data.

Creating the dashboard

In this section, we will create a new dashboard sheet, with the following visualizations:

- KPI with **Sales $**
- KPI with **Avg Discount %**
- KPI with **Orders #**
- Pie chart with sales by category
- Bar chart with sales by top 10 customers
- Geographical map with sales by country

Creating a new sheet for the dashboard

We will begin by creating a new sheet with the name `Dashboard`. The following steps will help us create and use a new sheet:

1. Open the app and click on **Create new sheet**:

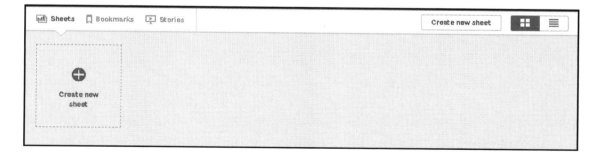

2. Set the **Title** of the sheet to Dashboard:

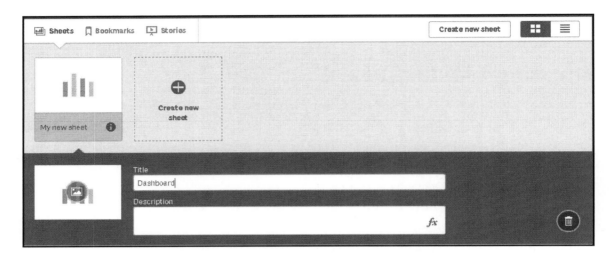

3. Click on the **sheet** icon to save the title, and open the sheet to start creating visualizations.

Creating KPI visualizations

The KPI visualization is used to get an overview of the performance values that are important to our company. We can show one or two measure values for comparison. For example, we can show a measure with sales for the year 2018, and a measure with sales for the year 2017, and see if the sales are increasing or decreasing year to year.

To add the KPI visualizations to the sheet, follow these steps:

1. Click on the **Edit** button located in the toolbar to enter the edit mode:

2. Click on the **Master items** button on the asset panel, which is on the left-hand side of the screen, and click on the **Measures** heading that was created in Chapter 4, *Working with Application Structure*:

3. Click on **Sales $** and drag and drop it into the empty space on the sheet:

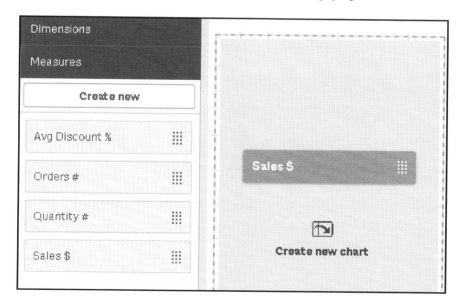

4. Qlik Sense will create a new visualization of the KPI type because we have selected a measure:

5. Resize the visualization toward the top-left of the sheet, as follows:

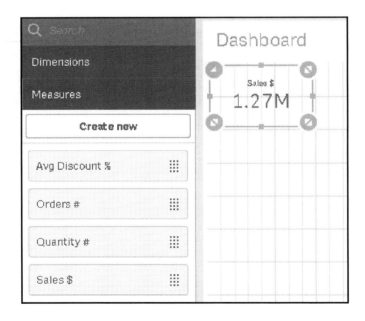

6. Repeat steps 1 through 5 to add two visualizations for the **Avg Discount** % and **Orders** # measures. Place the objects to the right of the previously added visualization. The sheet should look like this:

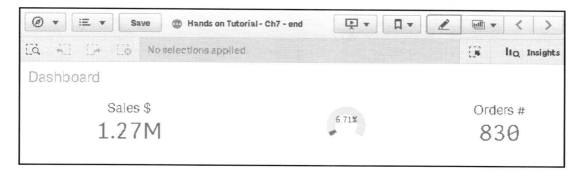

 For the **Avg Discount** % measure, Qlik Sense suggests the **Gauge visualization** instead of the KPI visualization, because the data is formatted with percentages.

7. To change the type of visualization from **Gauge** to KPI, click on the chart type selector, as follows:

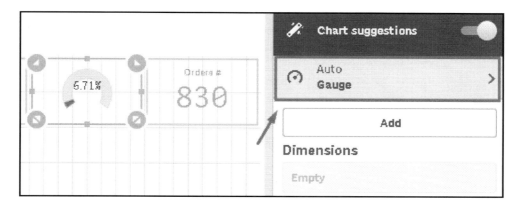

8. Select the **KPI** chart type that is depicted by the red arrow in the following screenshot:

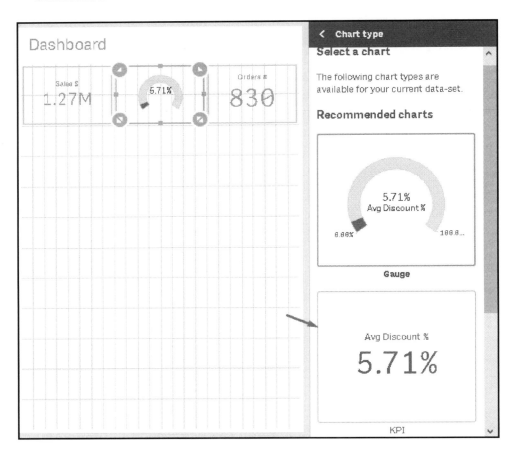

9. Now, all three of the measures are visualized as **KPI**:

Creating a pie chart with Sales $ by Categories

To add the pie chart with **Sales $ by Categories** onto the sheet, follow these steps:

1. Click on the **Charts** button on the asset panel, which is on the left-hand side of the screen, to open the chart selector panel.
2. Click on **Pie chart** and drag and drop it into the empty space on the sheet:

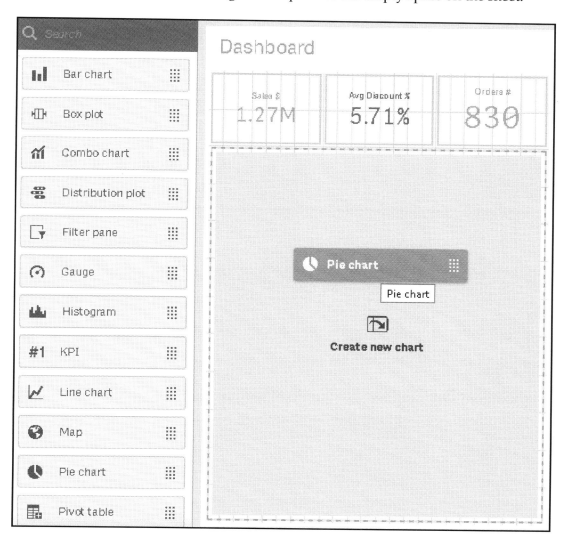

3. Click on the **Add dimension** button and select **Category** in the **Dimensions** section:

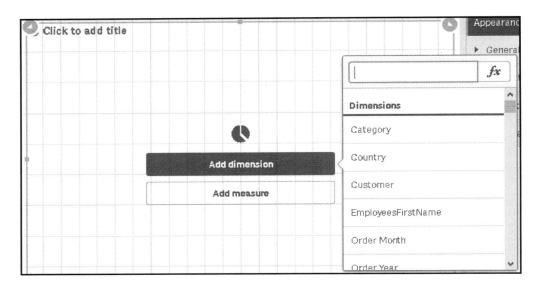

4. Click on the **Add measure** button and select **Sales $** in the **Measures** section:

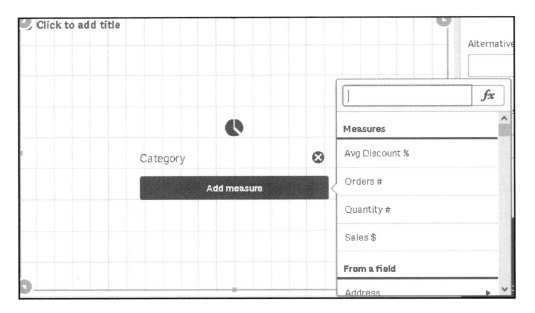

5. The pie chart will look like this:

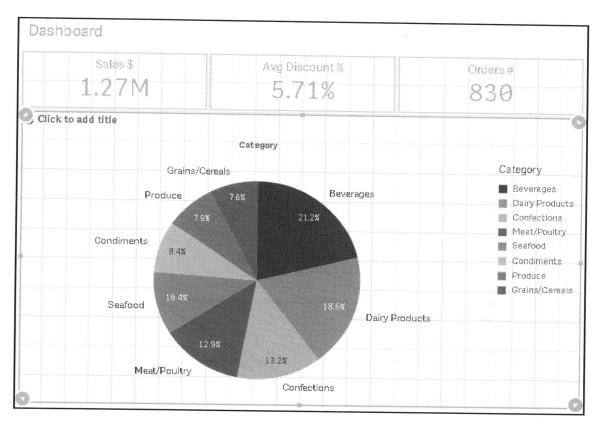

Now, we will enhance the presentation of the chart by removing the **Dimension label** and adding a title to the chart:

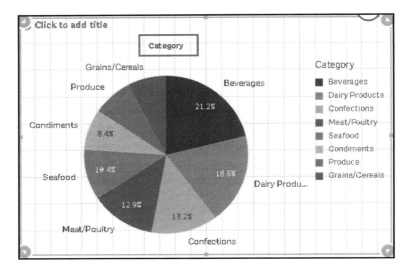

6. To remove the **Dimension label**, select the **Appearance** button that lies in the properties panel at the right-hand side of the screen and expand **Presentation**, under which you will find the **Dimension label**. Turn it off by simply clicking on the toggle button:

7. Click on the title of the object and type `Sales $ share by Category`:

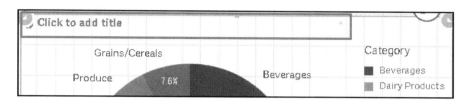

8. Click on **Done** in the toolbar to enter the visualization mode. The pie chart will look like this:

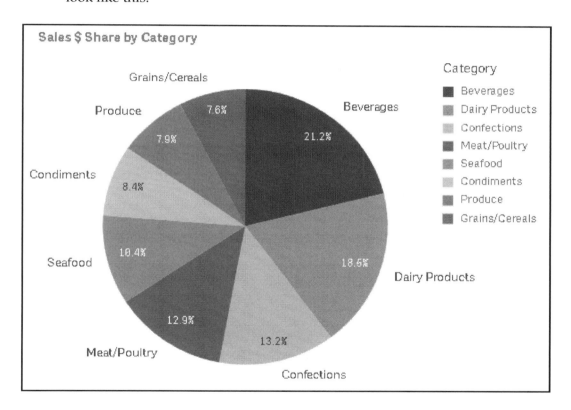

Creating a bar chart with Sales $ by Top 10 Customers

To add the bar chart with the top 10 customers by sales $ to the sheet, carry out these steps:

1. Before adding the bar chart, resize the pie chart by reducing the width and making room for the new chart on the right-hand side of the screen:

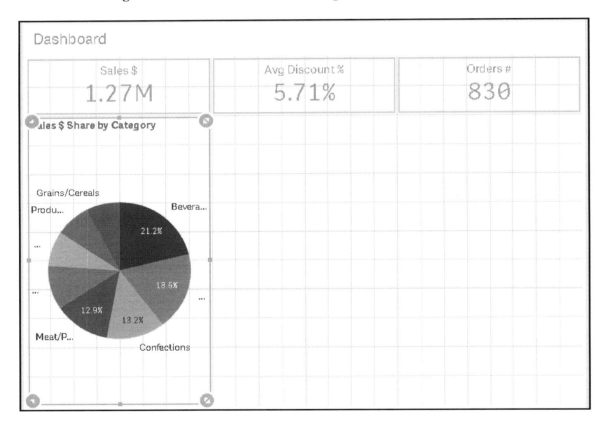

2. Click on the **Charts** button that lies on the asset panel, which is on the left-hand side of the screen, to open the chart selector panel.

3. Click on **Bar chart** and drag and drop it into the empty space in the center of the sheet:

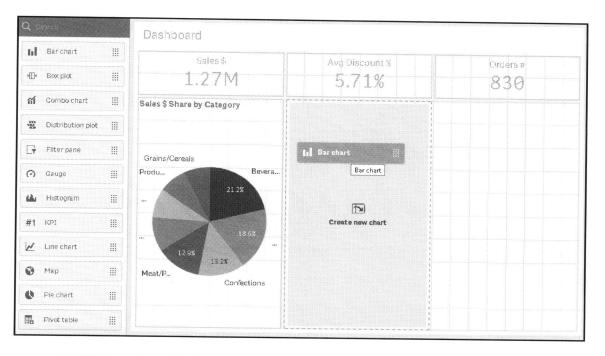

4. Click on the **Add dimension** button and select the **Customer** option in the **Dimensions** section.

5. Click on the **Add measure** button and select **Sales $** in the **Measures** section.

6. The bar chart will look like this:

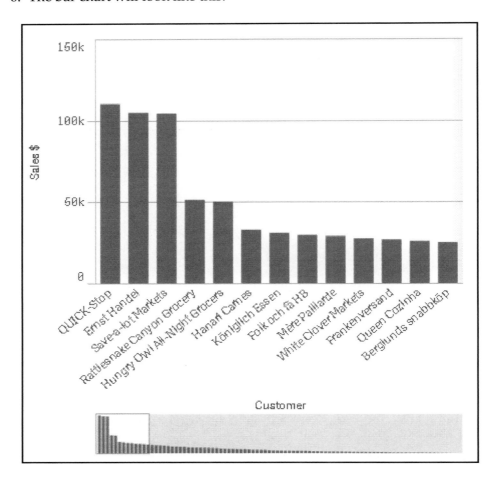

To enhance the presentation of the chart, we will limit the number of customers that are depicted in the chart to 10, and add a title to the chart.

To limit the number of customers, do the following:

1. Select **Data** in the properties panel on the right-hand side of the screen and expand the **Customer** dimension.
2. Set the **Limitation** values as **Fixed number**, **Top** and type `11` in the limitation box:

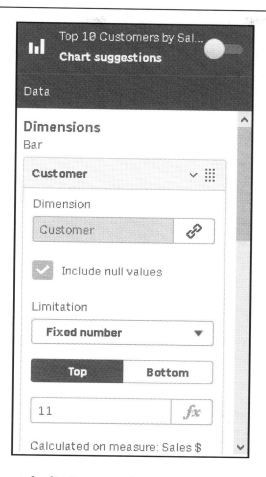

We need to set the limit to 11. This will show the first 10 bars for the customer name, and the last will be the others bar, grouping all of the other customers.

3. Click on the title of the chart and type `Top 10 Customers by Sales $`.

4. Click on **Done** to enter the visualization mode. The bar chart will look like this:

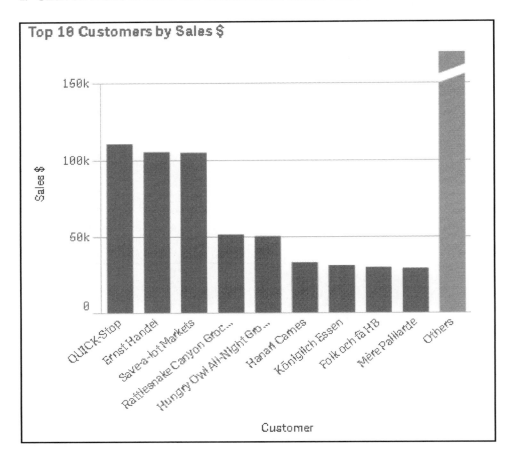

 Note that the gray bar depicts the values for others. You can eliminate the **Others** bar by deselecting the **Show Others** property in the **Customer** dimension.

Creating the geographical map of sales by country

To add the geographical map of sales by country to the sheet, follow these steps:

1. Before adding the map chart, resize the bar chart by reducing the width and making some room for the new chart at the bottom-right of the screen:

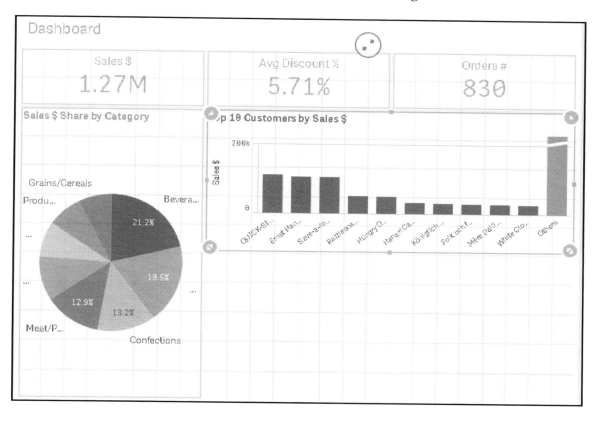

2. Click on the **Charts** button that lies on the asset panel, which is on the left-hand side of the screen, to open the chart selector panel.

3. Click on the **Map** button and drag and drop the chart into the empty space on the right-hand side of the sheet:

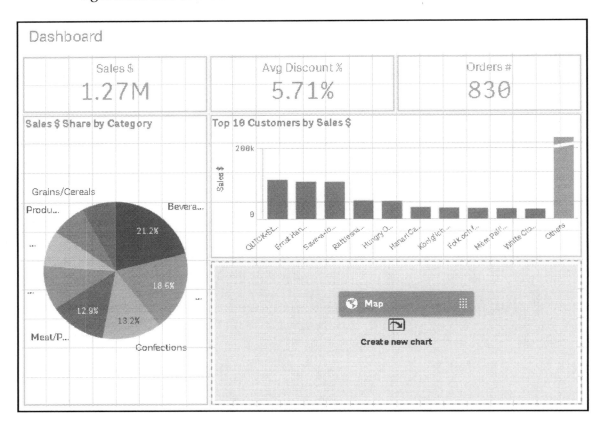

4. The map visualization will show a default world map with no data, as follows:

Here, we need to add an **Area layer** to plot the countries, and add a **Sales $** measure to fill in the area of each country with a color scale. Lower sales values will have lighter hues. Higher sales values will have darker hues.

To add the **Area layer,** follow these steps:

1. Click on the **Add Layer** button in the properties panel on the right-hand side of the screen:

2. Select the **Area layer:**

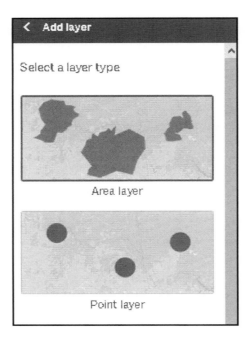

3. Add the **Country** dimension, as it contains the information to plot the area:

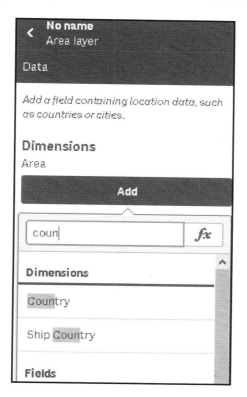

4. The map will show the country areas filled in with a single color, as follows:

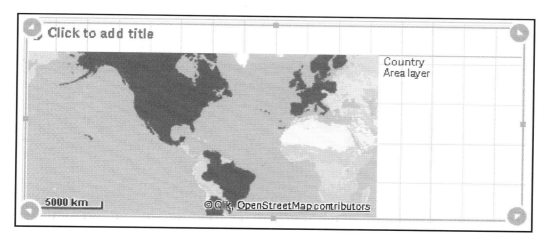

5. To add the **Sales $** measure to set the color scale for each country, go to the asset panel at the left-hand side of the screen and click on the **Master items** heading in the **Measures** section. Drag and drop the **Sales $** measure on top of the map:

6. In the pop-up menu for the map, select **Use in "Country"(Area Layer)**:

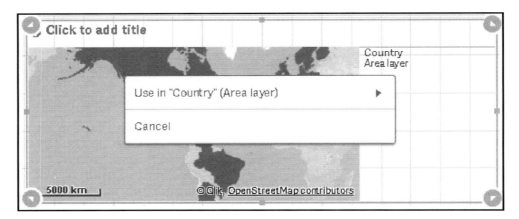

7. After that, select **Color by: Sales $**:

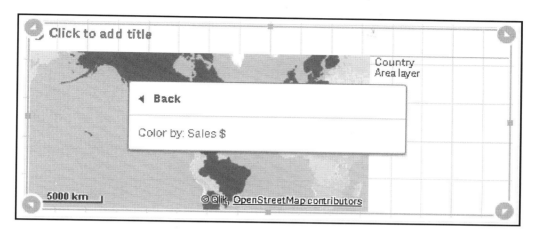

8. The map will now show the countries with more **Sales $** in a dark color, and those with lower **Sales $** in a light color:

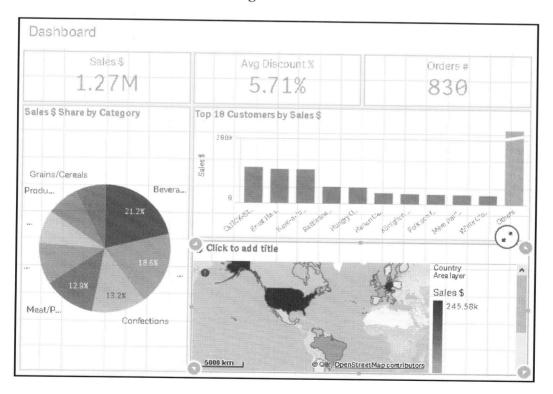

Note that Qlik Sense automatically detects whether a field contains a valid country. Qlik Sense can show countries as areas and cities or municipalities as points automatically with the point layer.

9. Now, click on the title of the object and type `Sales $ by Country`.

10. Click on the **Done** button to enter the visualization mode. The sheet will look like this, but it will vary according to your screen resolution:

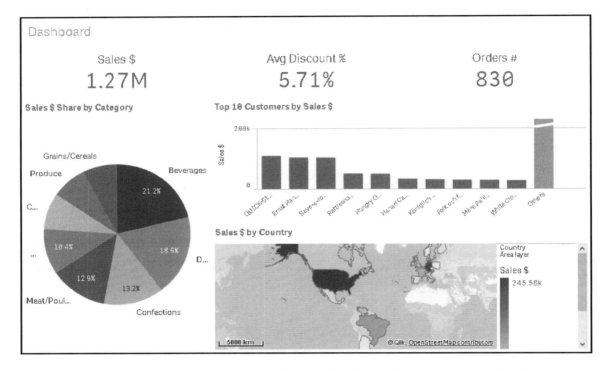

We now have a dashboard depicting the data of all of the order transactions for the entire years of 2016 to 2018. To finish the dashboard, we will add a filter panel to select the data by **Order Year** and **Order Month** (these fields are derived from the **Order Date** field).

Creating a filter pane with Order Year and Order Month fields

To add the filter pane to the sheet, follow these steps:

1. Before adding the filter pane, resize the KPI chart for **Sales $** by reducing the width by three cell columns and making some room on the left-hand side of the screen:

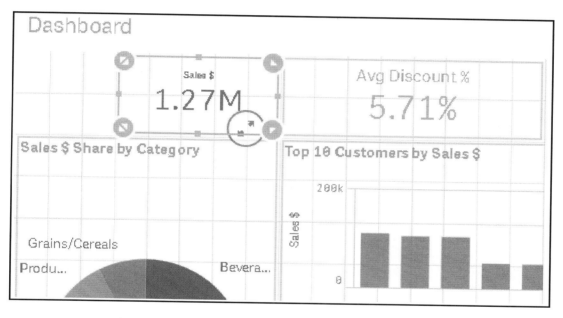

2. Click on the **Charts** button that lies on the asset panel, which is on the left-hand side of the screen, to open the chart selector panel.

3. Click on **Filter pane** and drag and drop it into the empty space to the left of the **Sales $** KPI on the sheet:

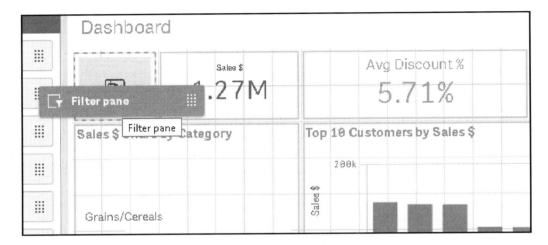

4. Open the **Data** section in the properties panel on the right-hand side of the screen:

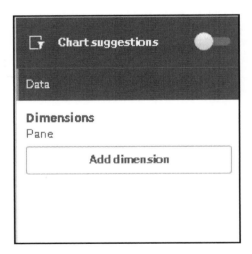

5. Click on the **Add Dimension** button and search for and select **Order Year**.
6. Repeat step 3 to add another dimension, then search for and select **Order Month**.
7. Fix the width of the other KPI objects to keep the font the same size.
8. Click on the **Done** button to enter the visualization mode. The sheet will look like what's shown in the following screenshot:

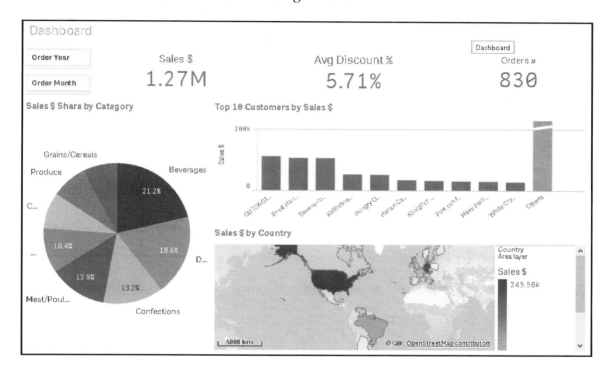

The dashboard depicts four things, as follows:

- KPI visualizations, showing the performance metrics for quick insight. We have **$1.27M** in sales for the whole period, with an average discount of **5.71%** and **830** orders processed.
- The pie chart compares the sales by category, showing the most relevant. We can see that **Beverages** is our top performing category.
- The bar chart shows the top performing customers, with the first three sales amounts being very close to each other.
- The map shows the distribution of sales by country. The USA and Germany are the top performers.

In the next section, you will learn how to create two analysis sheets: one for customer analysis, and another for product analysis.

Creating the analysis sheets

While the dashboard sheet shows information on several topics for a quick overview, the analysis sheet focuses on a single topic for data exploration.

We will create two new sheets: one for customer analysis, and the other for product analysis.

Each one will help us understand how the sales are performing.

For the customer analysis, we will create a Pareto analysis to find out who the most relevant customers are, with a share of 80% of our sales.

For the product analysis, we will create a scatter plot to find out how the average discount affects the sales performance.

Creating a customer analysis sheet

In this section, we will create a new analysis sheet with the following visualizations:

- A filter panel, with the following dimensions: **OrderYear**, **OrderMonth**, **Country**, **Customer**, **Category**, and **Product**
- **KPI Sales $**
- **KPI Avg Discount %**
- A combo chart for Pareto (80/20) analysis by customer
- A table with customer data

The customer analysis sheet will help our users to understand how the sales are performing, based on the customers, as well as which customers are the best ones. The user can explore the data, making selections on the filter pane and charts.

Creating a new sheet for customer analysis

We will start this section by creating a new sheet with the name Customer Analysis. The following steps will help us to create and use the new sheet:

1. Click on the **Sheet selection** button at the top-right of the screen to open the sheet overview panel.
2. Click on the **Create new sheet** button and set the title of the sheet to Customer Analysis.
3. To finish this example, click on the sheet icon to save the title, and open the sheet to start creating visualizations.

Adding a filter pane with main dimensions

We will start to build the customer analysis sheet by adding a filter pane. Follow these steps to do so:

1. Click on the **Edit** button to enter the edit mode.
2. Click on the **Charts** button on the asset panel, which is on the left-hand side of the screen, and find **Filter pane**.
3. Click on **Filter pane** and drag and drop it into the empty space on the sheet:

4. Click on the **Add dimension** button and select **Order Year** in the **Dimensions** section:

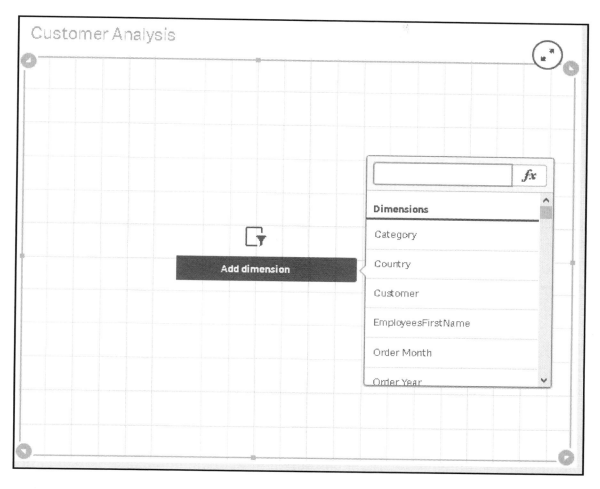

5. Since we need to add more dimensions to our **Filter pane**, click on the **Add dimension** button in the properties on the right-hand side of the screen, and select **Order Month** in the **Dimensions** section.

6. Repeat the previous step to add the **Country**, **Customer**, **Category**, and **Product** dimensions.

7. The **Filter pane** will look like what's shown in the following screenshot:

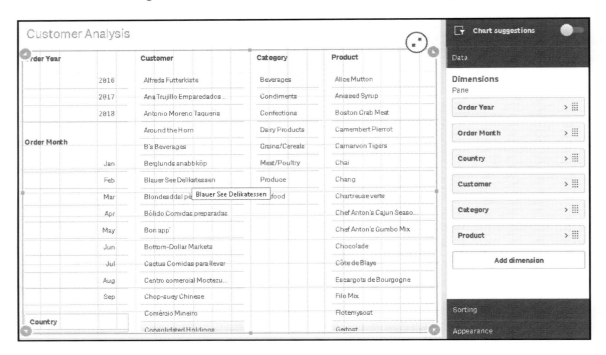

8. Now, resize the width of the filter panel to fit three columns of the grid:

We will keep the filter pane on the left-hand side of the screen as a standard for each analysis sheet.

We also need to add the **Filter pane** as a master visualization, which is to be reused across the analysis and reporting sheets that we will create next. Follow these steps to add it to the **Master items** library:

1. Right-click on the filter pane on the screen and select **Add to master items** in the menu:

2. Set the name of the master item to `Default Filter` and the description to `A filter pane to be reused across sheets`:

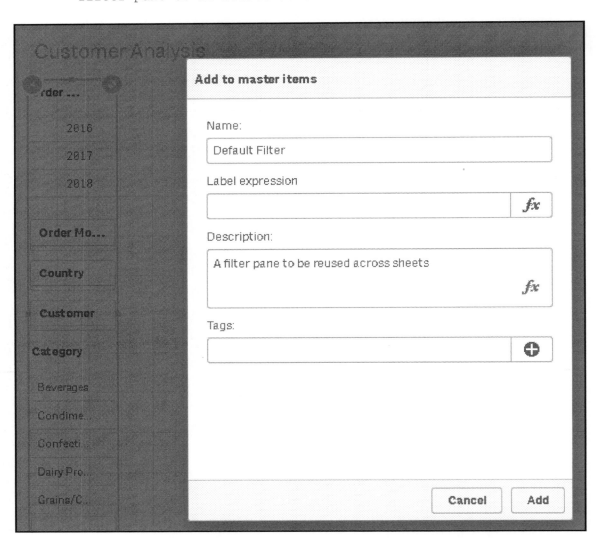

3. Click on the **Add** button:

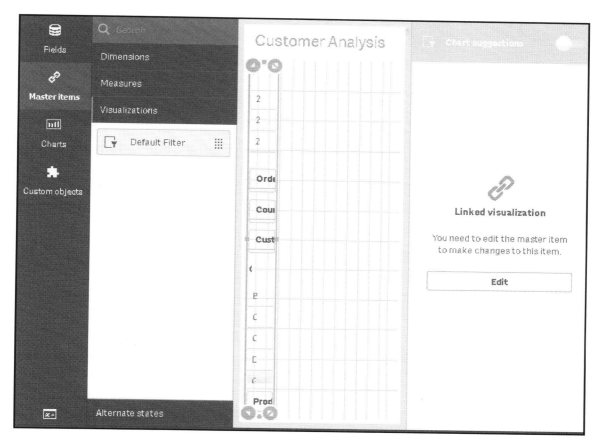

We now have a new visualization in the **Master items** library, and the properties panel is locked. The filter pane now became a **Linked visualization**. Linked visualizations can be added to several sheets. You can change the properties of the linked visualization by clicking on the **Edit** button. If you change the properties of the linked visualization, that change will be reflected on all of the sheets that it is added to.

Adding KPI visualizations

To add the KPIs of **Sales $** and **Avg Discount %** to the sheet, we have two options, as follows.

The first option is to add the KPI visualizations to the **Master items** library, and add them to the new sheet:

1. Go to the dashboard sheet.
2. Add the KPI visualizations of **Sales $** and **Avg Discount %** to the **Master item**.
3. Name them **KPI Sales $** and **KPI Avg Discount %**, respectively.
4. From the visualization section in the Master items library, simply drag and drop each of the KPIs into the top end of the sheet.

The second option is to copy and paste the KPI visualizations between sheets:

1. Go to the dashboard sheet.
2. Select the KPI visualization for **Sales $.**
3. Press *Ctrl + C* or right-click on the visualization object and select **Copy** in the context menu.
4. Go back to the **Customer Analysis** sheet.
5. Press *Ctrl + V* or right-click in the empty area of the sheet and select **Paste** in the context menu.
6. Repeat the same steps for **KPI Avg Discount %.**

Note that if the KPI visualization was created using chart suggestion, you will need to disable the chart suggestion switch to allow the visualization to be added to the **Master items** library.

The sheet editor will look like what's shown in the following screenshot:

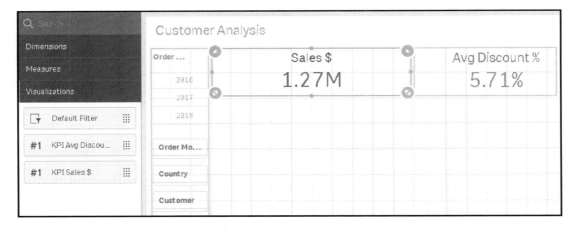

Creating a combo chart for Pareto (80/20) analysis

A Pareto analysis helps us to identify which groups of customers contribute to the first 80% of our sales. To create a Pareto analysis, we will use a combo chart.

The combo chart allows us to combine metrics with different shapes as bars, lines, and symbols. We will represent the data in two axes; the primary axis is found at the left-hand side of the chart, and the secondary axis is found at the right-hand side of the chart.

In our example, the chart has a bar for **Sales $** in the primary axis, as well as two lines: one for the **Cumulative %** of sales, and the other as static, with 80% in the secondary axis.

In the following screenshot, you can see the highlighted customers contributing to the first 80% of the sales. These are our best customers:

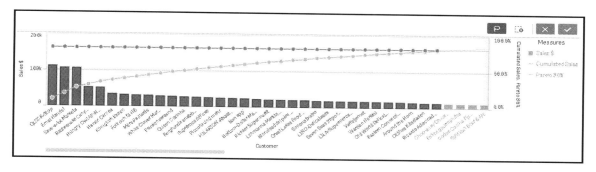

To create the Pareto analysis chart, follow these steps:

1. Click on the **Charts** button on the asset panel, which is on the left-hand side of the screen, and find the **Combo chart**.
2. Click on the **Combo chart** and drag and drop it into the empty space at the right-hand side of the sheet.
3. Click on **Add Dimension** and select **Customer** in the **Dimension** section.

4. Click on **Add Measure** and select **Sales $** in the **Measures** section.
5. The combo chart will look like this:

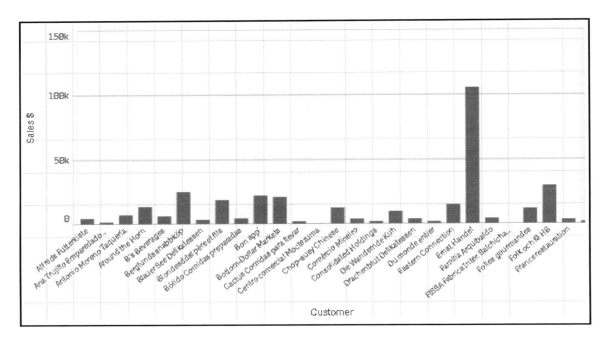

6. We need to add two other measures, represented by lines. The first is the cumulative percentage of sales, and the second is the reference line at 80%. To add the cumulative sales line, go to the properties panel, expand the **Data** section, and click on the **Add** button in **Measures**:

7. Click on the **fx** button to open the expression editor:

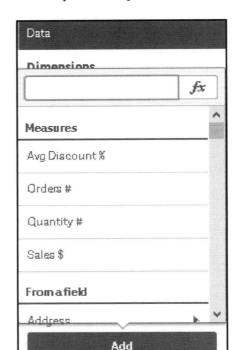

8. Type the following expression in the **Expression** editor:

```
RangeSum(Above(Sum(SalesAmount), 0, RowNo()))  /  Sum(total
SalesAmount)
```

This expression will calculate a cumulative ratio of the sales for each customer, over the whole amount of the sales of all customers.

We can break this expression down into two parts to understand how it works:

- `RangeSum(Above(Sum(SalesAmount), 0, RowNo()))`: In the first part of the expression, the `Rangesum()` function will summarize the numbers in an array of values returned by the `Above()` function. The array contains all of the preceding values in the chart, from row 0 (the second parameter) to the current row returned by the `RowNo()` function.

- **/ Sum(total SalesAmount)**: In the second part of the expression, the cumulative sum of the sales will be divided by the sum of the sales for all customers. We have to use the total qualifier inside of the `sum()` function to disregard the dimensions of the chart and to return the sales for all customers.

9. Click on the **Apply** button to close the expression editor and save the expression.
10. Set the **Label** of the new measure to **Cumulative Sales %**.
11. Check if the properties **Line** is selected and that **Secondary axis** is selected for the measure. The properties panel will then look like what's shown in the following screenshot:

12. Change the number formatting to **Number**, set the formatting option to **Simple**, and select **12.3%**:

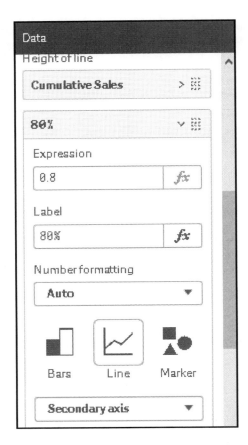

13. Now, find the **Add** button in the **Measure** pane to add another measure: the reference line for 80%.
14. Open the **Expression** editor, type 0.8, and click on the **Apply** button.
15. Set the **Label** to 80%.
16. Check if the properties **Line** is selected and that the **Secondary axis** is selected for the measure. The properties panel will look like what's shown in the following screenshot:

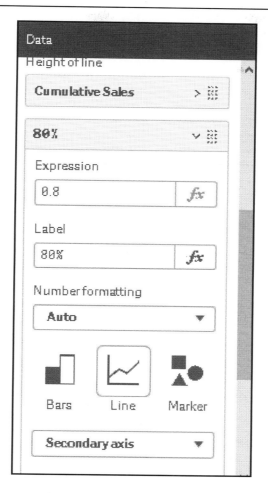

The combo chart is almost complete. We also need to fix the sort order into a descending fashion, by **Sales $**:

1. Go to the properties panel and expand the **Sorting** section.
2. Click on **Customer** to expand the **Sorting** configuration for the dimension.
3. Switch off the **Auto** sorting.
4. Click on the checkbox for **Sort by expression** to select the option.
5. Open the **Expression** editor and type the following:

$$sum(SalesAmount)$$

6. Click on **Apply** to close the expression editor and apply the changes.
7. Set the **Title** of the chart to `Pareto Analysis`.
8. Change the sorting order to **Descending**.
9. Deselect other sorting options if they are selected. The **Sorting** pane will look like this:

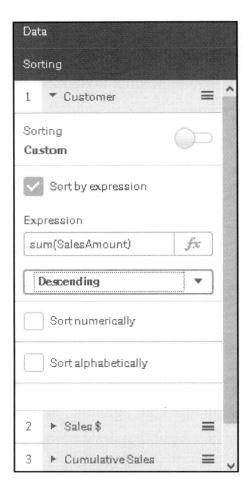

10. Finally, the combo chart will look like what's shown in the following screenshot:

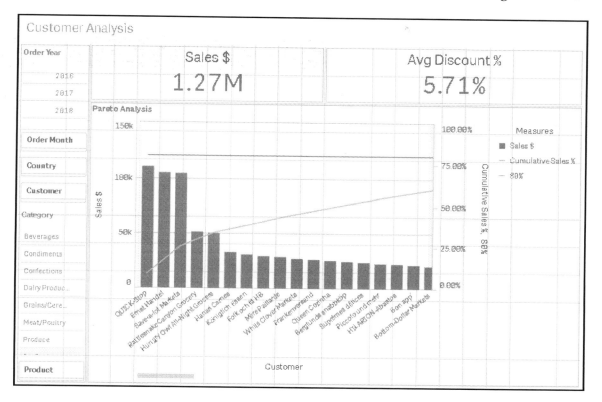

Creating a table chart with customer information

The next thing that we need to do is add a table with data about each customer. Follow these steps:

1. Click on the **Charts** button on the asset panel, which is on the left-hand side of the screen, and find the **Table visualization**.

2. Click on **Table** and drag and drop it into the empty space at the bottom end of the sheet to automatically adjust the previous chart and make room for the new one:

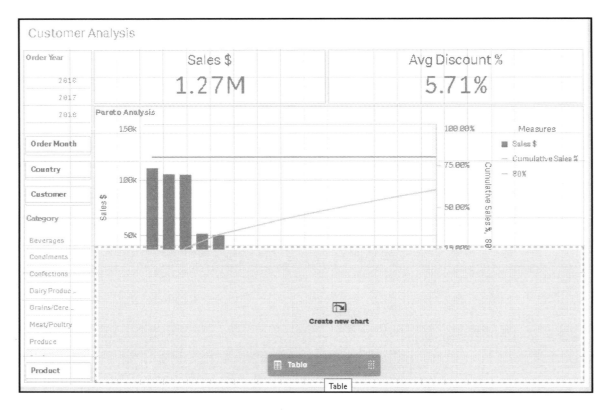

3. Click on **Add Dimension** and select **Customer** in the **Dimension** section.
4. Click on **Add Column** in the properties panel and select **Type** dimension.
5. Find and select the **Country** dimension.
6. Click on **Add Column** in the property pane and add the **City** field as a dimension.
7. Click on **Add Column** and add **Sales $** as a **Measure**.
8. Repeat step 7 to add **Orders #** and **Avg Discount %** as a **Measure**.
9. Click on **Add Column** in the properties panel and select the **Type Measure**.

10. Open the **Expression** editor and type the following expression:

```
Rank(total Sum(SalesAmount))
```

This expression calculates the ranking for each customer by sales amount, starting with 1 for the customer with the largest amount of sales and increasing the rank position for each customer based on a decreasing order of sales. The total qualifier is required to disregard all of the dimensions of the chart so that the rank is correctly calculated over the full segment of rows in the table.

11. Set the **Label** of the expression to **Rank**:

Customer	Country	City	Sales $	Orders #	Avg Discount %	Rank
Totals			1,265,793.04	830	5.71%	-
Alfreds Futterkiste	Germany	Berlin	4,273.00	6	5.90%	57
Ana Trujillo Emparedados y helados	Mexico	México D.F.	1,402.95	4	0.00%	84
Antonio Moreno Taquería	Mexico	México D.F.	7,023.98	7	6.10%	46
Around the Horn	UK	London	13,390.65	13	2.82%	31
B's Beverages	UK	London	6,089.90	10	0.00%	51
Berglunds snabbköp	Sweden	Luleå	24,927.58	18	6.59%	13

12. Change the formatting of the **Sales $** column to **Number with 2 decimal numbers**.
13. Set the **Table Title** to **Customer Data**.

The **Table visualization** will look like what's shown in the following screenshot:

Customer	Country	City	Sales $	Orders #	Avg Discount %	Rank
Totals			1,265,793.04	830	5.71%	-
Alfreds Futterkiste	Germany	Berlin	4,273.00	6	5.90%	57
Ana Trujillo Emparedados y helados	Mexico	México D.F.	1,402.95	4	0.00%	84
Antonio Moreno Taquería	Mexico	México D.F.	7,023.99	7	6.10%	46
Around the Horn	UK	London	13,390.65	13	2.82%	31
B's Beverages	UK	London	6,089.90	10	0.00%	51
Berglunds snabbköp	Sweden	Luleå	24,927.58	18	6.59%	13

The table shows some detailed information about the customers in the current selection: the customer's name, location, sales amount, number of orders, average discount, and a rank related to the sales amount.

In the end, the sheet will look like what's shown in the following screenshot:

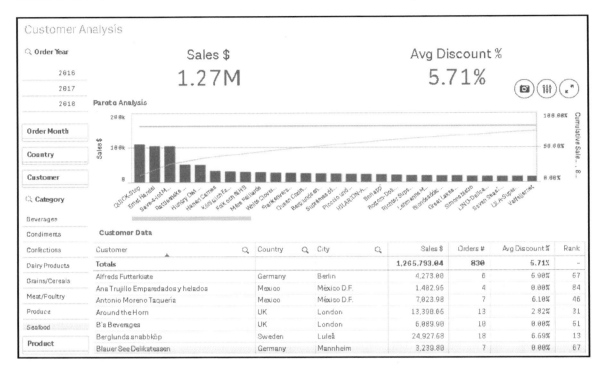

In the next section, you will learn how to create a product analysis sheet, exploring more charts and calculation expressions.

Creating a product analysis sheet

The product analysis sheet will help our users to understand how the sales are performing by product, and will highlight the products that are currently the best. The user will explore the data, making selections on the filter pane and charts.

In this section, we will create a new analysis sheet with the following visualizations:

- **KPI sales**
- **KPI % discount**
- A bar chart ranking **Sales $** by category and product (the **drill** dimension)
- A line chart, by month/year and category, with the **Sales $** measure
- A scatter chart, by sales and % discount by products and color by categories

Creating a new sheet for product analysis

Before adding the new visualizations, create a new sheet with a **Product Analysis** name. The following steps will help us to create and use the new sheet:

1. Click on the **Sheet selection** button at the top-right of the screen to open the sheet overview panel
2. Click on the **Create new sheet** button and set the title of the sheet to **Product Analysis**
3. To finish this example, click on the **sheet** icon to save the title, and open the sheet to start creating visualizations

Adding a filter pane

To create a product analysis sheet by adding the **Default Filter** pane that is present in the **Master items** library, follow these steps:

1. Click on the **Edit** button to enter the edit mode.
2. Click on the **Master items** button on the asset panel, which is on the left-hand side of the screen, and find the **Default Filter** in the **Visualization** section.

3. Click on the **Default Filter** pane and drag and drop it into the empty space to the left of the sheet:

4. Resize the width of the filter panel to fit three columns in the grid:

Adding KPI visualizations

We will now add the KPI visualizations to the sheet. Follow these steps:

1. Add the **KPI Sales $** from the **Master items** library and position it on the left of the screen, just before the panel filter:

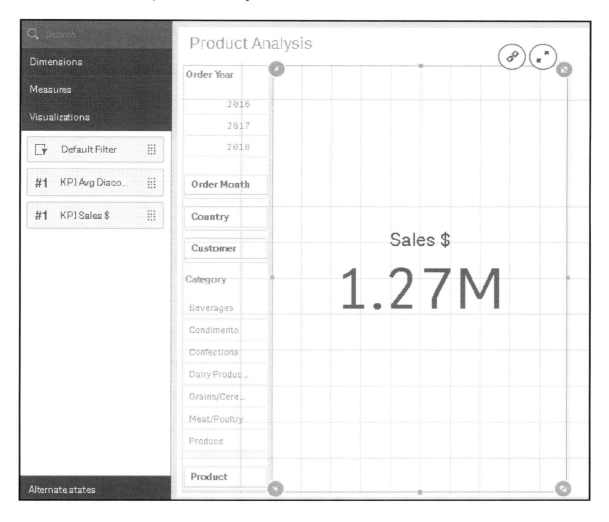

2. Add the **Avg Discount %** from the **Master items** library by adding the KPIs from the **Master items** library, and position it at the right end of the screen:

3. Resize the height of the two KPI objects to fit two rows in the grid:

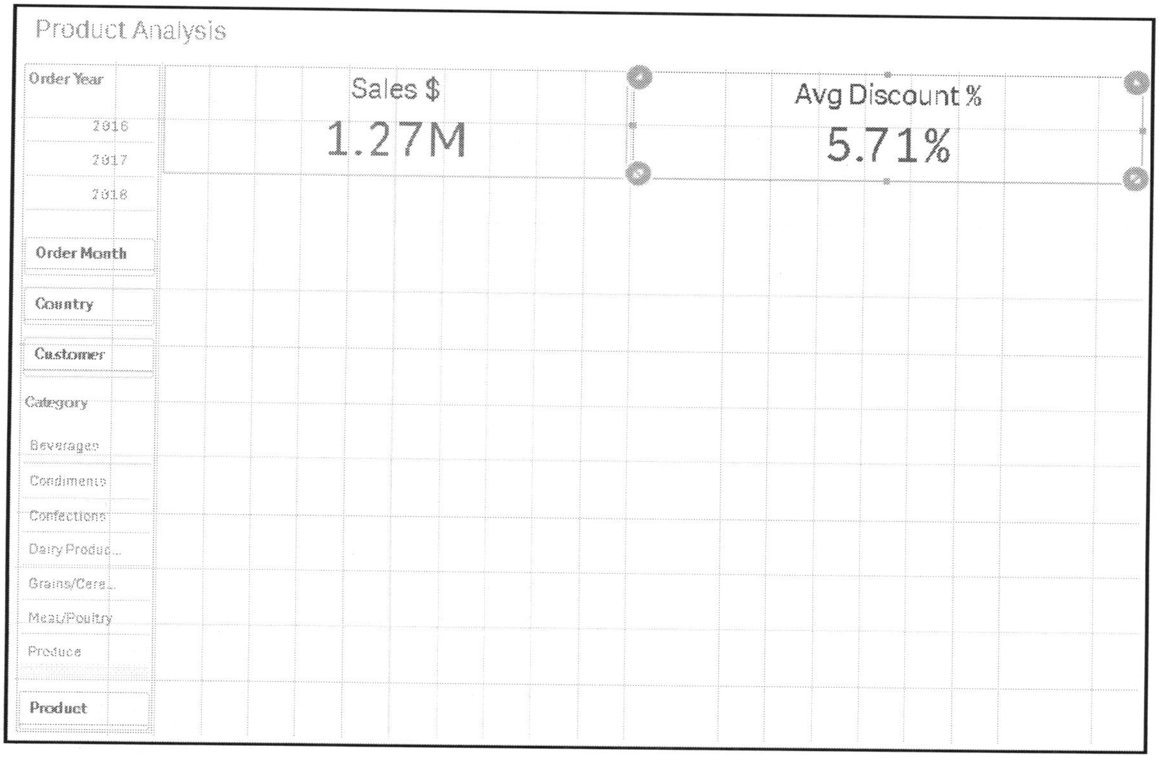

4. We need to add a new KPI visualization to the sheet. It will be **Quantity #**.
5. Click on the **Quantity #** measure from the **Master items** library and drag and drop it onto the sheet.

6. Resize the width of the KPI visualizations that already exist on the sheet to make room at the top-right of the screen. Set the width to seven columns of the grid for each one. The sheet will look like this:

Product Analysis

Order Year	Sales $	Avg Discount %	Quantity #
2016	1.27M	5.71%	51,32k
2017			
2018			

Order Month

Country

Customer

Category

Beverages
Condiments
Confections
Dairy Produc...
Grains/Cere...
Meat/Poultry
Produce

Product

Creating a bar chart with a drill-down dimension

A drill-down dimension allows you to go deeply into several dimensions on the same chart. Each time that you select an item in the chart, it will show you the items from the next dimension, following the order of the fields you selected when creating the dimension.

Now, we will add a bar chart with a drill-down dimension with the fields CategoryName and ProductName.

To create the **Drill-down** dimension for the category and products, follow these steps:

1. Click on the **Master items** button to open the **Master items** pane.
2. Click on the **Dimensions** heading to expand it.
3. Click on **Create new** to open the **Create new dimensions** dialog.
4. Select **Drill-down** as the dimension type.
5. Select the **CategoryName** field to add it to the **Field** list.
6. In the search box, type `product`. Here, you will only see fields with the word **product** in the name.
7. Select the **ProductName** field to add it to the field list.

8. Set the **Name** to `ProductDrill`. The configuration dialog will look like what's shown in the following screenshot:

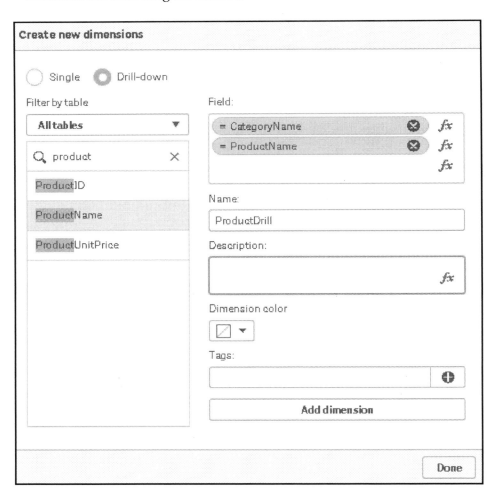

9. Click on the **Add dimension** button.
10. Click on the **Done** button to close the dialog.
11. A new dimension with the name **ProductDrill** will be added to the **Master items**:

Next, we will create the bar chart with the drill-down dimension. To create the chart, follow these steps:

1. Click on the **Charts** button on the asset panel, which is on the left-hand side of the screen.
2. Click on the bar chart and drag and drop it into the empty space at the left-hand side of the sheet.
3. Click on **Add dimension** and select **ProductDrill** in the **Dimension** section.
4. Click on **Add Measure** and select **Sales $** in the **Measures** section.

5. The bar chart will look like this:

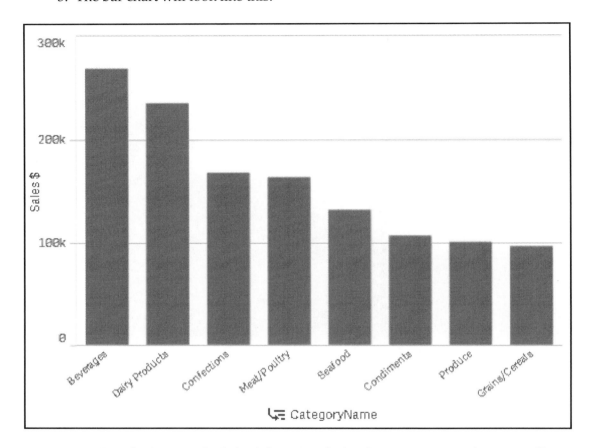

 Note the icon on the left of the axis title for **CategoryName**. This icon tells you that there is a drill-down dimension in that chart.

6. Click on **Done** to enter the visualization mode.
7. Click on the **Confections bar** and confirm the selection to drill down and show the products of the selected category. The chart will now look like what's shown in the following screenshot:

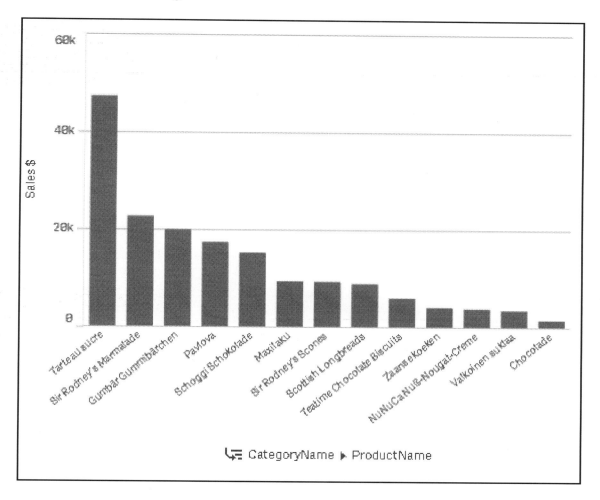

Creating a line chart by OrderMonthYear and Category

The next visualization that we will create is a line chart with the **Month/Year** and **Category** as dimensions. Create the chart with the following steps:

1. Before adding the new chart, resize the height of the bar chart to make some room on the sheet:

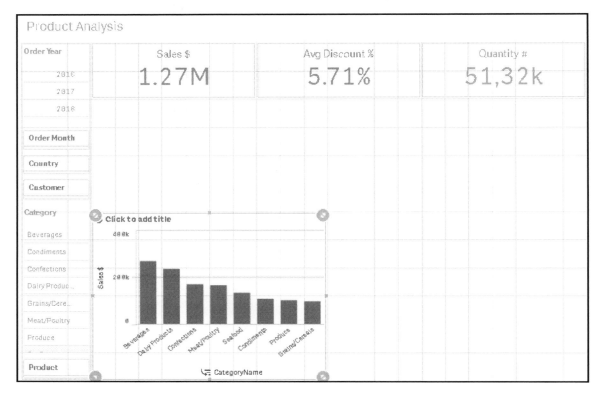

2. Click on the **Charts** button on the asset panel, which is on the left-hand side of the screen.
3. Click on **Line chart** and drag and drop it into the empty space between the KPI visualizations and the bar chart:

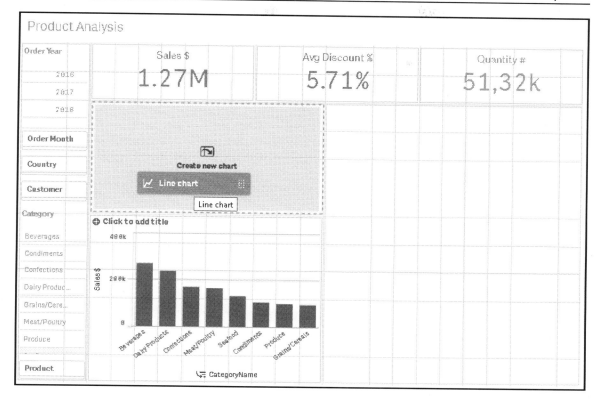

4. Expand the width of the new line chart to the right-hand side of the screen.
5. Click on **Add Dimension** and select **OrderMonthYear** in the **Fields** section.
6. Click on **Add Measure** and select **Sales $** in the **Measures** section.
7. The line chart will look like this:

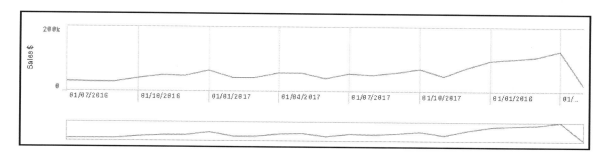

8. Now, click on the **Add** button in the **Dimensions** section of the **Data** properties panel at the right-hand side of the screen.
9. Select **Category** from the **Dimensions** list.
10. Now, each category will be presented as a line with a different color, as follows:

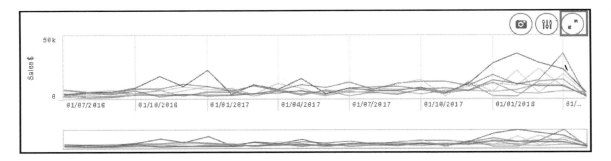

The chart has no legend, because there is not enough space to show it. To see the legend, hover the mouse over the top of the chart and click on the **expand** button. The **expand** button is found in the top-right corner, and it will expand the chart to full screen. The **expand** button is shown in the preceding screenshot.

We can also use another chart to help us create a legend for each color:

1. Click on the **Master items** button to open the **Master items** pane.
2. Click on the **Dimensions** heading to expand it.
3. Click on **Category** and drag and drop it on top of the bar chart.
4. Select **Color by: Category** in the menu.

The bar chart shows the categories with the same colors that are being used in the line chart. Now, we can see which color belongs to which category, using the bar chart as a chart legend. Consider the following screenshot:

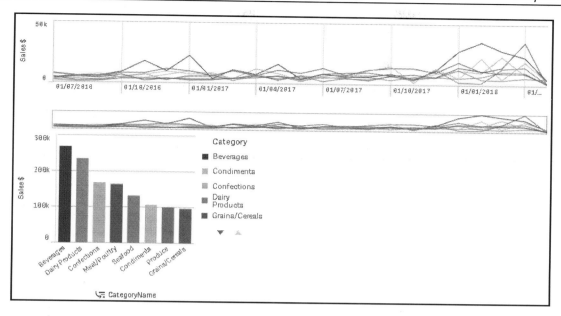

Creating a scatter plot

The scatter plot allows us to find a correlation, grouping, or outlier by plotting bubbles for each dimension item. This is done by using two measures: one for the y axis, and the other for the x axis. We can also add a third measure to set the size of the bubble, and a fourth measure to set a color. See the example that's shown in the following screenshot:

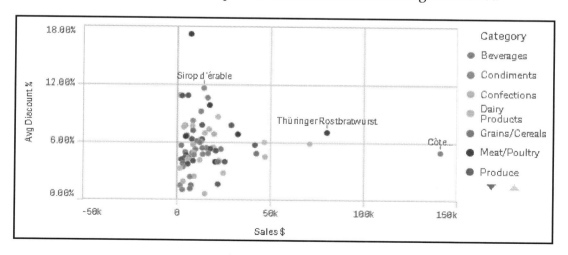

This example shows each product as a dot, and the **Category** defines the color of each dot. We can find some outliers: one for **Beverages** in the **Sales $** axis, and another for **Meat/Poultry** in the **Avg Discount %** axis. We can also find a concentration of sales up to **50k** on sales, and up to 12% of average discount.

To create the scatter plot chart, do the following:

1. Click on the **Charts** button on the asset panel, which is on the left-hand side of the screen, and find the **Scatter plot**.
2. Click on **Scatter plot** and drag and drop it onto the empty space on the right-hand side of the sheet.
3. Click on **Add Dimension** and select **Product** in the **Dimensions** section.
4. Click on **Add Measure** and select **Sales $** in the **Measures** section.
5. Click on **Add Measure** and select **Avg Discount %** in the **Measures** section.
6. The chart will look like this:

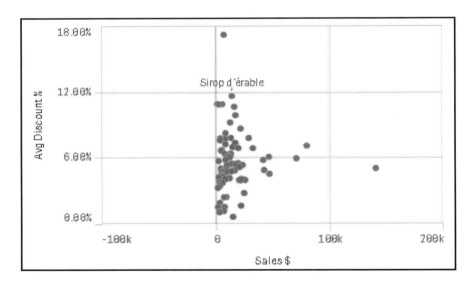

7. Click on the **Master items** button on the asset panel, which is on the left-hand side of the screen.
8. Find the **Category** dimension.
9. Drag and drop the **Category** on top of the scatter plot.
10. Select **Color by: Category** in the context menu.
11. Set the **Title** of the chart to **Products by Avg Discount $ x Sales $**.

The sheet will look like this:

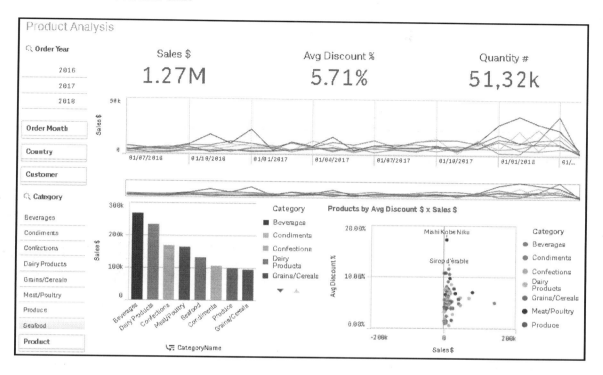

In the next section, you will learn how to create a reporting sheet to show some detailed information about the data.

Creating a reporting sheet

Reporting sheets allow the user to see the data in a more granular form. These reporting sheets are commonly displayed in the form of a table. This type of sheet provides information that allows the user to take action at an operational level.

In the following example, we will create a new reporting sheet with the following visualizations:

- A default filter pane with the main dimensions
- A table with data detailed by order transaction

Creating a new sheet

We will start this example by creating a new sheet with the name **Reporting**. The following steps will help us create and use the new sheet:

1. Click on the **Sheet selection** button at the top-right of the screen to open the sheet overview panel
2. Click on the **Create new sheet** button and set the **Title** of the sheet to Product Analysis
3. Click on the sheet icon to save the title, open the sheet to start creating visualizations, and enter the edit mode

Adding a default filter pane

We will start to build the reporting sheet by adding the default filter pane that has already been added to the **Master items** library:

1. Click on the **Edit** button to enter the edit mode.
2. Click on the **Master items** button on the asset panel, which is on the left-hand side of the screen, and find **Default filter** in the **Visualization** section.
3. Click on **Default filter pane** and drag and drop it into the empty space at the top of the sheet.
4. Resize the height of the filter pane to fit one row of the grid.
5. The sheet will then look like what's shown in the following screenshot:

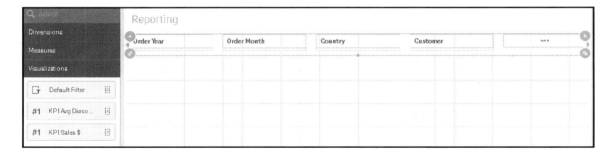

Next, we will add the table chart to the sheet, as follows:

1. Click on the **Charts** button on the asset panel, which is on the left-hand side of the screen, and find the **Table** visualization.
2. Click on **Table** and drag and drop it into the empty space at the center of the sheet.
3. Click on the **Add dimension** button and select **OrderID** from the **Field** list.
4. Click on **Add measure** and select **Sales $** from the **Dimensions** list.
5. Click on the **Master items** button on the asset panel, which is on the left-hand side of the screen, and click the **Dimensions** heading to expand it. We will then add more dimensions.
6. Drag and drop the **Customer** dimension on the table.
7. Select **Add "Customer"** from the floating menu.
8. Repeat the process, using the drag and drop feature to add the following dimensions to the table:
    - **Country**
    - **Category**
    - **Product**
    - **EmployeesFirstName**
9. Click on the **Measures** heading in **Master items** to expand it.
10. Drag and drop the following measures onto the table:
    - **Avg Discount %**
    - **Quantity #**
11. Select **Add** in the floating menu for each of the selected measure.
12. Click on the **Fields** button on the asset panel, which is on the left-hand side of the screen.
13. Find the **OrderID** field in the list.
14. Drag and drop the **OrderID** field onto the table.
15. Select **Add OrderID** from the floating menu.
16. Repeat the same steps to add the **OrderDate** field to the table.

The table will look like this:

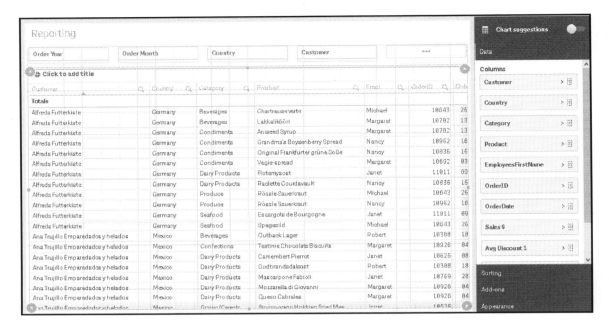

With these steps, we have created a table so that we can view detailed information about the orders at the transaction level.

Summary

In this chapter, you learned how to create a Qlik Sense application using the DAR methodology, which will help you to explore and analyze an application's information. You also learned how to create useful analyses, like a Pareto analysis with a combo chart, tables that show rankings, line charts for visualizing trends over time, and data dispersion with scatter plot charts. Additionally, we created master items to leverage the reusability of visualizations between sheets.

In the next chapter, you will learn about advanced expressions for enhancing the Qlik Sense app that we are building.

6
Interacting with Advanced Expressions

In this chapter, we are going to learn about the power of calculation engines. After reading this, you will understand how to create a calculation with conditions, as well as how to use the aggregation scope, inter-record functions, and advanced aggregation with the AGGR function. Finally, you will learn how to use Set Analysis to create a calculation with very specific data.

For each topic, we will create several visualizations to help us interact with the expressions and also use some additional functions to check whether there is selected data on fields.

The following topics will be covered in this chapter:

- Creating calculations with conditions
- Using TOTAL for aggregation scope
- Using some useful inter-record functions
- Using AGGR for advanced aggregation
- Leveraging Set Analysis for in-calculation selection

Technical requirements

For this chapter, we will use the app we created in Chapter 5, *Creating a Sales Analysis App Using Qlik Sense*, as a starting point with a loaded data model and visualizations. This will be done to eliminate the process and to recreate the application again.

You can also download the initial version of the .qvf file for this application, named Hands on Tutorial – Ch06 – start.qvf, from the book repository on GitHub at https://github.com/PacktPublishing/Hands-On-Business-Intelligence-with-Qlik-Sense/tree/master/Chapter06.

After downloading the app, follow these steps:

- If you are using Qlik Sense Desktop, place the app in the `Qlik\Sense\Apps` folder under your `Documents` personal folder
- If you are using Qlik Sense Cloud, upload the application to your personal workspace

Creating calculations with conditions

In `Chapters 4`, *Working with Application Structure* and `Chapter 5`, *Creating a Sales Analysis App Using Qlik Sense*, we created several calculations. These calculations were simple, showing data from current selection as well as numeric data.

Conditions can be used to select data used in an aggregate calculation, show different calculations, or even show a text according to the user selection.

In the following examples, we will learn how to use the `if()` function to create conditional calculations.

Before starting, we will create a new sheet named `Conditions`. The following steps will help us to create and use a new sheet:

1. Open the app and click on **Create new sheet**
2. Set the title of the sheet to `Conditions`
3. Click on the sheet icon to save the title and open the sheet to start creating

Condition to show a text message

Here, we will learn how to create a dynamic title in a text/image visualization using a condition to show the country name. If only one country is selected in the filter, it will display **Sales of** and the selected country name. If no county is selected in the filter, it will display the **Sales of All Countries** text. If two or more, but not all, countries are selected, it will display **Sales of Some Countries**.

We will add the following visualizations:

- **Filter pane** with **Country** dimension
- **Text & image** visualization with the **Sales $** measure

Follow these steps to create the visualizations:

1. Click on **Edit** button to enter the edit mode.
2. Click on the **Charts** button on the asset panel, which is on the left-hand side of the screen, and find the **Filter pane**.
3. Click on the **Filter pane**, and then drag and drop it into the empty space at the top of the sheet:

4. Click on the **Add dimension** button and select **Country** in the **Dimensions** section:

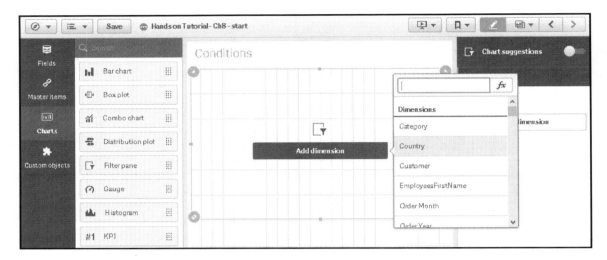

5. Resize the width and height of the filter panel to fit ten columns and one row of the grid:

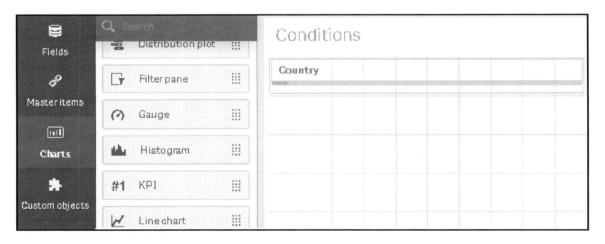

To create the **Text & image** visualization, follow these steps:

1. Click on the **Charts** button on the asset panel, which is on the left-hand side of the screen, and find the **Combo** chart.

2. Click on the **Text & image** visualization, and then drag and drop this into the empty space on the right-hand side of the sheet.

3. Click on **Add Measure** and select **Sales $** in the **Measures** section.

4. Fix the measure **Number formatting** to show a number with two decimal places.

5. Resize the width and height of the filter panel to fit ten columns and two rows of the grid. The **Text & image** chart will look like this:

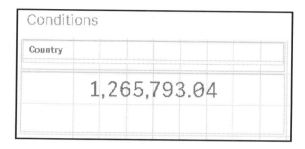

6. Select the **Text & image** chart and go to the properties panel.

7. Click on the **Appearance** heading, then click on the **General** section to expand it.

8. Switch on the **Show titles** property, as shown in the following screenshot:

9. Click on the *fx* button for the **Title** to open the expression editor, and then type the following expressions: `=if (GetSelectedCount(Country) = 1,' Sales of '&Country, if (GetSelectedCount(Country) = 0, 'Sales of all Countries', 'Sales of some Countries'))`.

10. Click on the **Apply** button to close the expression editor and save the expression.

11. If no country is selected, the screen will look like the following screenshot:

12. Click on the **Done** button to enter the visualization mode.

13. Select **Brazil** in the **Country** filter.

14. See how the title text changes when you select more countries in the **Country** field:

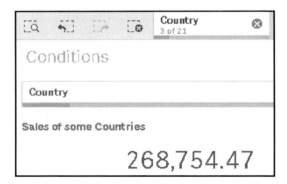

We learned how to create a nested `if` condition to evaluate three selection scenarios. First, we test whether one country is selected with the `GetSelectedCount(Country) = 1` condition. Then we test whether none of the countries are selected with the `GetSelectedCount(Country) = 0` condition. If none of these conditions are true, we show a text to say some countries are selected because there are two or more countries selected in the field.

Condition to show a different calculation

Here, we will learn how to create a dynamic measure in a table visualization using a condition to show the average price in the total heading and the sales amount for each category.

We will add the visualization, **Table** chart with dimension **Category**, and measure **Sales $**.

Follow these steps to create the visualizations:

1. Click on the **Edit** button to enter the edit mode.
2. Click on the **Charts** button on the asset panel, which is at the left-hand side of the screen, and find the **Table** chart.
3. Click on the **Table** chart, and then drag and drop it into the empty space at the bottom-left side of the sheet:

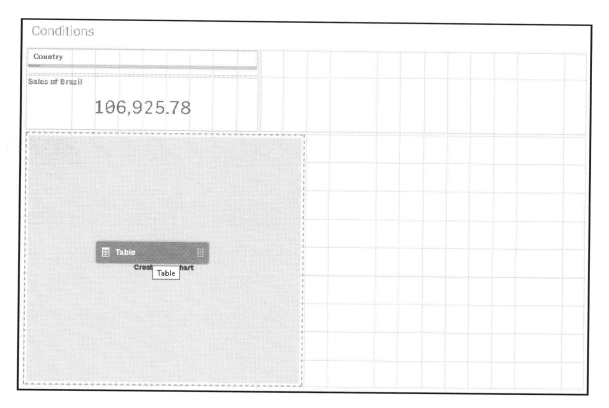

4. Click on **Add dimension** and select **Category** in the **Dimensions** section.
5. Click on **Add Measure** and select **Sales $** in the **Measures** section.
6. Click on the chain icon in the measure to unlink from the master measure and unlock the expression editor:

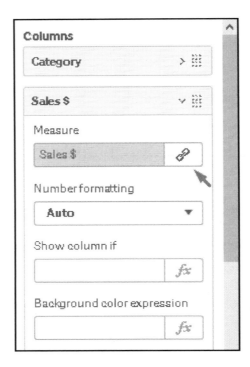

7. Click on the *fx* button to open the expression editor, then type the following expression: `if(rowno()=0,sum(SalesAmount)/sum(Quantity),sum(Sales Amount))`.
8. Click on the **Apply** button to close the expression editor and save the expression.
9. Fix the measure **Number formatting** to show the number with two decimal places.
10. Resize the width of the table to fit ten columns of the grid. The **Table** chart will look like this:

Category Q	Sales $
Total	**25.18**
Beverages	37,193.44
Condiments	11,180.76
Confections	11,436.10
Dairy Products	15,680.45
Grains/Cereals	6,121.55
Meat/Poultry	7,563.11
Produce	4,863.22
Seafood	12,887.13

11. Go to the properties panel.
12. Click on the **Appearance** heading and then the **General** section to expand it.
13. Switch on the **Show titles** property and type `Sales by Category and Total Average Price`.
14. Click on the **Presentation** section to expand it.
15. In the **Totals** labels property, type `Total Average Price`. The **Table** chart will look like this:

Sales by Category and Total Average Price	
Category Q	Sales $
Total Average Price	**25.18**
Beverages	37,193.44
Condiments	11,180.76
Confections	11,436.10
Dairy Products	15,680.45
Grains/Cereals	6,121.55
Meat/Poultry	7,563.11
Produce	4,863.22
Seafood	12,887.13

The sheet now looks like the following screenshot:

We learned how to create a different calculation condition for the total heading of the table. This calculation shows the average price of the products sold for the current selection.

 We used the `rowno()` = 0 condition to test whether the line of the table is the total line. The total line is always row 0, even it is shown at the bottom of the table. The dimension values start at row 1.

Condition to filter data on a measure

Here, we will learn how to create a measure in a table visualization using a condition to show only the sales amount for orders shipped the next day of the order date.

We will add the visualization, **Table** chart with dimensions **OrderID**, **ShippedDate**, **OrderDate**, and measure with **Sales Amount** with the shipped date condition.

Follow these steps to create the visualizations:

1. Click on the **Edit** button to enter the edit mode.
2. Click on the **Charts** button on the asset panel, which is on the left-hand side of the screen, and find the **Table** chart.
3. Click on the **Table** chart, and then drag and drop it into the empty space on the right-hand side of the sheet:

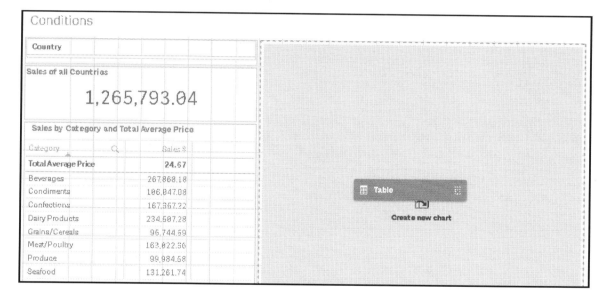

4. Click on **Add dimension** and select **OrderID** in the **Dimensions** section.

5. Add the **OrderDate** and **ShippedDate** fields as dimensions.

6. Click on the **Add Measure** button.

7. Click on the *fx* button to open the expression editor, and then type the following expression: `sum(if(ShippedDate<=OrderDate+1,SalesAmount))`.

8. Click on the **Apply** button to close the expression editor and save the expression.

9. In the **Label** of the measure, type `Sales $`.

10. Fix the measure **Number formatting** to show a number with two decimal places.

11. To remove rows with zero (that is, rows that don't match the date criteria), click on the **Add-Ons** heading in the properties panel.

12. Click on the **Data handling** section to expand it.

13. Clear the **Include zero values** property, as shown in the following screenshot:

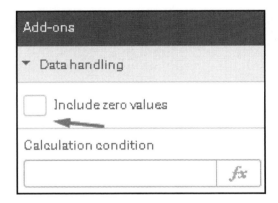

14. Click on the **Done** button.

15. Clear all selections. The **Table** chart will look like this:

OrderID	OrderDate	ShippedDate	Sales $
Totals			**17,395.89**
10270	01/08/2016	02/08/2016	1,376.00
10381	12/12/2016	13/12/2016	112.00
10388	19/12/2016	20/12/2016	1,228.80
10459	27/02/2017	28/02/2017	1,669.20
10538	15/06/2017	16/06/2017	139.80
10573	19/06/2017	20/06/2017	2,082.00
10631	14/08/2017	15/08/2017	55.80
10649	28/08/2017	29/08/2017	1,434.00
10673	18/09/2017	19/09/2017	412.35
10690	02/10/2017	03/10/2017	862.50
10732	06/11/2017	07/11/2017	360.00
10774	11/12/2017	12/12/2017	868.75
10783	18/12/2017	19/12/2017	1,442.50
10846	22/01/2018	23/01/2018	1,112.00
10884	12/02/2018	13/02/2018	1,378.07
10944	12/03/2018	13/03/2018	1,025.33
11013	09/04/2018	10/04/2018	361.00
11046	23/04/2018	24/04/2018	1,485.80

16. Go to the properties panel.
17. Click on the **Appearance** heading, and then click on the **General** section to expand it.
18. Switch on the **Show titles** property if disabled.
19. Click on the *fx* button to open the expression editor.
20. Type the following expression: `='There are '&count(distinct if(ShippedDate<=OrderDate+1,OrderID))&' Orders delivered next day'`.

The **Table** chart will look like this:

OrderID	OrderDate	ShippedDate	Sales $
There are 18 Orders delivered next day			
Totals			**17,395.89**
10270	01/08/2016	02/08/2016	1,376.00
10381	12/12/2016	13/12/2016	112.00
10388	19/12/2016	20/12/2016	1,228.80
10459	27/02/2017	28/02/2017	1,659.20
10538	15/06/2017	16/06/2017	139.80
10573	19/06/2017	20/06/2017	2,082.00
10631	14/08/2017	15/08/2017	55.80
10649	28/08/2017	29/08/2017	1,434.00
10673	18/09/2017	19/09/2017	412.35
10690	02/10/2017	03/10/2017	862.50
10732	06/11/2017	07/11/2017	360.00
10774	11/12/2017	12/12/2017	868.75
10783	18/12/2017	19/12/2017	1,442.50
10846	22/01/2018	23/01/2018	1,112.00
10884	12/02/2018	13/02/2018	1,378.07
10944	12/03/2018	13/03/2018	1,025.33
11013	09/04/2018	10/04/2018	361.00
11046	23/04/2018	24/04/2018	1,485.80

We have now learned how to create a table chart that only shows orders that meet the date criteria: **ShippedDate** on the next day of **OrderDate**.

The rows with no matching criteria have a zero value in the **Sales $** column, so we cleared the **Include zero values** property to remove them.

We created a dynamic title to show how many orders match the criteria. We used the count () function on the **OrderID** field with the distinct clause to count orders without repeating values.

The finished sheet now looks like the following screenshot:

| | | | No selections applied | | | | | Insights |

Conditions

Country

Sales of all Countries

1,265,793.04

Sales by Category and Total Average Price

Category	Q	Sales $
Total Average Price		24.67
Beverages		267,868.18
Condiments		106,047.08
Confections		167,357.22
Dairy Products		234,507.28
Grains/Cereals		96,744.69
Meat/Poultry		163,022.36
Produce		99,984.58
Seafood		131,261.74

There are 18 Orders delivered next day

OrderID Q	OrderDate Q	ShippedDate Q	Sales $
Totals			17,395.89
10270	01/08/2016	02/08/2016	1,376.00
10381	12/12/2016	13/12/2016	112.00
10388	19/12/2016	20/12/2016	1,228.80
10459	27/02/2017	28/02/2017	1,659.20
10638	16/06/2017	16/06/2017	139.80
10673	19/06/2017	20/06/2017	2,082.00
10631	14/08/2017	15/08/2017	55.80
10649	28/08/2017	29/08/2017	1,434.00
10673	18/09/2017	19/09/2017	412.35
10690	02/10/2017	03/10/2017	862.50
10732	06/11/2017	07/11/2017	360.00
10774	11/12/2017	12/12/2017	868.75
10783	18/12/2017	19/12/2017	1,442.60
10846	22/01/2018	23/01/2018	1,112.00
10884	12/02/2018	13/02/2018	1,378.07
10944	12/03/2018	13/03/2018	1,025.33
11013	09/04/2018	10/04/2018	361.00
11046	23/04/2018	24/04/2018	1,485.80

Using TOTAL for aggregation scope

When creating calculations on a chart, we usually create expressions that calculate the value of aggregation for each dimensional value. In some situations, you may want to disregard the dimension in the calculation by changing the aggregation scope. To achieve this, we use the TOTAL qualifier inside the aggregation function.

The TOTAL qualifier may be followed by a list of one or more field names within angular brackets. These field names should be a subset of the chart dimensions. In this case, the calculation is made by disregarding all chart dimension variables except those listed. This means that one value is returned for each combination of field values in the listed dimension fields.

Before starting the examples, we will create a new sheet with the name Total Qualifier. The following steps will help us to create and use a new sheet:

1. Open the app and click on **Create new sheet**
2. Set the title of the sheet to Total Qualifier
3. Click on the sheet icon to save the title, and then open the sheet to start creating

Calculating the relative share over the total

Here, we will learn how to create a relative share of products over the total amount.

To start, we will add the visualization, **Table** chart with the dimension **Product** and master measure **Sales $**.

Follow these steps to create the visualizations:

1. Click on the **Edit** button to enter the edit mode.
2. Click on the **Charts** button on the asset panel, which is on the left-hand side of the screen, and find the **Table** chart.
3. Click on the **Table** chart, and then drag and drop it into the empty space at the top of the sheet:

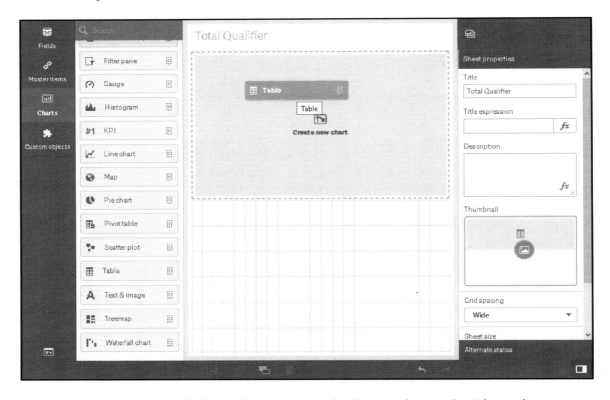

4. Click on the **Add dimension** button and select **Product** in the **Dimensions** section.
5. Click on the **Data** heading in the properties panel to expand it.

6. Find the **Add column** button, click on it, and choose **Measure**:

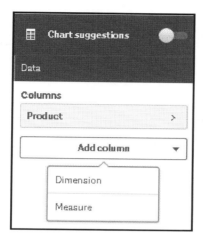

7. Select **Sales $** in the **Measures** section:

8. Click on the **Add column** button to add the second measure.

9. Click on the *fx* button to open the expression editor, and then type
   `sum(SalesAmount)/ sum(TOTAL SalesAmount)` for the new measure.

10. Click on the **Apply** button to close the expression editor and save the expression.

11. In the **Label** of the measure, type `Share %`.

12. Fix the measure **Number formatting** to show the number as a percentage with two decimal places:

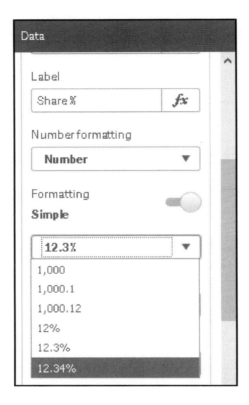

The **Table** chart will look like the following screenshot:

Total Qualifier		
Product 🔍	Sales $	Share %
Totals	**1,265,793.04**	**100.0%**
Alice Mutton	32,698.38	2.6%
Aniseed Syrup	3,044.00	0.2%
Boston Crab Meat	17,910.63	1.4%
Camembert Pierrot	46,825.48	3.7%
Carnarvon Tigers	29,171.87	2.3%
Chai	12,788.10	1.0%
Chang	16,365.96	1.3%
Chartreuse verte	12,294.54	1.0%
Chef Anton's Cajun Seasoning	8,567.90	0.7%
Chef Anton's Gumbo Mix	5,347.20	0.4%

Here, we learned how to calculate a relative share over total. In the preceding screenshot, we can see the calculation of the share ratio of each product compared to the total amount. The share is calculated within the current selection. If we select a specific country or group of products, the share-ratio calculation changes, showing the share with regards to the specific selection.

Calculating the relative share over a dimension

Here, we will learn how to create a relative share of products over the total amount of each category they belongs to.

To start, we will add the visualization, **Table** chart with dimension **Product** and **Category** and master measure **Sales $**.

Follow these steps to create the visualizations:

1. Click on the **Edit** button to enter the edit mode.
2. Click on the **Charts** button on the asset panel, which is on the left-hand side of the screen, and find the **Table** chart.
3. Click on the **Table** chart, and then drag and drop it into the empty space at the bottom of the sheet:

4. Click on the **Add dimension** button and select **Product** in the **Dimensions** section.
5. Click on the **Data** heading in the properties panel to expand it.
6. Find the **Add column** button, and then click on it and choose **Dimension**:

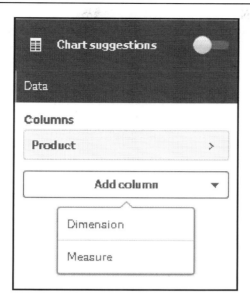

7. Select **Category** in the **Dimensions** section.
8. Find the **Add column** button, then click on it and choose **Measure**.
9. Select **Sales $** in the **Measure** section.
10. Click on the **Add column** button again to add the second measure.
11. Click on the *fx* button to open the expression editor, and then type the expression for the new measure, sum (TOTAL <CategoryName> SalesAmount).
12. Click on the **Apply** button to close the expression editor and save the expression.
13. In the **Label** of the measure, type Category Sales.
14. Fix the measure **Number formatting** to show a number with two decimal places.
15. Click on the **Add column** button again to add the third measure.
16. Click on the *fx* button to open the expression editor, and then type the expression for the new measure, sum (SalesAmount)/sum (TOTAL <CategoryName> SalesAmount).
17. Click on the **Apply** button to close the expression editor and save the expression.
18. In the **Label** of the measure, type Category Share %.

19. Fix the measure **Number formatting** to show a number as a percentage with two decimal places. The **Table** chart will look like this:

Product	Category	Sales $	Category Sales	Category Share %
Totals		1,265,793.04	1,265,793.04	100.00%
Alice Mutton	Meat/Poultry	32,698.38	163,022.36	20.06%
Aniseed Syrup	Condiments	3,044.00	106,047.08	2.87%
Boston Crab Meat	Seafood	17,910.63	131,261.74	13.64%
Camembert Pierrot	Dairy Products	46,825.48	234,507.28	19.97%
Carnarvon Tigers	Seafood	29,171.87	131,261.74	22.22%
Chai	Beverages	12,788.10	267,868.18	4.77%
Chang	Beverages	16,355.96	267,868.18	6.11%
Chartreuse verte	Beverages	12,294.64	267,868.18	4.59%
Chef Anton's Cajun Seasoning	Condiments	8,567.90	106,047.08	8.08%
Chef Anton's Gumbo Mix	Condiments	5,347.20	106,047.08	5.04%

We learned how to calculate a more sophisticated relative share, this time over a specific group dimension. The **Category** dimension added to the table is referenced in the TOTAL qualifier to calculate the total amount of each category disregarding the product dimension. We can see the calculation of the share ratio of each product compared to the total amount of the category it belongs to. The share is calculated within the current selection. If we select a specific country or group of products, the share-ratio calculation changes, showing the share considering the specific selection.

Using some useful inter-record functions

When creating calculations on a chart, in some situations, you may want to reference a value of a previous record in the chart, or reference a column in a table chart with a predefined expression. We can use an inter-record function to help us with this requirement.

These are the inter-record functions we will learn:

- Above()
- Column()

Before starting the examples, we will create a new sheet with the name Inter-Record. The following steps will help us to create and use a new sheet:

1. Open the app and click on **Create new sheet**
2. Set the title of the sheet to Inter-Record
3. Click on the sheet icon to save the title, and then open the sheet to start creating

Calculating sales variance year over year

Here, we will learn how to create a sales variance analysis year over year. A year over year variance calculates the difference between the current year and previous years to determine whether sales are increasing or decreasing. We will use a **Table** chart to understand the calculation in a simpler manner, but this function can be used in others charts, such as **Bar**, **Line**, and **Combo**.

We will add the visualization, **Table** chart with the dimension **OrderYear** and master measure **Sales $**.

Go through the following steps to create the visualizations:

1. Click on the **Edit** button to enter the edit mode.
2. Click on the **Charts** button on the asset panel, which is on the left-hand side of the screen, and find the **Table** chart.
3. Click on the **Table** chart, and then drag and drop it into the empty space at the top of the sheet:

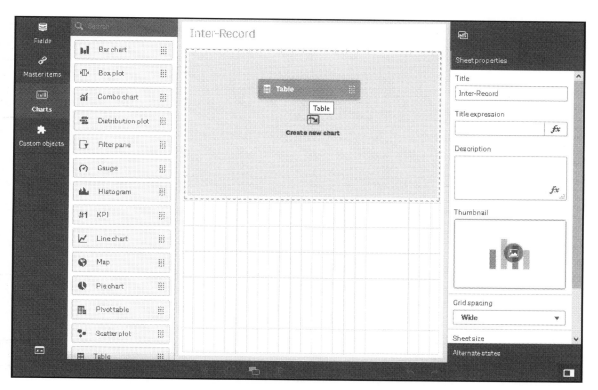

4. Click on the **Add dimension** button and select **Year** in the **Dimensions** section.
5. Click on the **Data** heading in the properties panel to expand it.
6. Find the **Add column** button, click on it and choose **Measure**.
7. Select **Sales $** in the **Measure** section.
8. Fix the measure **Number formatting** to show a number with two decimal places.
9. Click on the **Add column** button again to add the second measure.
10. Click on the *fx* button to open the expression editor, and then type the expression for the new measure, Above (sum(SalesAmount)).
11. Click on the **Apply** button to close the expression editor and save the expression.
12. In the **Label** of the measure, type Sales LY.
13. Fix the measure **Number formatting** to show a number with two decimal places.
14. Click on the **Done** button to enter the visualization mode. The **Table** chart will look like this:

Order Year Q	Sales $	Sales LY
Totals	1,265,793.04	–
2016	208,083.97	–
2017	617,085.20	208,083.97
2018	440,623.87	617,085.20

15. Click on the **Edit** button to enter the edit mode.
16. Go to the properties panel and click on the **Data** heading to expand it.
17. Click on the **Add column** button again to add the third measure.
18. Click on the *fx* button to open the expression editor, and then type the following expression for the new measure: Column(1)/Above(sum(SalesAmount)).
19. Click on the **Apply** button to close the expression editor and save the expression.
20. In the **Label** of the measure, type Sales Variance.

21. Fix the measure **Number formatting** to show the number as a percentage with two decimal places. The **Table** chart will look like this:

Order Year	Sales $	Sales LY	Sales Variance
Totals	1,265,793.04	-	-
2016	208,083.97	-	-
2017	617,085.20	208,083.97	296.56%
2018	440,623.87	617,085.20	71.40%

We learned how to calculate a year over year variance. We used the `Above()` function in the **Sales LY** column to retrieve the value of the previous record; that is, the previous year. The **Sales Variance** calculates the percentage between the value from the current record and the previous record. On this column, the value for the current record was retrieved using the `Column(1)` function with the number 1 as a parameter to get the value from the first measure.

You can only use the `Column()` function to reference measure columns.

Using AGGR for advanced aggregation

So far, we have learned how to use several aggregation functions, such as `sum`, `max`, `min`, and `avg`. When used in a measure of a chart or table, these functions aggregate values over the dimension stated in that chart or table.

Sometimes you need to create a second aggregation based on the result of the first. An example of this could be the average value of sales over a sum of categories. Another example is to find the highest value for product sales in each category.

In these situations, we need to use the AGGR function.

Before starting the examples, we will create a new sheet with the name AGGR. The following steps will help us to create and use a new sheet:

1. Open the app and click on **Create new sheet**
2. Set the title of the sheet to AGGR
3. Click on the sheet icon to save the title, and then open the sheet to start creating

Calculating the top sales product over each category

Here, we will learn how to create a calculation to retrieve the top sales product value over each category and the corresponding name of the top sale product. The value is **Sales Amount**.

We will start by adding the visualization, **Table** chart with dimension **Category**, and master measure **Sales $**.

Follow these steps to create the visualizations:

1. Click on the **Edit** button to enter the edit mode.
2. Click on the **Charts** button on the asset panel, which is on the left-hand side of the screen, and find the **Table** chart.
3. Click on the **Table** chart, and then drag and drop it into the empty space at the top of the sheet:

4. Click on the **Add dimension** button and select **Category** in the **Dimensions** section.
5. Click on the **Data** heading in the properties panel to expand it.
6. Find the **Add column** button, click on it, and choose **Measure**.
7. Select **Sales $** in the **Measure** section.
8. Fix the measure **Number formatting** to show a number with two decimal places.
9. Click on the **Add column** button again to add the second measure.
10. Click on the *fx* button to open the expression editor, and then type the expression for the new measure, `max(aggr(sum(SalesAmount), CategoryName, ProductName))`.
11. Click on the **Apply** button to close the expression editor and save the expression.
12. In the **Label** of the measure, type `Top Sales Product Value`.
13. Fix the measure **Number formatting** to show a number with two decimal places.
14. Click on the **Done** button to enter the visualization mode. The **Table** chart will look like this:

AGGR

Category	Sales $	Top Sales Product Value
Totals	1,265,793.04	141,396.73
Beverages	267,868.18	141,396.73
Condiments	106,047.08	16,701.09
Confections	167,357.22	47,234.97
Dairy Products	234,507.28	71,155.70
Grains/Cereals	95,744.59	42,593.06
Meat/Poultry	163,022.36	80,368.67
Produce	99,984.58	41,819.65
Seafood	131,261.74	29,171.87

15. Click on the **Edit** button to enter the edit mode.
16. Go to the properties panel and click on the **Data** heading to expand it.
17. Click on the **Add column** button again to add the third measure.
18. Click on the *fx* button to open the expression editor, and then type the expression for the new measure, `Firstsortedvalue(ProductName, -aggr(Sum(SalesAmount), CategoryName, ProductName))`.

19. Click on the **Apply** button to close the expression editor and save the expression.
20. In the **Label** of the measure, type `Top Sales Product Name`.
21. Find the **Totals** function property in the measure and select **None** to not display a value in the total heading. The **Table** chart will look like this:

Category	Sales $	Top Sales Product Value	Top Sales Product Name
Totals	1,265,793.04	141,396.73	-
Beverages	267,868.18	141,396.73	Côte de Blaye
Condiments	106,047.08	16,701.09	Vegie-spread
Confections	167,357.22	47,234.97	Tarte au sucre
Dairy Products	234,507.28	71,155.70	Raclette Courdavault
Grains/Cereals	95,744.59	42,593.06	Gnocchi di nonna Alice
Meat/Poultry	163,022.36	80,368.67	Thüringer Rostbratwurst
Produce	99,984.58	41,819.65	Manjimup Dried Apples
Seafood	131,261.74	29,171.87	Carnarvon Tigers

We can now use the AGGR function to retrieve information about the top-performing product in each category on the sales amount.

The AGGR function works like the script load with a group by creating a virtual table with one measure (first parameter) and one or more dimensions as the second to *n*th parameter. In this example, the aggregation dimension is **Category** and **Product**.

By combining `Max()` and `AGGR()`, we found the highest value for the **Sales Amount** of a product in each category they belong to.

We used `FirstSortedValue(value, sorting_argument)` to show the corresponding product with the highest value for the **Sales Amount**. This returns the value (product) that corresponds to the result of the sorting argument. In general, the sorting argument is a field, but we can also use an `AGGR()` expression. We add a minus sign in front of the sorting argument to start the sorting from highest to lowest, and not from lowest to highest, which is the default sorting criteria.

Leveraging Set Analysis for in-calculation selection

By default, all calculations refer to the current selection state. In some specific situations, you may need to show data from a different selection. We can define a **Set Analysis** in calculations to help us modify the selection state for one or more fields.

Set Analysis is a unique feature in Qlik Sense. Each set contains a group of selected dimensional values. The sets allow the users to create independent selections, other than the one being used in the active Qlik Sense objects. The set expression is defined inside curly brackets ({}). The set identifiers are separated from the modifiers by angular brackets (< >).

A Set Analysis expression consists of three main parts:

- **Set identifiers** define the relationship between the set expression and the field values or the expression that is being evaluated. Some examples include $, 1, and 1-$ - (Qlik, help).
- **Set modifiers** (optional) are made up of one or several field names, each followed by a selection that should be made on the field (Qlik, help).
- **Set operators** (optional) are used to refine the set of data by specifying how the sets of data represented by the identifiers or modifiers are combined to create a subset or superset of data. The most common operators are + (union), - (subtraction), and / (intersection) (Qlik, help).

For example, to summarize the sales from 2017 for two countries, we can write the following Set Analysis expression: `Sum({$<OrderYear={2017},Country={Brazil, 'United Kingdom'}>}SalesAmount)`.

When using set modifiers, you need to specify sets of elements. The sets of elements can be enclosed in single quotation marks. Here's an explanation of single quotation marks usage:

- For numerical elements, you don't need to use single quotation marks
- For string elements with a single word, single quotation marks are optional
- For string elements with two or more words, such as United Kingdom, you need to enclose them in single quotation marks
- For date or time elements, you must enclose them in single quotation marks

You can also create a set of elements with a search expression using the same syntax used in a filter panel in your dashboard interface. In this case, it's mandatory to enclose the set using double quotation marks.

Before starting the examples, we will create a new sheet with the name `Set Analysis`. The following steps will help us to create and use a new sheet:

1. Open the app and click on **Create new sheet**
2. Set the title of the sheet to `Set Analysis`
3. Click on the sheet icon to save the title, and then open the sheet to start creating

Selecting a specific country for comparison

In this section, we will learn how to create an expression to retrieve the sales amount of a specific country so that we can use this value to compare it against all other countries.

To start, we will add a **Table** visualization to the sheet, **Table** chart with dimension **Country**, and master measure **Sales $**.

Follow these steps to create the visualizations:

1. Click on the **Edit** button to enter the edit mode.
2. Click on the **Charts** button on the asset panel, which is on the left-hand side of the screen, and find the **Table** chart.
3. Click on the **Table** chart, and then drag and drop it into the empty space at the top of the sheet:

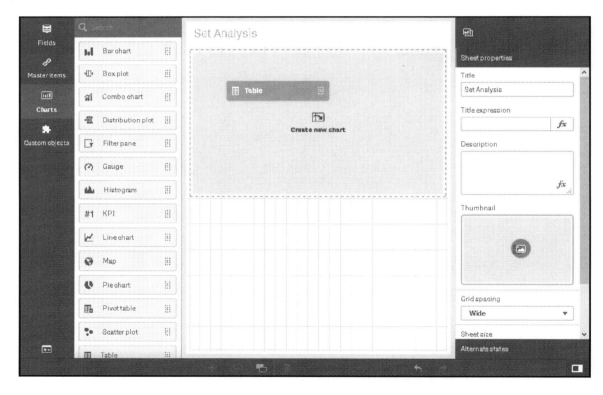

4. Click on the **Add dimension** button and select **Country** in the **Dimensions** section.

5. Click on the **Data** heading in the properties panel to expand it.
6. Find the **Add column** button, click on it, and choose **Measure**.
7. Select **Sales $** in the **Measure** section.
8. Fix the measure **Number formatting** to show a number with two decimal places.
9. Click on the **Add column** button again to add the second measure.
10. Click on the *fx* button to open the expression editor, and then type the following expression for the new measure: `sum({<Country={Brazil}>} SalesAmount)`.
11. Click on the **Apply** button to close the expression editor and save the expression.
12. In the **Label** of the measure, type `Brazil Sales $`.
13. Fix the measure **Number formatting** to show a number with two decimal places.
14. Click on the **Done** button to enter the visualization mode. The **Table** chart will look like this:

Set Analysis

Country	Sales $	Brazil Sales $
Totals	**1,265,793.04**	**106,925.78**
Argentina	8,119.10	0.00
Austria	128,003.84	0.00
Belgium	33,824.85	0.00
Brazil	106,925.78	106,925.78
Canada	50,196.29	0.00
Denmark	32,661.02	0.00
Finland	18,810.05	0.00
France	81,358.32	0.00
Germany	230,284.63	0.00
Ireland	49,979.90	0.00
Italy	16,770.15	0.00
Mexico	23,582.08	0.00
Norway	5,735.15	0.00
Poland	3,531.95	0.00
Portugal	11,472.36	0.00
Spain	17,983.20	0.00
Sweden	54,495.14	0.00
Switzerland	31,692.66	0.00
UK	58,971.31	0.00
USA	245,584.61	0.00
Venezuela	56,810.63	0.00

We can only see **Brazil** with its value. To create the calculation of the value on Brazil, the **Sales $** column needs to be repeated along all other countries. We will fix this by adding the TOTAL qualifier, as follows:

1. Click on the **Edit** button to enter the edit mode.
2. Go to the properties panel and click on the **Data** heading to expand it.
3. Find the **Brazil Sales $** measure.
4. Click on the *fx* button to open the expression editor, and then replace the expressions with the following: sum(TOTAL {<Country={Brazil}>} SalesAmount).
5. Click on the **Apply** button to close the expression editor and save the expression.
6. Find the **Totals** function property in the measure, and then select **None** to not display a value in the total heading. The **Table** chart will look like this:

Country Q	Sales $	Brazil Sales $
Totals	1,265,793.04	-
Argentina	8,119.10	106,925.78
Austria	128,003.84	106,925.78
Belgium	33,824.85	106,925.78
Brazil	106,925.78	106,925.78
Canada	50,196.29	106,925.78
Denmark	32,661.02	106,925.78
Finland	18,810.05	106,925.78
France	81,368.32	106,925.78
Germany	230,284.63	106,925.78
Ireland	49,979.90	106,925.78
Italy	15,770.15	106,925.78
Mexico	23,582.08	106,925.78
Norway	5,735.15	106,925.78
Poland	3,531.95	106,925.78
Portugal	11,472.36	106,925.78
Spain	17,983.20	106,925.78
Sweden	54,495.14	106,925.78
Switzerland	31,692.66	106,925.78
UK	58,971.31	106,925.78
USA	245,584.61	106,925.78
Venezuela	56,810.63	106,925.78

To create the comparison calculation, add another measure column:

1. Click on the *fx* button to open the expression editor, and then replace the expressions with the following: `Column(1)-Column(2)`.
2. Click on the **Apply** button to close the expression editor and save the expression.
3. In the **Label** of the measure, type `Variance`.
4. Fix the measure **Number formatting** to show a number with two decimal places.
5. Click on the **Done** button to enter the visualization mode. The **Table** chart will look like this:

Set Analysis

Country	Sales $	Brazil Sales $	Variance
Totals	**1,265,793.04**	–	**1,158,867.26**
Argentina	8,119.10	106,925.78	-98,806.68
Austria	128,003.84	106,925.78	21,078.06
Belgium	33,824.86	106,925.78	-73,100.92
Brazil	106,925.78	106,925.78	0.00
Canada	50,196.29	106,925.78	-56,729.49
Denmark	32,661.02	106,925.78	-74,264.75
Finland	18,810.05	106,925.78	-88,115.72
France	81,358.32	106,925.78	-25,567.45
Germany	230,284.63	106,925.78	123,358.86
Ireland	49,979.90	106,925.78	-56,945.87
Italy	15,770.16	106,925.78	-91,155.62
Mexico	23,582.08	106,925.78	-83,343.70
Norway	5,735.15	106,925.78	-101,190.63
Poland	3,531.95	106,925.78	-103,393.83
Portugal	11,472.36	106,925.78	-95,453.41
Spain	17,983.20	106,925.78	-88,942.58
Sweden	54,495.14	106,925.78	-52,430.64
Switzerland	31,692.66	106,925.78	-75,233.12
UK	58,971.31	106,925.78	-47,954.47
USA	245,584.61	106,925.78	138,658.83
Venezuela	56,810.63	106,925.78	-50,115.15

We learned how to use a Set Analysis modifier, `{<Country={Brazil}>}`, in the `sum()` function to summarize sales only for Brazil, but the resulting value was only applied to a single row. To repeat the result on all the other rows in the table, we used the `TOTAL` qualifier to disregard the dimension. To calculate the variance between **Sales $** and Brazil's **Sales $**, we used the `Column()` function to reuse the calculations already created in the first two measures of the table, so we don't need to repeat all the formulas again.

Summary

In this chapter, we learned how to effectively create expressions with conditions and aggregation. We looked at how to use the AGGR function. We also learned how to use data already loaded in charts to create calculations with inter-record functions, and finally, we explored using Set Analysis to create set modifiers for in-calculation selections.

In the next chapter, you will learn how to create narratives with your data using the Stories feature.

Further reading

To learn more about the functions used in this chapter, check out the Qlik Sense online help at `https://help.qlik.com/en-US/sense/November2018/Subsystems/Hub/Content/Sense_Hub/ChartFunctions/visualization-expressions.htm`

You can find more useful tips and tricks to use with AGGR and Set Analysis in *Qlik Sense Cookbook - Second Edition*, Packt Publishing (`https://www.packtpub.com/big-data-and-business-intelligence/qlik-sense-cookbook-second-edition`).

7
Creating Data Stories

The whole idea of storytelling when applied to **business intelligence (BI)** is to take an idea or an insight and turn it into an appealing story to show what we think about it. The story makes our insight more interesting. This also happens in everyday life; stories have always been the go-to method to grab someone's attraction.

Aristotle, the Greek philosopher from the third century BC, argued that to convince people, we need the following:

- **Ethos**: We have the right to say something about a matter when we are ethical (this word comes directly from *ethos*) and we have the credibility to talk about that subject because we have a strong background or knowledge about that matter.
- **Logos**: We appeal to logical reasoning (the word *logic* comes directly from *logos*) because we are using facts and numbers.
- **Pathos**: We persuade an audience by appealing to their emotions. This is why we tell a story. Modern neuroscience tells us that when we tell a story, we activate the limbic system, which is related to our emotions. To activate this area, we have to capture the audience's attention using images, videos, different colors, and so on.

Qlik Sense has a built-in feature called **stories** that allows users to present their data discoveries and insights as a slideshow, creating an effective mode of communication across the organization. Stories allow users to share their data discoveries using well-known presentation tools, similar to those of Microsoft PowerPoint, but with a lot of improvements.

In this chapter, we are going to look at an effective way to communicate insights using a Qlik Sense feature called **storytelling** by covering the following topics:

- An overview of stories
- Creating snapshots
- Planning and organizing presentations

- Creating and editing stories
- Sharing stories

An overview of stories

A **story** is structured as a timeline of slides. Each slide consists of one or more elements (snapshots, text, images, and shapes) that are combined to tell you something about the data and your analysis of it. A **slide** is a part of a story and corresponds to a screen, or in other words, a collection of text, images, and other objects. A **snapshot** is an image (a table, graph, or **key performance indicator** (**KPI**)) that represents the state of a data object at a certain point in time.

The process to create and publish a story is shown in the following workflow:

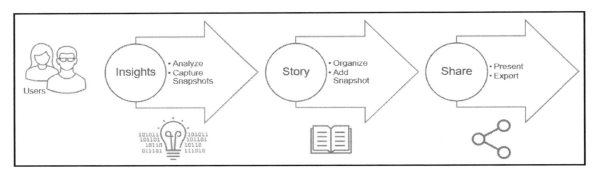

The user does the following:

- Uses the application, applying filters and getting insights
- Collects insights when they find something that should be added to their story (graphs, tables, or KPIs)
- Creates a story
- Adds snapshots to the story by adding one or more slides
- Adds explanatory text, images, or other decorations
- Uses the story to make a presentation or exports it as a PDF or presentation form

Creating snapshots

Snapshots are static representations of the state of an object from one Qlik Sense application at a certain point in time. A snapshot is a copy of that object, even though the original object might have been deleted or changed, or the underlying data reloaded. The snapshot keeps the context, format, and value of the original object.

For every Qlik Sense object, any changes made to the **filter pane** and the extensions can be captured as a snapshot in a very simple and intuitive way. When you place your cursor over the object, an icon with a camera appears, which looks like this:

When you click the icon, the object's state is captured and a form is displayed, giving you the opportunity to describe the snapshot using an annotation, as shown in the following screenshot (this is very useful for organizing your snapshot library):

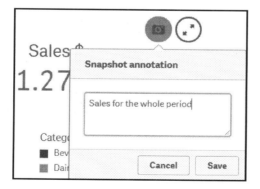

You can add an annotation to help you remember the selections that were made when the snapshot was taken.

Now, let's take two more snapshots so that we can create a story later on. Place your cursor over the following two graphs and take snapshots:

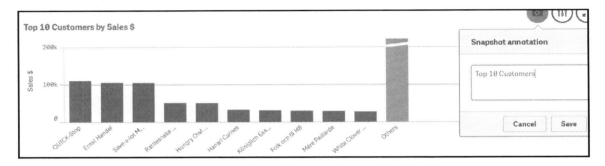

The following is the pie chart:

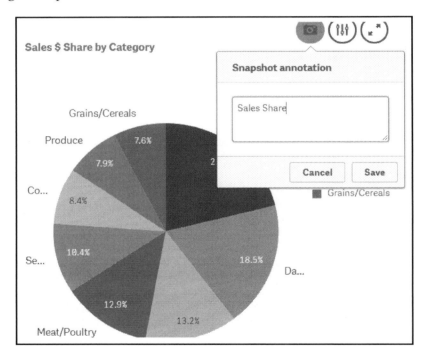

In this section, we've seen how to use snapshots and have learned how this can help us analyze data. For every insight that we want to add to our presentation (story), we take a snapshot to show that data.

When editing your story, you can always come back and take more snapshots of the required graphs. Don't worry about capturing all the insights at once.

Planning and organizing your presentation

Before starting your presentation, take a few minutes to think about how to create and format your presentation. This book is not intended to be a complete guide on how to create presentations, but here are a few useful tips:

- **Keep it small**: Don't add dozens of slides and prints. *Less is more*. Brevity in communication is more effective than verbosity. Get straight to the point.
- **Use visual aids**: We are using a visual analytics platform, so use the snapshots feature to add graphs and corroborate the insights you want to share. For example, instead of *writing* that Beverages is the top selling category for a particular region, *add a bar chart* that demonstrates this information. People are smart: if you show information in a suitable manner, they will draw their own conclusions. Using Qlik Sense stories, you can add shapes, images, and effects to make your slides more appealing.
- **Use the rule of three**: There's a Latin phrase that goes *omne trium perfectum* (everything that comes in threes is perfect). People are more likely to remember information you are sharing as a group of three because using three entities combines both brevity and rhythm (the information is not too simple, but there is not too much of it either). You might notice that throughout literature, a lot of stories use this concept, including the *Three Little Pigs* and the *Three Musketeers*. Similarly, many important mottos also use this rule: *Faster, Higher, Stronger* (Olympics), *veni, vidi, vici* (Julius Caesar), and *Life, Liberty, and the Pursuit of Happiness* (*The Declaration of Independence*). Consider organizing your presentation into three sections (a beginning, an explanation, and a conclusion).

Creating stories

Using the snapshots we took previously, let's create our first story by going through the following steps:

1. From the app overview, or sheet view, click the small **Stories** icon that lies at the top of the screen. This icon looks as follows:

2. Click on the **Create new story** button, as shown in the following screenshot:

3. A story named **My new story** is created. We can rename it, add a description and a thumbnail image, or even delete the story using the form shown in the following screenshot:

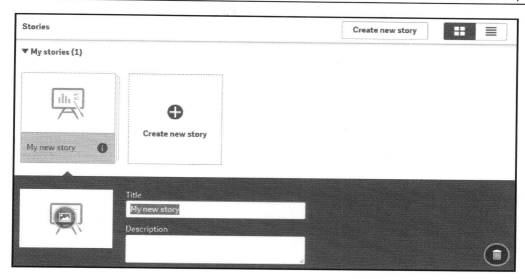

4. This brings us to the following screen, which allows us to manage our story:

As you can see, we have four major areas:

- **The left area**: Here, we can see a preview of all our slides, as shown in the following screenshot. We can either rearrange the slides, add more slides, or delete the existing ones:

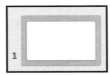

- **The right area**: Here, we can access the following:
    - **Snapshot library**: All the snapshots that we take are located here
    - **Text objects**: This allows us to add text objects (titles and paragraphs)
    - **Shapes library**: This is used to add shapes to make our story more compelling
    - **Effects library**: This is used to add effects to snapshots (we will see how this works in the *Editing your story* section)
    - **Media library**: This is used to add images from a previously loaded library or to upload images to use
    - **Sheet library**: This is used to add a whole sheet to the presentation

- **The area at the bottom**: Here, we can access icons that help us cut, copy, paste, and delete objects (snapshots, shapes, images, or text), as shown in the following screenshot:

- **The central area**: The central area is the blank white screen in which you edit each of your slides.

Let's get back to creating the story:

1. Begin by dragging the snapshot of the KPI from the **Snapshot library**, as shown in the following code:

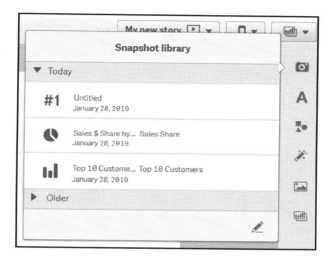

2. Add a square shape and a title so that we can create a bar on top and add some text, as shown in the following screenshot:

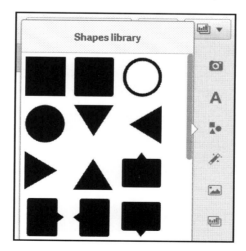

3. Use the **Title** object, as shown in the following screenshot:

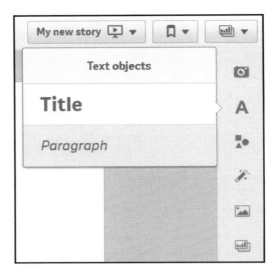

4. You will see something that looks as follows:

5. Drag and drop the box, reposition it, and change its color so that it looks like a top bar, as shown in the following screenshot:

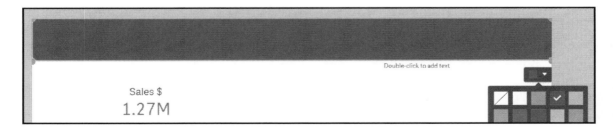

6. Double-click the title and change the content to `Qlik Sense Story`, as shown in the following screenshot:

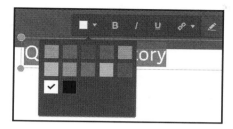

7. Change the color to white and then move it to the appropriate position, as shown in the following screenshot:

8. The slide should then look as follows:

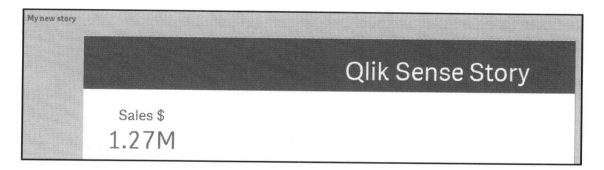

9. Add a description of the KPI using an arrow (from the shapes library) and a paragraph (from the text objects), as shown in the following screenshot:

10. Resize the arrow (using the circles next to the borders) and change the color to a light gray, as shown in the following screenshot:

11. Change the text paragraph to **Sales for the whole period** and adjust the position using your mouse or the arrow keys on your keyboard, as shown in the following screenshot:

12. Add the two other snapshots that we collected in the *Creating snapshots* sections. Go to the **Snapshots library** and drag and drop them into your slide, creating a screen that looks as follows:

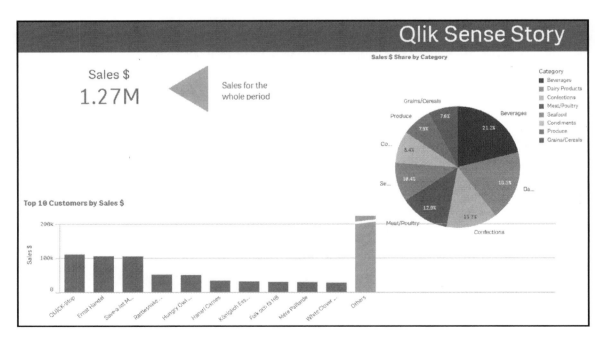

13. Do you remember the rule of three? Look at the previous slide: we added three graphs, with descriptions. Keep it small, keep it simple.

14. The first slide is now ready. Play it using the **Play the story** button, as shown in the following screenshot:

Qlik Sense Enterprise will enter presentation mode, showing a page that looks as follows:

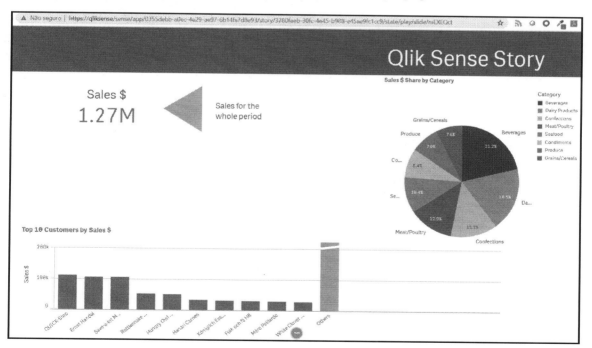

You can use this page to deliver your presentation and tell a story about the data and your insights.

Keep in mind that any time you have to explain any details about your data, you can right-click on your graph and go to the source, and you will be redirected to your application with your object surrounded by a blue box, as shown in the following screenshot:

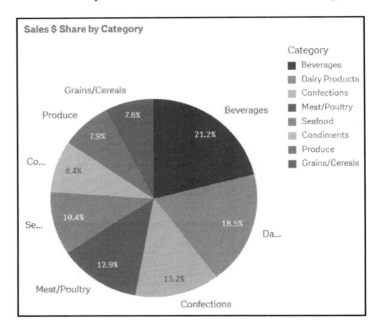

The next section will look at editing and improving the story we created in this section.

Editing your story

In the last section, *Creating your story*, we discussed the process of creating and telling a story, which is basically as follows:

- Take a snapshot
- Add it to a slide
- Add decorations and more information
- Play your story

Now, let's add some more insights to the story by collecting some snapshots from the Qlik Sense application using the following steps:

1. Go to the **Product Analysis** sheet and select the **Beverages** option under the **Category** section, as shown in the following screenshot:

2. The bar chart will show the products from this category. Place your cursor over this chart and take a snapshot, renaming it as **Top products for Beverage**, as shown in the following screenshot:

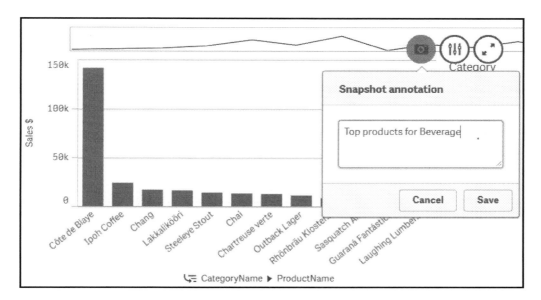

3. Using the same process, collect a snapshot from the scatter graph, renaming it as **Products Discount x Sales for Beverages**, as shown in the following screenshot:

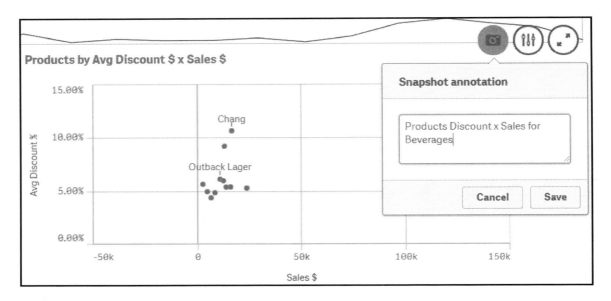

4. Collect a snapshot from the time series chart, renaming it as **Beverages Sales over period**, as shown in the following screenshot:

Once we have three snapshots (remember the rule of three?), let's include them in the story, as follows:

1. Go to the **Stories** menu and click on **My new story**, which will allow us to edit the story as we want, as shown in the following screenshot:

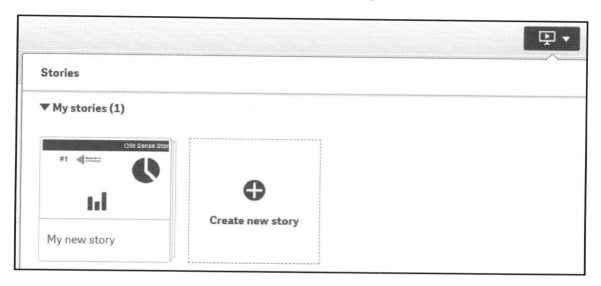

2. Since we already have a top bar, we can reuse it here. Duplicate this by right-clicking on our first slide and using the **Duplicate** option, as shown in the following screenshot:

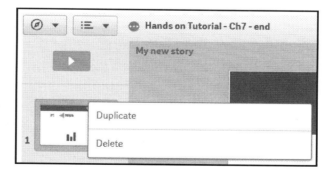

3. Remove all graphical objects but leave the top bar and the title. Change the title to **Beverages Analysis**, as shown in the following screenshot:

4. Drag the snapshots that pertain to the **Beverages** category onto our sheet, as shown in the following screenshot:

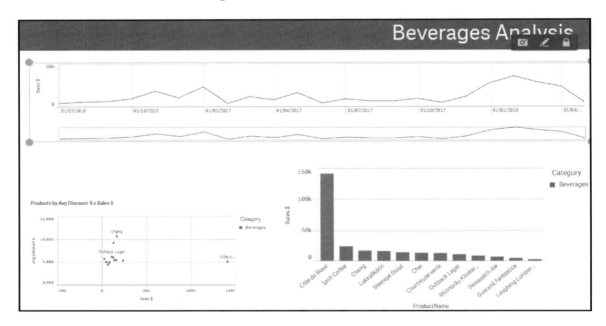

5. Add a text object of the **Paragraph** type and a shape to describe some elements and add some information. Use the color gray, as shown in the following screenshot:

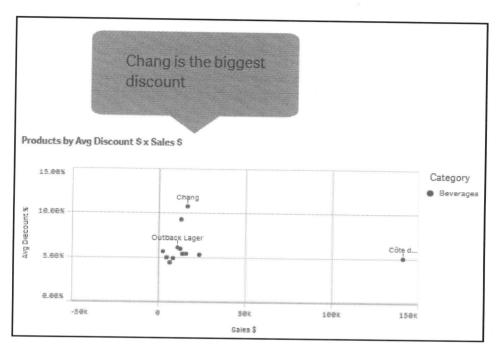

6. Sometimes, the object may be superimposed. In this case, right-click and change the order of the objects, as depicted in the following screenshot:

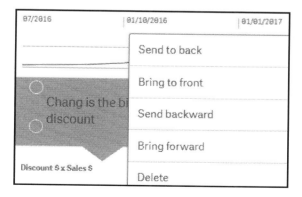

7. Add an effect to the bar chart by highlighting the product that has the highest sales, as shown in the following screenshot:

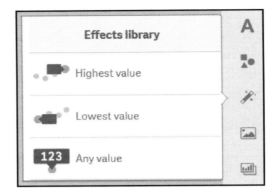

8. To do this, choose the highest value effect and drag and drop it over the graph, as shown in the following screenshot:

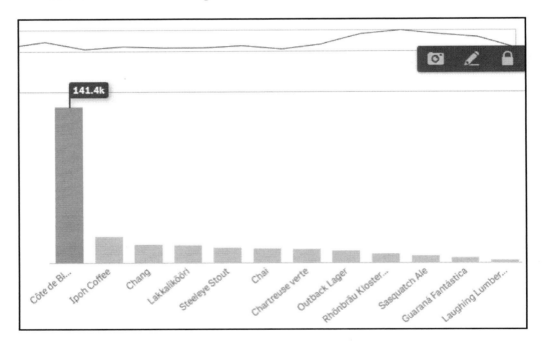

9. The slide should look as follows:

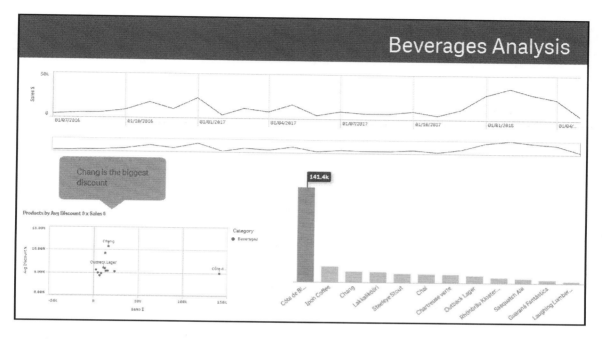

Use the **Play the story** button to see how the story is displayed. You can navigate through the slides using the keyboard (the left arrow goes to the previous slide and the right arrow advances to the next slide).

To test this feature, go to the source by moving the mouse over the bar chart. This is done to ensure that it is the exact selection that was made when the snapshot was taken, as shown in the following screenshot:

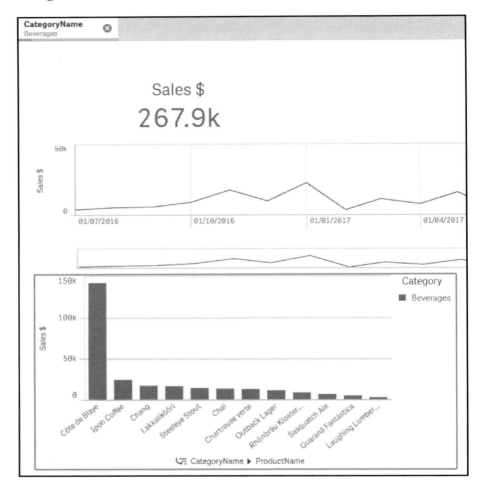

We can also insert a whole sheet from our app into our story. To do this, go to the menu on the right and select an option from the **Sheet library**, as shown in the following screenshot:

The selected options will be shown as in the following screenshot:

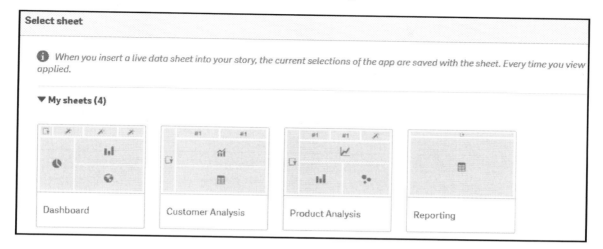

You can choose from three alignment options, as shown in the following screenshot:

Please note that when you add a whole sheet to your story, it is *live data*, so any data changes in your app will be reflected in your story. This is the opposite of a snapshot, which captures the values from the time when it was taken.

Sharing stories

In the previous sections, we built our story using the features provided by Qlik Sense. It's now time to deliver the presentation and tell the story.

As we have seen, the most common way of sharing insights is by using the **Play the story** button, as shown in the following screenshot. This will change your story from being in edit mode to play mode:

You can directly access your story in play mode using your browser URL. The form is `https://[hostname]/sense/app/[YourAppID]/story/[YouStoryID]/state/play`.

 Go into play mode and save the link in your browser.

While in play mode, there are various features that you can use to make it easier to deliver your presentation, as described in the following list:

- **Keyboard shortcuts**: Use the arrow keys to navigate to the next or the previous slide.

- **Highlight a section of your data**: Click on a slice of a pie chart or a bar of a bar chart to visualize that particular value, as shown in the following screenshot:

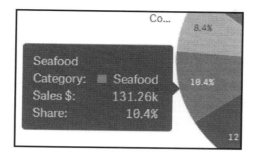

- **Go to source**: Right-click on a graph and you will be redirected to the exact place in which the snapshot was taken.
- **Fast navigation**: Use the small button at the bottom to go directly to a specific slide, as shown in the following screenshot:

- **Export**: You can export your story as a PDF or PowerPoint file, as shown in the following screenshot:

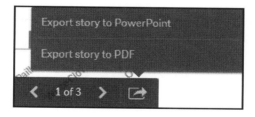

If your target audience has no access to Qlik Sense, you can download a copy of your story (as a PDF or a PowerPoint document) and share it using email.

Summary

In this chapter, we learned about an effective method of sharing insights from our data called storytelling. It is a way of sharing your thoughts and adding information about the data you have in a Qlik Sense application.

We also learned some presentation techniques and how to create a story, collect snapshots, and add them to slides in our presentation.

We also saw how to make a presentation and export our story to a PDF file or a Microsoft Office PowerPoint presentation.

In the next chapter, you will learn how to create a summarized application. This application will be capable of analyzing a database that contains the data of a million bike trips without sacrificing too much RAM.

Further reading

- Qlik Sense Documentation (https://help.qlik.com/en-US/sense/November2018/Subsystems/Hub/Content/Sense_Hub/StoryTelling/use-data-storytelling.htm)
- *Effective Presentation Techniques – The Top 10* (https://www.presentationmagazine.com/effective-presentation-techniques-the-top-10-149.htm)
- *The Power of Three: Why Fairy Tales Often Feature a Triple* (https://fairytalez.com/blog/the-power-of-three-why-fairy-tales-often-feature-a-triple/)
- *Ethos, Pathos, and Logos Definition and Examples* (https://pathosethoslogos.com/)
- *The Limbic System* (https://webspace.ship.edu/cgboer/limbicsystem.html)

Section 4: Additional Features

4

Here, you will learn a number of additional features available in Qlik Sense Enterprise Server.

This section compromises the following chapters:

- Chapter 8, *Engaging ODAG*
- Chapter 9, *Creating a Native Map Using Geo Analytics*
- Chapter 10, *Working with Self-Service Analytics*
- Chapter 11, *Data Forecasting Using Advanced Analytics*
- Chapter 12, *Deploying Qlik Sense Apps for Mobile/Tablets*

8
Engaging On-Demand App Generation

On-demand App Generation (ODAG) is one technique that Qlik Sense Enterprise platforms have to create fresh new apps on-demand based on user selections. This feature is used mainly in situations where the size of your data is much bigger than your Qlik Sense Enterprise server's RAM memory.

Using the ODAG feature enables users to analyze billions of records without retrieving the whole dataset into memory. The idea behind this concept is that it is not necessary (or sometimes not even possible) to load all detailed data inside your Qlik Sense box RAM memory. We may simply summarize a sample of our data that leverages users to analyze business metrics. If a detailed version is needed, Qlik Sense will generate a fresh new application with that data.

In this chapter, we will learn how to create a summarized application, which is a regular Qlik Sense app where the fact table is aggregated. This application is capable of analyzing a database that contains the data of a million bike trips without sacrificing too much RAM. By integrating a template, we leverage the capability to dig into detailed information. When the user needs to see the detailed Qlik Sense data, we will use the template to generate another application with the detailed data that the user has requested.

The following topics will be covered in this chapter:

- How Qlik Sense handles large data volumes
- Setting up Google BigQuery Account
- Configuring Qlik Sense for ODAG applications
- Building a summarized application
- Building a detailed application
- Integrating the summarized and detailed applications

Technical requirements

The technology used in this chapter is as follows:

- Qlik Sense Enterprise access with admin rights
- **Qlik Sense Management Console (QMC)** knowledge
- Google BigQuery

How Qlik Sense handles large volumes of data

The usual Qlik in-memory approach does a really good job of handling usual datasets (millions of records). Obtaining the answer in a sub-second upon user selection is a regular experience.

Qlik Indexing Engine (QIX) is Qlik's patented in-memory data-indexing technology. This approach loads and keeps the user dataset (databases, files, and data lakes extracts) in server memory. It does this using a compression algorithm that can compress data down to 10% of original data. Let's understand how this works; while the data is being loaded by your script or data manager internally, Qlik engine creates some tables to accommodate your data. First, Qlik creates a **symbol table** for each field with two fields (pointer and value); then the engine loads only distinct values to this table and creates a pointer with the smallest bit representation for how many distinct values were loaded. This table has only one row for each distinct value and the smallest binary representation of that number. Let's see some examples of the symbol table.

Let's suppose we are loading a small table such as this:

Gender	Age
Male	0-1 years
Other	100
Female	110
Male	001
... (more rows)	...
Male	001

The following is the symbol table for the gender field (only one record for each distinct value and a the smallest binary representation of the value) would be:

Value	Pointer
Female	00
Male	01
Other	10

The following is the symbol table for the age field (only one record for each distinct value and the smallest binary representation of the value) would be:

Value	Pointer
0-1 years	000
2-5 years	001
6-10 years	010
11-15 years	011
16-24 years	100
25-40 years	101
More than 40 years	110

Qlik engine now recreates the original data table with just the pointers (binary representation stored from symbol tables):

Gender	Age
01	000
10	100
00	110
01	001
... (more rows)	...
01	001

As you can see, this approach leads to a much more compact representation of the loaded data, which creates a very optimized dataset. Please check `https://community.qlik.com/ t5/Qlik-Design-Blog/Symbol-Tables-and-Bit-Stuffed-Pointers/ba-p/1475369` to find a more detailed description of this model.

But how can we handle a really big dataset that contains billions of rows? While adding more RAM is an option, this might not always be feasible. To handle this situation, we now have four approaches to handle big datasets in Qlik technology, which can be used together or apart:

- **Segmentation**: Segmentation is the process of splitting one huge Qlik application into several applications. For example, instead of having one huge application with information on the entire country, we can split it into one app for each state of data.
- **Chaining**: Chaining is an approach that is usually attached to segmentation. This refers to the linking of multiple segmented Qlik applications, which maintains some sense of selection. This means that when a user selects something that is related to another application, they are redirected to that application with the same selections, keeping the selections made so that the experience is smooth and natural. As observed in the following diagram, when a user makes a selection in **SegApp1**, they will be redirected to the respective application, keeping the current selections, so the user can even think they are using the same application:

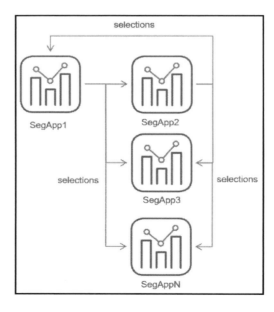

- **Direct discovery**: Using this approach, a SQL statement is executed against the original data source for each uncached selection made by a user. In this case, the values from dimensions are usually pre-populated and for each calculation the SQL is reevaluated. This approach is being deprecated, giving way to ODAG.

- **ODAG**: In the June 2017 version, Qlik Sense Enterprise launched a new way of handling really big datasets. This method is called ODAG. In this scenario, we have a **summarized application** (as we can see in the following diagram) that is refreshed by a schedule, which retrieves a consolidated view of the data (rolling up by date, product). This application is loaded in-memory and, if the user wants more detailed information, all selections that were made are passed to the **detailed application template script** that retrieves only the required detailed subset from the **Data Lake**:

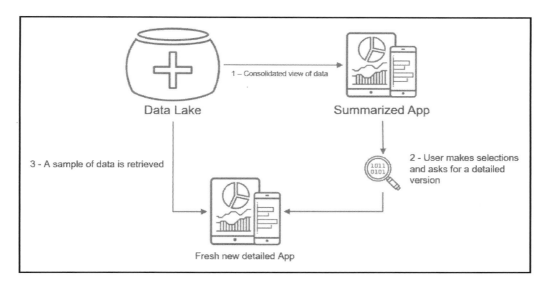

This approach allows you to analyze billions of data records through a summarized view (something that Apache Hive, Impala, Redshift, BigQuery, or alternatives do very well) and if the user wants to analyze a detailed version of the scenario, a fresh new application with a custom query can retrieve the records that were selected.

Setting up a Google BigQuery account

Google's BigQuery (`https://cloud.google.com/bigquery/`) is a service provided by Google as part of Google Cloud Platform as a serverless enterprise data warehouse. This can be deployed in minutes and tested using a free tier. They have a data sample that we can use. Perform the following steps to set up an account:

1. Set up the data lake access using `https://cloud.google.com/bigquery/` and click on **TRY BIGQUERY FREE**. From here, you will be redirected to your Google account login form:

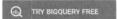

GOOGLE BIGQUERY

A fast, highly scalable, cost-effective, and fully managed cloud data warehouse for analytics, with built-in machine learning.

> TRY BIGQUERY FREE

View documentation for this product.

> If you don't have a Google account, please create a new one for the purpose of this chapter. You're going to receive a $300.00 credit, which is valid for 12 months.

Once you are redirected to **Google Cloud Platform** (`https://console.cloud.google.com`), which is the Google **Software as a Service (SaaS)** ecosystem home, we can see where the BigQuery console resides:

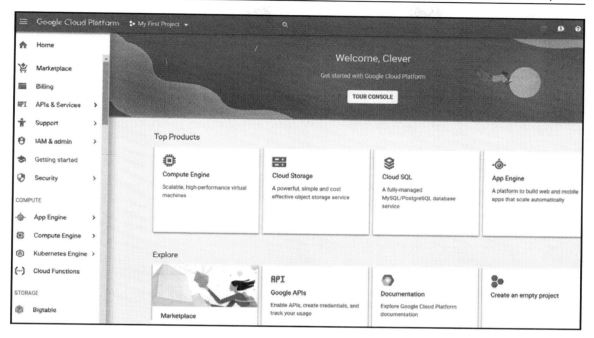

2. To the left side of our screen, find the **BIG DATA** section, under which we can see the **BigQuery** section. Click on **BigQuery**:

3. **Open** `https://console.cloud.google.com/bigquery?p=bigquery-public-data d=new_york_citibike,` **which redirects you to a screen that should look like this:**

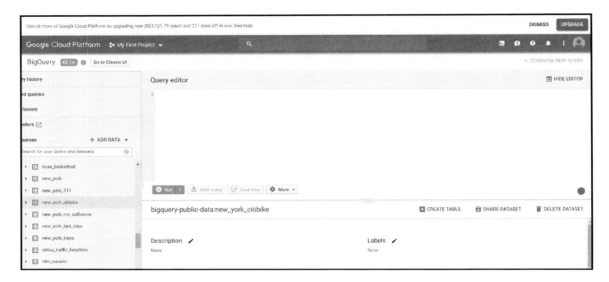

4. On the left-hand side, click in `new_york_citibike,` expanding the view so you can see **citibike_trips**. Click on **citibike_trips**:

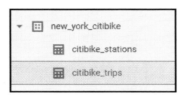

5. Press the **QUERY TABLE** option:

6. A template of SQL query will be inserted into editor and is similar to the following query:

```
SELECT FROM 'bigquery-public-data.new_york_citibike.citibike_trips'
LIMIT 1000
```

Exchange the template script with the following script (you can find it at `https://github.com/PacktPublishing/Hands-On-Business-Intelligence-with-Qlik-Sense/blob/master/Chapter08/01%20-%20First.sql`). This script below will retrieve data aggregated for every month with start and end stations, number of trips and total duration of the trips. The resulting data will be the base for our Qlik Sense summarized app:

```
SELECT
 TIMESTAMP_TRUNC(starttime, month) AS trip_month
 ,start_station_name
 ,end_station_name
 ,sum(tripduration) AS tripduration
 ,count(starttime) AS trips
FROM 'bigquery-public-data.new_york.citibike_trips'
GROUP BY
 TIMESTAMP_TRUNC(starttime, month)
 ,start_station_name
 ,end_station_name
 limit 100
```

Please note the `limit 100` clause, so we can test our SQL for syntax errors using the **Run Query** button.

Configuring Qlik Sense for ODAG applications

ODAG is not enabled on Qlik Sense Enterprise by default. Instead, you have to enable it in the QMC.

To enable it, follow these steps:

1. Log into your Qlik Sense with administrator rights and go to QMC:

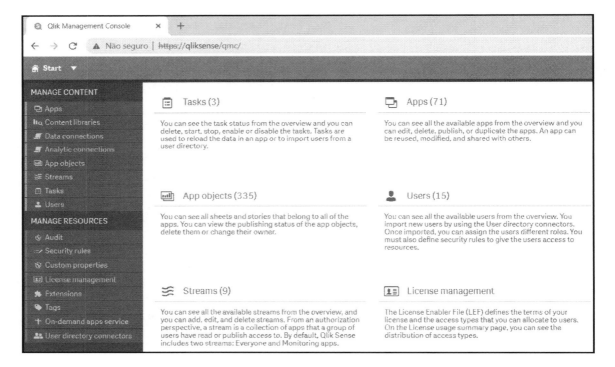

2. Find the option to enable **On-demand apps service** under **MANAGE RESOURCES**:

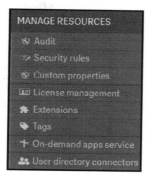

When you select that option, you're going to see this screen:

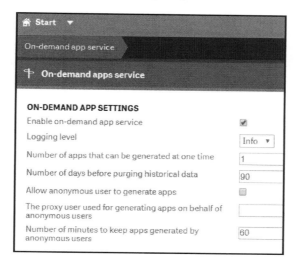

The most important option here is the first one, where you enable the service that handles on-demand requests. The other options are as follows:

- **Logging level (Off-through Trace)**: This is where we set how verbose our log messages will be.

- **Number of apps that can be generated at one time**: This option is important if we have a large user base, so you can configure how many apps (and requests) are generated at once. The default number is 1 and the maximum is 10. This affects the response time and user experience. If our database queries are slow, we could incur poor performance if we set too many applications.

- **Number of days before purging historical data**: This parameter sets the number of days an application is preserved before it is removed. Set this parameter to 0 so it never deletes anything (90 default, 365 maximum).
- **Allow anonymous users to generate apps**: If our Qlik Sense license permits an anonymous user, enable this option to permit them to generate applications.
- **The proxy user used for generating apps on behalf of anonymous users**: The parameter will set the username that will serve as the proxy user for anonymous users if the previous parameter is enabled. Choose a regular user with permission to create on-demand applications.
- **Number of minutes to keep apps generated by anonymous users**: Set how many minutes an app generated by an anonymous user will be kept. If set to 0, this will persist for 365 days. The limit is measured from the last data load.

Building a summarized application

We'll now connect the Qlik Sense Enterprise to Google BigQuery and run the SQL created in the *Setting up a Google BigQuery account* section. We're going to create an analysis that provides a way to analyze the results. We start by creating the application and connecting to Google's BigQuery, and then we add our SQL to it. Be sure to use a professional licensed user account with permission to create an application.

Creating a connection

Use the following steps to create a connection to Google BigQuery:

1. At your Qlik Sense hub, use the **Create new app** option and give an appropriate name to the new application.
2. At the add data step, we're forced to use the **Script editor** since data manager does not currently allow SQL statements:

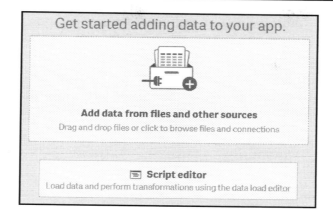

3. Create a connection to Google BigQuery using the provided connector, named **Google BigQuery** (marked in the following screenshot). Choose the **Create new connection** option and then select the **Google BigQuery** option:

4. Click **Sign In** and be sure to disable the popup blocker on your browser:

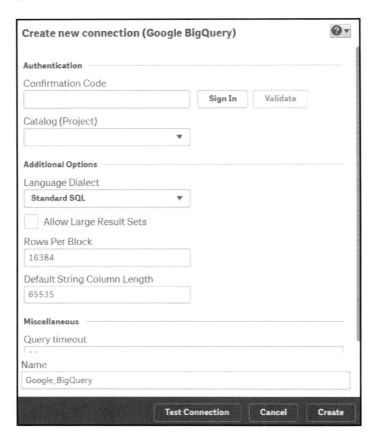

5. A Google account form will be displayed. Please log in with the appropriate Google credentials.
6. A form with the **Qlik Web Connectors (BigQuery) wants to access your Google Account** message will be displayed. Please use the **Allow** option:

7. A long string with a code will be generated. Copy this to your clipboard:

8. Paste the string into the **Authentication** field of the **Create new connection** form.
9. Click the **Validate** button.
10. Click the **Create** Button.

The right-hand side of the screen will now contain a connection with a Google logo:

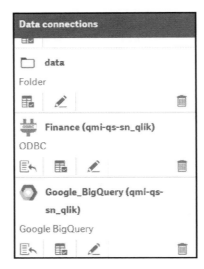

Press the small icon just beneath **Google BigQuery** so the Qlik Sense Script editor will add a line just after your script:

```
LIB CONNECT TO 'Google_BigQuery';
```

Adding a script to retrieve data

Now let's add the SQL to the script. The code that can be found at https://github.com/ PacktPublishing/Hands-On-Business-Intelligence-with-Qlik-Sense/blob/master/ Chapter08/02%20-%20Retrieve%20Script.qvs. Please copy and paste it into the Script editor:

```
//Precedent load to format the field trip_month
NYC_Bike_trips:
load
   date(trip_month) as trip_month
   ,line_counter
   ,start_station_name
   ,end_station_name
   ,tripduration
   ,trips;
SQL // SQL to retrieve summarized data
SELECT
    TIMESTAMP_TRUNC(starttime, month) AS trip_month // Converts a date to
month
```

```
     ,start_station_name
     ,end_station_name
     ,sum(tripduration) AS tripduration // aggregates the total duration
     ,count(starttime) AS trips // aggregates the total count of trips
     ,sum(1) as line_counter // line counter
FROM `bigquery-public-data.new_york.citibike_trips`
GROUP BY
       TIMESTAMP_TRUNC(starttime, month) // Converts a date to month
     ,start_station_name
     ,end_station_name;
```

This script connects using our newly-created connection, then executes a SQL statement with a GROUP BY clause summarizing our data by month and start/end stations, summing up the duration and counting how many trips were done.

Save the script and run the code. It will take no more than a few minutes to retrieve approximately 3,000,000 records:

```
Started loading data

Connected
NYC_Bike_trips << QueryResult
Lines fetched: 2,999,575
Creating search index
Search index creation completed successfully

App saved

Finished successfully
0 forced error(s)
0 synthetic key(s)
```

 Keep in mind that I've used the Insight Advisor to generate these graphs.

Create a dashboard with graphs, a filter panel, some KPIs, and a bar chart, similar to the following. We left all expressions, such as sum (tripduration), as headers to make it easier to reproduce them. This application can be downloaded from the GitHub (https://github.com/PacktPublishing/Hands-On-Business-Intelligence-with-Qlik-Sense/blob/master/Chapter08/NYC%20Bikes.zip).

There's a sample on-demand app installed in your Qlik Sense Enterprise box. This is located in `ProgramData\Qlik\Examples\OnDemandApp\sample`.

Building the detailed application

We're going to prepare an application that would be used as a template for on-demand requests. This app will have a special script that will recover the values passed as parameters from the summarized app. This will enable the business users to retrieve detailed data from a source without needing further knowledge about SQL or other tools. We have to prepare our script to collect the selections made by the user and then use them to create a script that will retrieve only the records the user is interested in.

Binding expressions in on-demand template apps

Qlik Sense encapsulates all values passed as selections from the summarized application into some special variables. Those variables have a special name and content, and they are usually referred to as **binding variables**.

Let's assume you've made some selections (`Central Partk S & 6th Ave` and `West St & Chambers St`) in the `start_station_name` field. Qlik will encapsulate all values into a variable called `ods_start_station_name`. The `ods` prefix means on-demand selected values. There are other prefixes that we can choose, based on which information we need to retrieve:

Pattern	Meaning
`$(ods_start_station_name)`	Selected values of the `start_station_name` (green values) field
`$(odo_start_station_name)`	Optional values of the `start_station_name` (white values) field
`$(odso_start_station_name)`	Selected or optional values of the `start_station_name` field
`$(od_start_station_name)`	Same of `ods` (only green values)

Usually, if we want to create SQL using a value passed in as the selected value of `start_station_name`, we can write the following code:

```
SELECT *
FROM 'bigquery-public-data.new_york.citibike_trips'
WHERE
start_station_name into ($(odso_start_station_name){"quote": "'",
"delimiter": "."})
```

Qlik Sense will parse your variable and consider an example where the user has selected the `Central Park S & 6 Ave` and `West St & Chambers St` values. The SQL will be rewritten as follows:

```
SELECT *
FROM 'bigquery-public-data.new_york.citibike_trips'
WHERE
start_station_name into ('Central Partk S & 6 Ave', 'West St & Chambers
St')
```

Here, the quote parameter represents how values should be surrounded and the delimiter refers to how values have to be split.

If we have only numeric values, we can use `$(odso_some_numeric_field){"quote": "", "delimiter": "."}`. Consequently, a list with our numeric values should be returned.

Recovering a long list of selected (or possible) values

If a user selects too many values from a field (dozens of stations, for example), the regular approach will not work. Instead, it will generate an error because the variable that handles the selection becomes too long.

The way to work around this is by populating a table with all values, so you can use a regular concatenation script to retrieve all values. The script can be generated as follows:

```
StartStations:
LOAD concat(Station,chr(39)&','&chr(39)) as concatenated_stations Inline [
    Station
    $(odso_start_station_name){"quote": "", "delimiter": ""}
];
Let vStartStations='';
if NoOfRows('StartStations') > 0 then
```

```
          LET vStartStations = chr(39)&Peek('concatenated_stations')&chr(39);
Endif
Drop Table StartStations;
```

In this script, we're generating an inline table with all values passed into our binding variable. We then apply a `concat` function that joins all values, separated by commas. Finally, we check whether there is at least one selected value, which creates a variable that contains a string with all values.

Adding restrictions

We can add some restrictions that make it possible to control how many selections the user will be required to make in order to generate the details:

```
$(odso_start_station_name)[1-10]
```

In this example, it is essential that the user makes at least one selection in `start_station_name` and no more than ten selections.

It's important to create some limits that require the user to make some selections. Avoid the temptation to retrieve all data and break all efforts to plan how much data is loaded. If you retrieve more data that the server can load into RAM, this could lead to a system failure.

Creating a dynamic SQL

Let's put all these concepts (binding variables with a possible long list of selections) together to create a script that will recover the detailed records from BigQuery according to the selected values of some fields.

Let's assume that the user can make selections into `trip_month`, `start_station_name`, and `end_station_name`, and that we're applying some restrictions:

```
// Numbers in [] will force the user to make selections
// [1-10] at least one value selected and no more than 10

// Restriction Setup
//$(odso_trip_month)[1-4]
//$(odso_start_station_name)[1-10]
//$(odso_end_station_name)[1-10]


Trace Collecting values for selected values;
```

```
// Concatenating all selections from field "StartStations" and delimiting
with a quote
StartStations:
LOAD concat(Station,chr(39)&','&chr(39)) as concatenated_stations Inline [
Station
$(odso_start_station_name){"quote": "", "delimiter": ""}
];
Let vStartStations='';
if NoOfRows('StartStations') > 0 then
 LET vStartStations = chr(39)&Peek('concatenated_stations')&chr(39);
Endif
Drop Table StartStations;



// Concatenating all selections from field "EndStations" and delimiting
with a quote
EndStations:
LOAD concat(Station,chr(39)&','&chr(39)) as concatenated_stations Inline [
Station
$(odso_end_station_name){"quote": "", "delimiter": ""}
];
Let vEndStations='';
if NoOfRows('EndStations') > 0 then
 LET vEndStations = chr(39)&Peek('concatenated_stations')&chr(39);
Endif
Drop Table EndStations;



// Concatenating all selections from field "TripMonths" and delimiting with
a quote
// We have to adjust date format so we're using subfield to convert to
YYYY-MM-DD
TripMonths:
LOAD concat(
 SubField(TripMonths,'/',3) & '-'
 & SubField(TripMonths,'/',1) & '-'
 & SubField(TripMonths,'/',2)
 ,chr(39)&','&chr(39)) as concatenated_months
 Inline [
TripMonths
$(odso_trip_month){"quote": "", "delimiter": ""}
];
Let vMonths='';
if NoOfRows('TripMonths') > 0 then
 LET vMonths = chr(39)&Peek('concatenated_months')&chr(39);
Endif
Drop Table TripMonths;
```

Now we are creating the final SQL query that will be submitted to Google BigQuery:

```
Trace Creating dynamic SQL;
// Basic SQL for retrieve all fields
SET SQL = 'SELECT * FROM 'bigquery-public-data.new_york.citibike_trips'
WHERE 1=1 ';

// If the user has selected StartStations we add a condition
IF Len(vStartStations) > 0 Then
 LET SQL = SQL & chr(10) & ' AND start_station_name in
($(vStartStations))';
Endif

// If the user has selected vEndStations we add a condition
IF Len(vEndStations) > 0 Then
 LET SQL = SQL & chr(10) & ' AND end_station_name in ($(vEndStations))';
Endif

// If the user has selected TripMonths we add a condition
IF Len(TripMonths) > 0 Then
 LET SQL = SQL & chr(10) & ' AND TIMESTAMP_TRUNC(starttime, month) in
($(vMonths))';
Endif
```

And now we are executing the script:

```
Trace Executing SQL $(SQL);
LIB CONNECT TO 'Google_BigQuery (qmi-qs-sn_qlik)';
SQL $(SQL);
```

After pasting all this code, please save your application using *Ctrl + S*.

Integrating the summarized and detailed applications

Now we are going to put all the pieces together by linking our summarized application to the detailed one and configuring how the integration between them will be done. We will set additional parameters to make sure that our user will make selections and that those selections will be passed to the template script.

Let's begin by adding **App navigation links** to our summarized application. As discussed in the *Building a summarized application* section, an on-demand app loads a summarized sample of the data usually using a GROUP BY clause in the SQL or a LOAD statement. To link the summarized app to the template, we need to create **App Navigation Links**. Let's take a look at how to create these:

1. On the left-hand side of the screen in edit mode, you can see an option to create an app link:

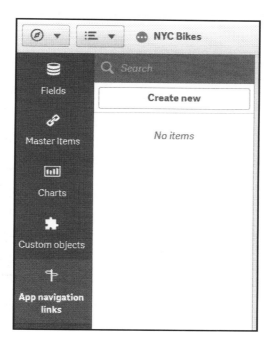

2. Click on **Create new**, which will show you the following form:

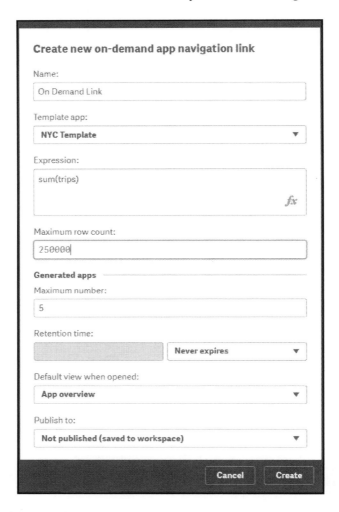

Fill in the form and create the app link according to the previous image and the following explanation:

- Give the link a user-friendly name that makes it easier for users to identify what this link is about.
- Select the template we created in the *Building the detailed application* section.

- Set an expression that calculates the total number of detailed records that correspond to the current selections made by the user. The expression usually uses the `sum` function to calculate this value. In our case, we're using `sum(trips)` since we created this field especially for this.

- Set the maximum value from the last expression set. This is important to prevent the user from retrieving too many rows at once.

- Set the maximum number of apps the user can create; this is important to control how many apps will be created for each user.

- Set a retention time for the generated app. After that time has expired, Qlik Sense will clean up the app. Set it to **Never expires** if you want to allow the user to manage the apps by themselves.

- Set the default view for the app; you can set it to **App overview** or a specific sheet.

- Establish whether you want the app to be deployed to a user's work area or a specific stream.

3. Drag and drop your application's navigation link to your sheet, placing it in the far bottom of the sheet. Click **Done** to exit the edit mode:

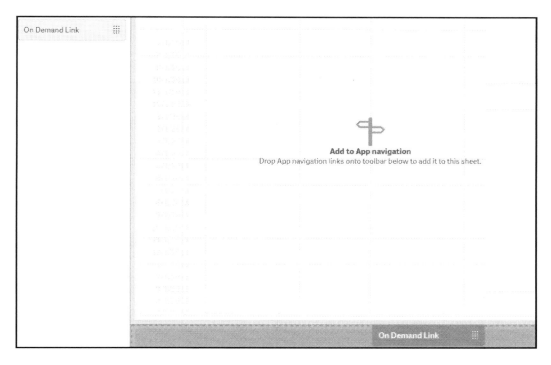

Testing our on-demand application

Now that we have everything set up, let's test our applications to make sure everything is correct.

When we see an app that uses ODAG, we will see a small circle at the bottom-left corner with the name of the app navigation link that we just created.

As the user makes selections, that circle is filled with the green color, indicating that a detailed version of the app can be generated:

This means that some selections were made, but the total row count still extrapolates the threshold set in **Maximum Row count**:

This green circle means that row count is less than the total maximum set.

Please follow the next steps to create your detailed application:

1. Click on the small arrow on the right side of the link:

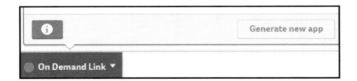

The red icon indicates that some restrictions are not yet satisfied. Please refer to the *Adding restrictions* section to check how they were set.

2. Click on that red icon. Qlik Sense will show the whole set of restrictions:

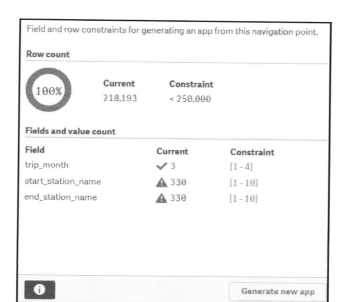

In this case, the current selections would retrieve 218,193 rows (less than the set maximum of 250,000). The selections made to **trip_month** are within the threshold set (3 for a maximum of 4) and the selections made to **start_station_name** and **end_stations_name** are not okay.

Let's make some selections to those fields and see what happens when you click on the green circle:

- Select `Central Partk S & 6 Ave` **and** `West St & Chambers St` **for** `start_station_name`.
- Select `1 Ave & E 15 St`, `1 Ave & E 16 St` **and** `1 Ave & E 18 St` **for** `end_station_name`.

- **Select** `1/1/2016` **for** `trip_month`:

Now press the icon for information (small black rounded **i**):

Qlik Sense is showing that all four constraints are attained:

- Row count, we have 7 of a minimum 250,000
- 1 selection for **trip_month**
- 2 selections for **start_station_name**
- 2 selections for **end_station_name**

Now that all the restrictions are satisfied, the **Generate new app** button becomes dark, indicating that the user can create a detailed app of the selected data. When you click on it, a monitoring screen will be shown so you can check the progress of the request:

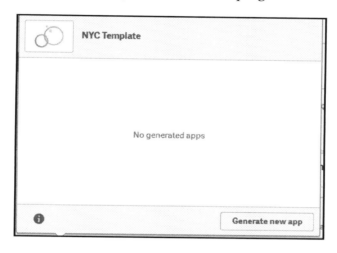

When the process has finished, Qlik Sense will enable a popup button on the right-hand side of the screen, giving you access to the new app loaded with the data. When you click that icon, the new app will open in another browser tab:

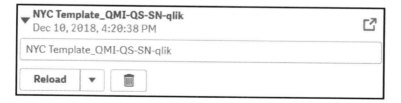

Summary

In this chapter, we learned an efficient way to analyze huge volumes of data in Qlik Sense. This feature, called ODAG, completes the toolset that a Qlik Data Architect can use to manage big data.

For our example, we used Google BigQuery tables; then we connected to it to retrieve a summarized sample of data and created a template to enable users to analyze detailed versions of data.

In the next chapter, we will work on creating a self-service analysis application.

Further reading

You can find more information on this topic at the following links:

- **Symbol Tables and Bit Stuffed Pointers**: https://community.qlik.com/blogs/qlikviewdesignblog/2012/11/20/symbol-tables-and-bit-stuffed-pointers
- **Qlik Community Tutorial**: https://community.qlik.com/t5/Qlik-Sense-Enterprise-Documents/On-demand-App-Generation-ODAG-in-QlikSense/ta-p/1479247

9
Creating a Native Map Using GeoAnalytics

GeoAnalytics is an add-on to Qlik Sense and QlikView. This product has mapping capabilities that leverage Qlik Sense to analyze data that has geospatial naming conventions, exposing geographic relationships between data points.

We are going to use these capabilities to analyze vehicular collisions that have occurred in New York City.

In this chapter, we will cover the following topics:

- Concepts of GeoAnalytics
- Creating a map
- Heatmap layer
- Adding information to the map

Technical requirements

The dataset that we will be using is available at the following link:

```
https://cloud.google.com/bigquery/public-data/nypd-mv-collisions
```

Concepts of GeoAnalytics

GeoAnalytics for Qlik Sense is provided as a group of extensions, which, once installed into Qlik Sense Enterprise or Desktop, enables the user to create geographical analysis and a connector that provides load time operations. Some of these extensions are as follows:

- **Map**: A map in GeoAnalytics for Qlik Sense consists of a **base map** and one or more **layers** that add significance to the map.
- **Layers**: Layers can be added to represent information over the base map. By using GeoAnalytics, you can add layers of several types, as follows:
  - **Bubble layer**: The bubble layer is used when you want to use points (a latitude and longitude pair) that can be colored and scaled by measures.
  - **Line layer**: The line layer is used when you have the concept of a **starting point** and **ending point** (two pairs of latitude and longitude). In this case, the layer will display lines from a start point to an end point. You can control the line width and the color using measures. Optionally, lines can have arrows or curves.
  - **Area layer**: The area layer is used when you want to show areas (such as polygons, or a collection of at least three pairs of latitude and longitude) using colors controlled by measures.
  - **Heatmap layer**: The heatmap layer is used when you have a lot of points that can't be correctly displayed using a bubble layer (due to the overlapping of points). In this layer, a point density with a color scale is displayed with a color gradient, representing how many points (a latitude and longitude pair) there are in that region.
  - **Geodata layer**: The geodata layer is used when you want to plot a background map that comes from a file or a tile web service, such as GeoJSON. The URL parameter is evaluated at each selection and data is reloaded when the URL changes.
- **Locations**: Locations are geographical data that GeoAnalytics can use to plot information on the map. They can be represented in several ways, as follows:
  - Location IDs are feature names that can be used instead of coordinates. Usually, they are country names, regions, airports codes, postal codes, and so on. They are converted by GeoAnalytics location service into coordinates, so that the developer does not have to take care of this translation.

- Geometries are strings that have coordinates within brackets. For example, [-75.3924409, 40.0879543] is a point (Qlik Headquarters in King of Prussia, PA, USA), and [[-0.128, 51.507],[2.3477, 8.8566]] is a line coordinate from London to Paris.
- Latitude and longitude decimal values can be used directly by some layers (such as a bubble layer and a line layer)

- **Projections**: A map projection is a transformation of a location's coordinates (latitude and longitude) from the Earth into locations on a plane. All map projections distort the surface in some way because we have to convert a sphere into a plane.

The most common projection is the **Mercator**; any maps you have seen (including Google Maps or Bing) are probably adaptations of this projection. Mercator, however, has an issue, which is that the further away from the equator an area is, the bigger that area seems to be when compared to its real measures. For example, Greenland seems to be as large as South America through the Mercator projection, whereas the real proportion is about 1:8 between Greenland and South America, as demonstrated in the following screenshot:

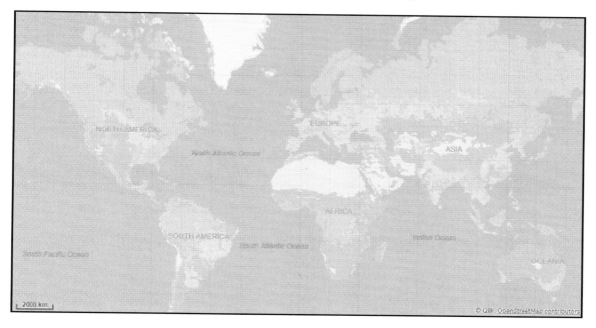

GeoAnalytics implements other projections called **Adaptive**, which fix a small part of this distortion using different projections when you zoom in or out, as shown in the following screenshot:

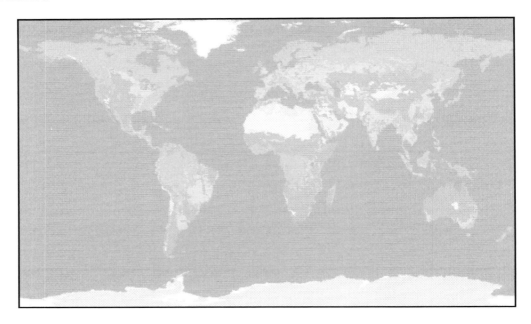

Creating a map

Let's use a base map supplied by Google BigQuery that has all of the vehicular collisions that occurred in New York City. We are going to see whether there are any geographical relations between different types of collisions.

Loading geographical data

First of all, we need to change our script so that we can extract the coordinates (latitude and longitude) from each vehicular collision that happened in New York according to the dataset. The Google BigQuery dataset provides the latitude and longitude values for each collision, so we're going to use them in our SQL. Qlik Sense provides a function called `GeoMakePoint()`, which consolidates a pair of latitude and longitude values in a single field (a geometry), making the data model more compact.

Please refer to Chapter 11, *Data Forecasting Using Advanced Analytics*, **and On-demand App Generation (ODAG)** on how to connect and use a BigQuery table, as follows:

```
LIB CONNECT TO 'Google_BigQuery';
// We have to make a small adjustment, since GeoAnalytics recognizes
Brooklyn as Kings County
Borough:
mapping load * Inline [
From, To
BROOKLYN, KINGS
];
MAP borough USING Borough;
Collisions:
Load
 collision_date,
 borough,
 latitude,
 longitude,
 zip_code,
 contributing_factor_vehicle_1,
 number_of_cyclist_injured,
 number_of_cyclist_killed,
 number_of_motorist_injured,
 number_of_motorist_killed,
 number_of_persons_killed,
 number_of_persons_injured,
 unique_key,
 vehicle_type_code1,
 vehicle_type_code2,
 GeoMakePoint(latitude,longitude) as collision_point;
SELECT DATETIME_TRUNC(TIMESTAMP, DAY) AS collision_date,
 borough,
 latitude,
 longitude,
 zip_code,
 contributing_factor_vehicle_1,
 number_of_cyclist_injured,
 number_of_cyclist_killed,
 number_of_motorist_injured,
 number_of_motorist_killed,
 number_of_persons_killed,
 number_of_persons_injured,
 unique_key,
 vehicle_type_code1,
 vehicle_type_code2
FROM `bigquery-public-data.new_york_mv_collisions.nypd_mv_collisions`
WHERE NOT LOCATION IS NULL AND LENGTH(borough)>0;
```

```
Collisions_Vehicle:
load unique_key,vehicle_type_code1 as vehicle_type Resident Collisions;
Collisions_Vehicle:
load unique_key,vehicle_type_code2 as vehicle_type Resident Collisions;
```

Adding the base map

To add a base map, follow these steps:

1. Create a new sheet on the application and switch to **Edit** mode, as demonstrated in the following screenshot:

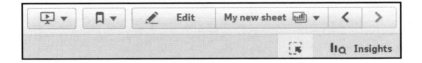

2. Add a custom object of type **GeoAnalytics Map** to your sheet by dragging and dropping the extension, as shown in the following screenshot:

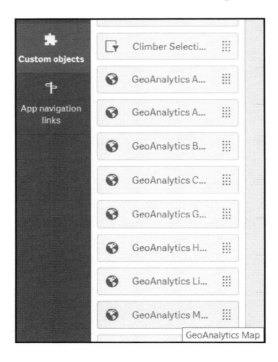

3. Check whether the main settings are set as per the values presented in the following screenshot:

4. The most important setting is the **Base Map** setting, where we can find the following options:

Basically, they are a combination of projections (Mercator or Adaptive) and background images, and include the following:

- **Empty (WGS-84)**, **Empty (undefined meters)** and **Empty (Mercator)**—these base maps do not have a background image, but they apply projections. Empty background maps are useful if you want to use your own background using a geodata layer.
- The **Default** option (the base map) is a greenish background map using the Mercator projection.
- The **Plain Map** option is a pale background map with a few details using the Mercator projection.
- **Default Server Rendered** displays the similar map as the **Default** option, but it is rendered at the server, which can be more efficient in some device, such as smartphones.
- **Plain Adaptive** is the same as **Plain Map**, and uses the Adaptive projection.
- **Default Adaptive** is the same as the **Default** map, and uses the Adaptive projection.

A few other settings are as follows:

- **Server URL**: If you're using GeoAnalytics installed on premise, check if this parameter is set to your installation. If not, then leave it blank.
- **Map ID**: This read-only field shows the ID of your map. This is only meaningful if you have two or more maps on the same sheet, so you can set your layers accordingly with the help of this ID.
- **Show Labels**: When unchecked, the labels in the client-rendered base maps are turned off.
- **Zoom to Selection**: When checked, if the user make selections to the application, the map zooms according to the selections.
- **Auto Select**: When checked, zooming and panning will make selections based on visible area. This option only works if the *spatial index operation* from the GeoAnalytics connector was used while your data was loaded. This operation is beyond the scope of this book and can be found in the GeoAnalytics documentation.

Adding layers

Now that we have a map, we can start adding information with layers to it.

Area layer

First, let's add an area map for each borough, so that we can check which regions have more collisions, as follows:

1. Drag and drop a custom object of type **Area Layer**, as shown in the following screenshot:

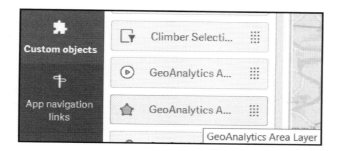

2. Configure the dimension of our layer; let's choose the **borough** field, as demonstrated in the following screenshot:

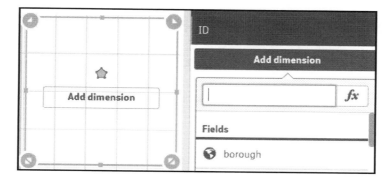

3. As you can see, you don't have to worry about the **borough** coordinates, GeoAnalytics is smart enough to understand your data and use this field as a geometry, as shown in the following screenshot:

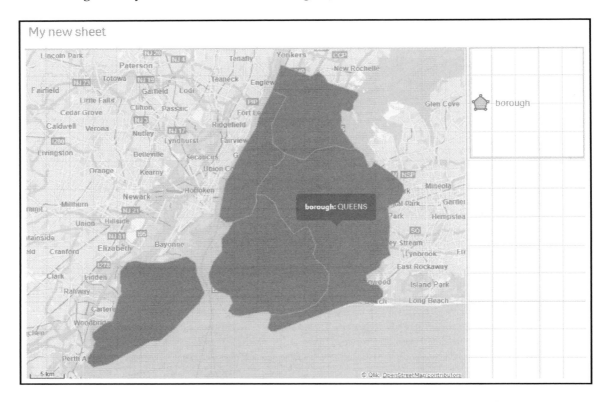

Here, GeoAnalytics plots the base map, zooms into the corresponding area (because we have checked **Zoom to Selection** in the base map), plots the borough boundaries, and fills the limits with a blue color. Now, let's add more information. We will create a color gradient that is based on the collisions that occurred in the **borough**, as follows:

1. Select the **Appearance** section from the layer. Here, you're going to see a subsection called **Colors**, uncheck the **Auto** option, choose the **By measure** option, and select **Collisions** as a measure. You can set the transparency too, so that the colors are not so solid, as demonstrated in the following screenshot:

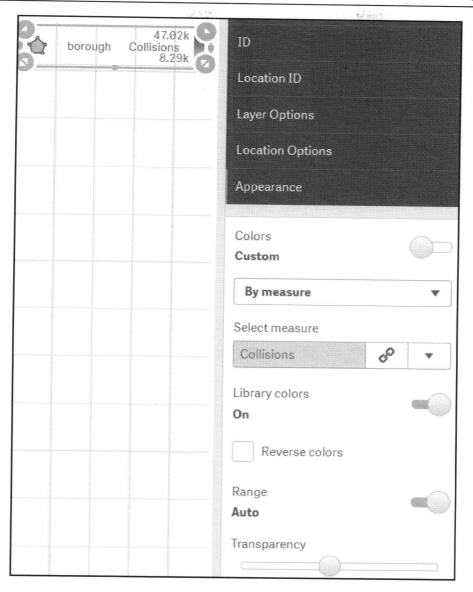

2. Your screen should look like the following:

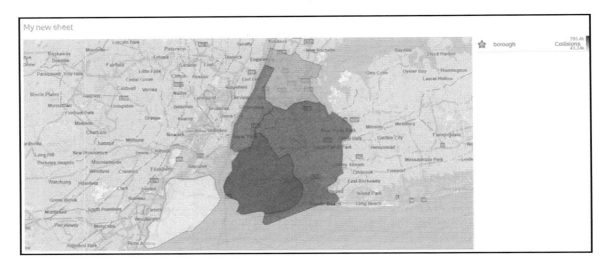

Let's now add more information. We're going to enable our user to drill-down from the borough to the ZIP area, so that the user can conduct a deeper analysis. The easiest way to do this is by using a Qlik Sense native feature, called **Drill-Down Dimension**.

In order to create a dimension, perform the following steps:

1. Go to the **Master items** library under the **Dimensions** section. Here, you're going to see a **Create new** button, as demonstrated in the following screenshot:

2. In the **Create new dimensions** form, select the **Drill-down** option; then, select **borough** and **zip_code** as fields, and name your dimension. After this, click on **Add dimension** and then **Done**, as depicted in the following screenshot:

3. Drag and drop this new dimension over your area layer, you will then be prompted by Qlik Sense to do what you want to do. Please choose the **Replace 'borough'** option, as shown in the following screenshot:

To test the map, follow these instructions:

1. Clear all selections. Your screen should then look like the following:

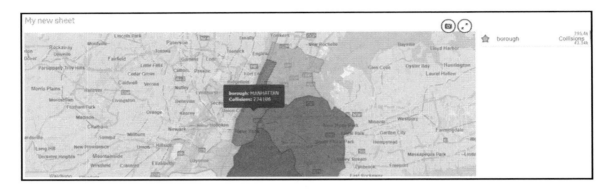

2. Click on **Manhattan**. You can see that the borough value is **MANHATTAN** and that all ZIP areas are shown. The map zooms in to show only the Manhattan area that has had collisions, as shown in the following screenshot:

If you clear your selections again, you're going to see that the map zooms out and only the borough borders are shown.

Heatmap layer

Now, let's show exactly where the collisions happened. We could use a bubble layer to show the points, but as we saw in the *Concepts of GeoAnalytics* section, when you have too many points, it is usually advisable to use a heatmap since this map does not hide overlapping points (two or more close points are shown in a *warmer* color, so you know where more collisions happened).

To add a heatmap layer, follow these steps:

1. Drag and drop a custom object of type **Heatmap Layer**, as demonstrated in the following screenshot:

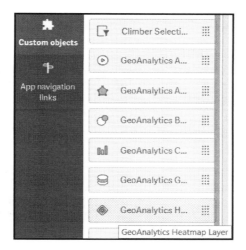

2. Choose the dimension for our layer and choose our field, `collision_point`, as shown in the following screenshot:

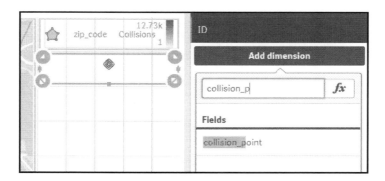

Now, we are going to see a map like the following screenshot:

There are some issues with this, however. Let's look at them before we begin tackling these issues:

1. We did not set which measures were meant to be evaluated, so GeoAnalytics will calculate the gradient over the points plot and we are interested in how many collisions took place (the same crossing could have more than one collision).
2. The heatmap layer is being shown for all selections. Since we require more precise information, we're going to show this layer when there's only one ZIP code selected.
3. Due to performance limitations, only 1.000 points were evaluated.

Let's work on each of these points now, as follows:

1. Go to the **Location** | **Weight** section of the heatmap layer. GeoAnalytics expects that the first parameter should be the location (geometry), and the second should be the measure being evaluated. This order is important; configure both measures (clicking **Add measure** first) as the following screenshot depicts. This will fix the first issue, so that now the measure being evaluated shows how many collisions happened and not how many points have had collisions:

2. Configure the layer to show only when there's one ZIP code selected, and let the layer show more than 1.000 points. Go to the **Layer Options** section, change the value of **Maximum Number of Objects** to `100000` points, and set **Calculation Condition** to `count(DISTINCT zip_code) = 1`. Uncheck the **Include in Auto Zoom** option because the **Auto Zoom** feature will be evaluated only for ZIP areas borders (this is faster to calculate than for each point), as shown in the following screenshot:

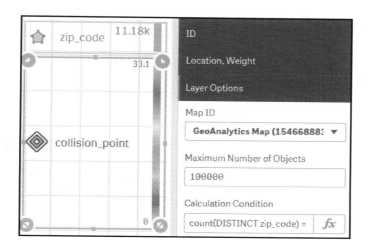

3. To test our map again, clear all of the selections, and check if the maps are plotted as before. Then, select **MANHATTAN** as we did previously. The behavior of the maps (before the selection) should be equal to the last version of the map without the heatmap. It should appear only after a selection into the **zip_code** field (remember our **Calculation Condition** parameter). You may notice that an exclamation mark appears over the layer, indicating that it isn't being calculated:

4. Select (click in a **zip_code** area, for example 10,035). Here, you're now going to see that our heatmap appears to show how many collisions happened in every region. You can scroll using your mouse or pitch your tablet, so that you can zoom in your map showing the collisions over the street crossings. Remember that the heatmap layer does not have a bubble layer with additional information:

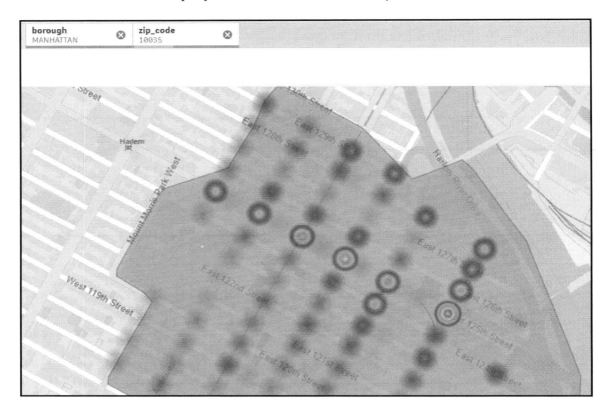

In the next section, we will see how to add more information to our map.

Adding more information to the map

A map can have more information than just colored boundaries. We can add more information to our map using Info Bubbles (all layer types have these) and Labels, aggregating even more data in our map.

Label

Most layer types have a subsection called **Label** in the **Appearance** section, which is composed of a checkbox to enable/disable the label, an expression that you can use to set what to show over a region, and an option called **Outer resolution limit** that sets the maximum zoom that enables the label to be shown. The following screenshot depicts all of these parameters:

Setting this box into our area layer will render the name of our borough over the map, as shown in the following screenshot:

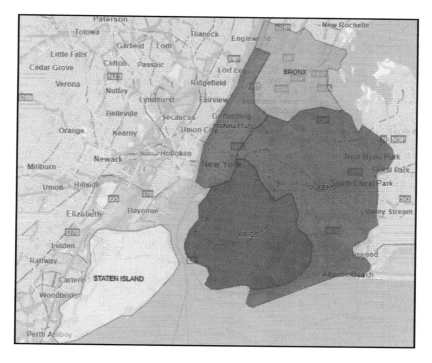

You can add more information by concatenating strings. For example, if you use

`=borough & ' ' & count(unique_key) & ' Collisions'` as the expression, you will see how many collisions happened in each region:

Info Bubble

Most layers type layers have a subsection called **Info Bubble** in the **Appearance** section. This control is what is shown when the mouse is passed over a region or point. The standard behavior is to display the dimension value (if it is set in the information) and the value of the measures (in this case **Collisions**), as shown in the following screenshot:

Let's see how to configure this using the following option:

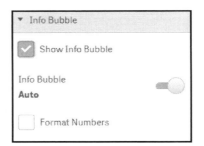

You can enable/disable the bubble by adjusting the **Show Info Bubble** checkbox. You can also enable/disable the default **Format Numbers** option, as shown in the preceding screenshot.

In our case, the **Format Numbers** option is important, because our zip codes are numeric. Take a look at the changes in formatting shown in the following screenshot:

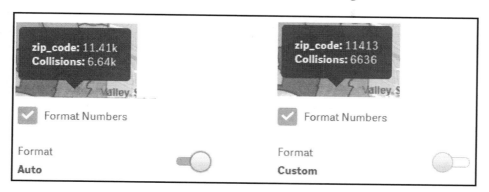

Summary

In this chapter, we saw how to create maps using GeoAnalytics, enabling users to analyze information that have a geographical relationship. We loaded data from New York City car collisions and plotted the information into a map, enabling users to discover which areas and crossings have more collisions.

In the next chapter, you will discover how to explore the self-service analytics features provided by Qlik Sense Enterprise and Qlik Sense Cloud Business.

Further reading

- **Product documentation:** https://help.qlik.com/en-US/geoanalytics/ Content/Home.htm
- *Qlik Sense – Getting Started with Qlik GeoAnalytics*: https://www.youtube.com/ watch?v=N9ckza8oPrc
- *Map projections*: https://en.wikipedia.org/wiki/Map_projection

10
Working with Self-Service Analytics

Qlik Sense is tailored to drive self-service analytics with business users in mind. Business users can create their own analyses, freeing up the IT department to create queries and reports that usually change every time. However, this only works with a strong foundation of data and security governance, allowing users to access the data freely. With a lot of content being created by business users some analysis can be promoted so that it is accessible to a wide audience and can be incorporated into the original app. This enables interaction between developers and business users, so that they can co-develop the analysis. These key points are important to guaranteeing the adoption of self-service analytics.

In this chapter, you will discover how to explore the self-service analytics features provided by Qlik Sense Enterprise and Qlik Sense Cloud Business. When using Qlik Sense Enterprise, you will learn how to build new sheets and create new visualizations by using the Master items library. You will also learn how to share insights with other users, creating community sheets and approving an analysis sheet to act as a baseline for developers. In Qlik Sense Cloud Business, you will learn how to co-create apps with other users in the same workspace.

The following topics will be covered in this chapter:

- Creating self-service analytics
- Sharing insights by using community sheets
- Approving sheets to add them to a baseline
- Co-creating apps in Qlik Sense Cloud Business

Technical requirements

In this chapter, we will use the Sales Analysis app that we created in Chapter 5, *Creating a Sales Analysis App Using Qlik Sense*, as a starting point, with a loaded data model and visualizations; this will eliminate the process of creating the application again.

You can also download the initial version of the .qvf file for this application, called CH10_start.qvd, from the book repository on GitHub, at https://github.com/PacktPublishing/Hands-On-Business-Intelligence-with-Qlik-Sense/tree/master/Chapter10.

You will also need access to one of the following two environments to import the application:

- For Qlik Sense Enterprise, you will need an account with a root admin or a content admin role to access the **Qlik Management Console (QMC)** with the URL https://<servername>/qmc
- For Qlik Sense Cloud Business, you will need an account with a subscription and a workspace admin role

After downloading the application, take one of the following steps:

- For Qlik Sense Enterprise, open the QMC and use the **import** button in the **Apps Management** section to import the sample application
- For Qlik Sense Cloud Business, upload the application to a personal workspace

Creating self-service analytics

In the previous chapters, we developed a Sales Analysis app with several sheets and visualizations in the personal workspace. The **personal workspace** is a private area where we create our apps, and no other users have access to it unless they are published to the stream. The **stream** is a place to publish applications that is available to selected users that are allowed access.

In the following examples, you will learn how to publish an application and how to interact with a published application so that you can create new sheets and visualizations.

Publishing an application

To enable users to access the application, we need to publish it to a stream. To publish an application to a stream, we need to provide publishing access. For that reason, we will use the Everyone stream, in which everyone has publishing access.

In this example, we will publish the Sales Analysis application to the Everyone stream.

The following steps will allow us to publish the application:

1. Open the Qlik Sense hub at the URL `https://<servername>/hub`. You will see the **Sales Analysis** app in the personal workspace.
2. Right-click on the **App** icon and select **Publish** from the menu.
3. In the dialog window, select the **Everyone** stream from the **Stream** list.
4. Click on the **Publish** button to publish the app. A message at the bottom of the screen will be displayed when the publishing process has completed.
5. Click on the **Everyone** stream to see the published app.

When a Qlik Sense app is published to the stream for the first time, it will be moved from the personal workspace to the stream that's selected. We can duplicate the app from the stream in which it was published, and have a copy in our personal workspace. If we follow this process, the next time we publish the app to the same stream, it will automatically update the app when we choose to replace the existing app.

A published app is also displayed in the published area of our personal workspace. It contains links to the apps that we have published, enabling us to keep track of our published apps.

Creating a new sheet in a published app

As a self-service tool, Qlik Sense provides capabilities to enable users to create their own analyses in a governed environment. Users can create new analyses by creating new sheets and new visualizations, using existing dimensions and measures from the Master items library or duplicating an existing sheet to modify existing visualizations.

In the following example, you will learn how to create a new sheet. Follow these steps to create a new sheet:

1. Click on the **Everyone** stream to open the published app:

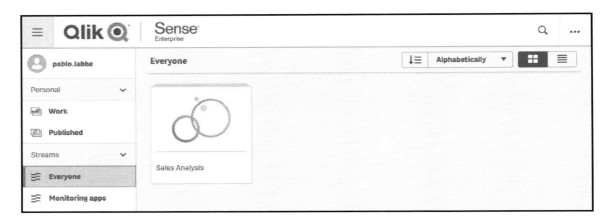

2. Click on the **Sales Analysis** app to open it.
3. In the app overview, click on the **Create new** button:

4. Set the name of the sheet as `Salesperson Analysis`:

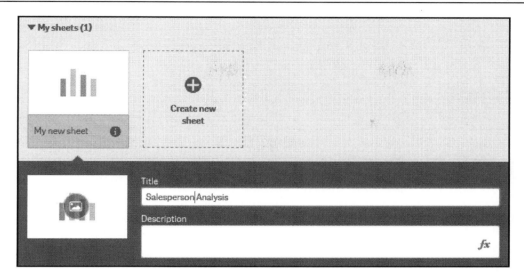

5. Click on the sheet icon to close the title window and open an empty sheet:

6. Click on the edit button to start editing the sheet.
7. Click on the **Master items** button in the asset panel, which is on the left-hand side of the screen, and find the filter pane.

8. Click on the **Visualizations** section to expand it.
9. Click on the **Default Filter** visualization and drag and drop it into the empty space at the top of the sheet:

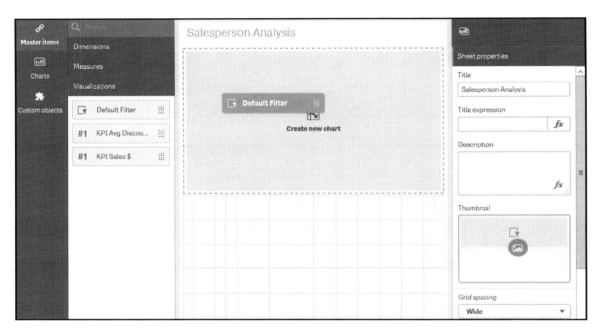

10. Resize the width and the height of the filter panel, so that you have ten columns and one row:

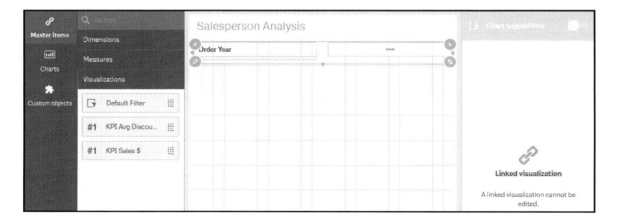

Now, we will add a bar chart to analyze the performance of the salespeople by sales and average discount. This will show us which salespeople have low sales and high average discounts. Follow these steps:

1. Click on the **Charts** button in the asset panel, which is on the left-hand side of the screen.
2. Click on **Bar chart** and drag and drop it into the empty space at the center of the sheet.
3. Click on **Add dimension** and select EmployeesFirstName in the **Dimensions** section.
4. Click on **Add measure** and select Sales $ in the **Measures** section.
5. Fix the measure number formatting to show a number with two decimal places.
6. The sheet will look as follows:

7. In the **Bar chart**, go to the **Properties** panel.
8. Click on the **Appearance** heading and click on the **General** section to expand it.

9. Switch on the **Show titles** property, as shown in the following screenshot:

10. Set the **Title** as `Salesperson performance by Sales $ and Avg Discount`.

11. We will now add the **Average Discount**. Click on the **Master items** button in the asset panel, which is on the left-hand side of the screen, and click on the **Measures** heading:

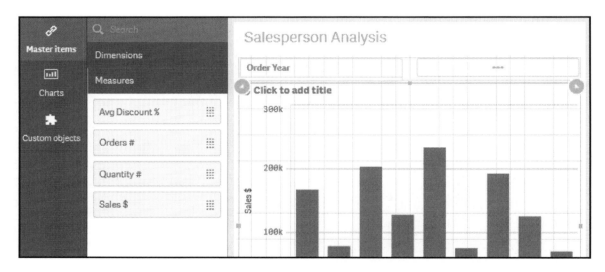

12. Click on the **Avg Discount %** measure and drag and drop it over the bar chart.

13. Click on **Color by: Avg Discount %** in the pop-up menu:

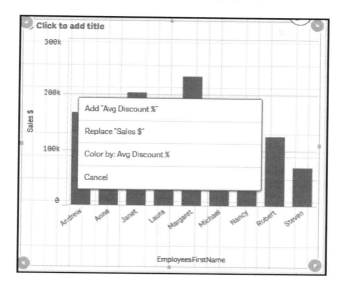

14. Set the sorting order of the bars from the highest to lowest by **Sales $**. To do this, go to the Properties panel on the right and click on the **Sorting** heading:

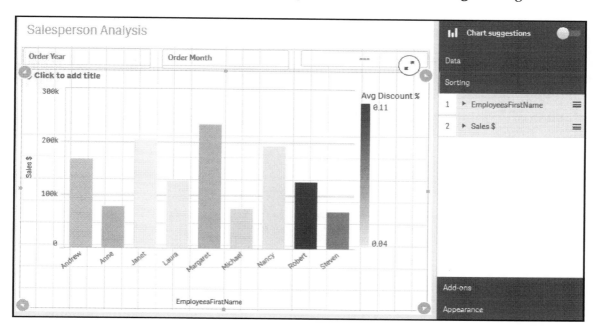

15. To change the sorting order of the bars, drag the **Sales $** measure to the top of the **Sorting** section. The bar chart will then be updated and sorted by **Sales $**:

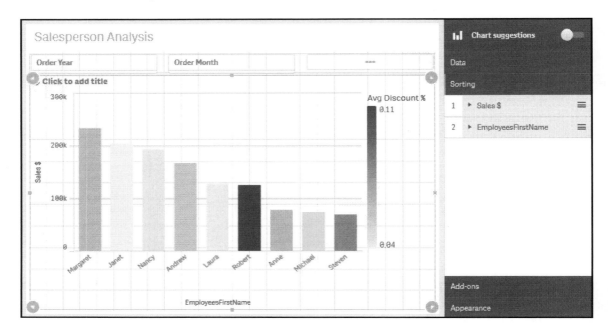

16. Click on the **Done** button to enter the visualization mode and interact with the visualization.

The chart depicts a comparison of the sales made, from the salesperson with the highest sales to the salesperson with the lowest sales. The colors show us the average discount given by each. We can see that **Robert** is in the sixth position by **Sales $**, but he has the highest average discount. We can therefore infer that a high average discount does not guarantee good sales.

We can also create a new sheet by duplicating an existing sheet and changing the existing visualizations. The following example explains how to do this:

1. Click on the sheet name button to open the sheet navigator.
2. Right-click on the **Reporting** sheet and select **Duplicate** from the pop-up menu.
3. We now have a copy of the **Reporting** sheet, under the **My sheets** section. We can freely change the content of the sheet by modifying the existing visualization, or by adding new visualizations.

Sheets created in the published app are placed in the **My sheets** section. Sheets that were already created by the developer before publishing are placed in the **Base sheets** section.

When creating a visualization in a published app, only predefined dimensions and measures that were created in the Master items library are available to the user. The base fields are hidden from the main interface, but they are available to be used if you create a dimension or measure expression using the expressions editor (the *fx* button).

Sharing insights with community sheets

In this section, you will learn how to share insights on a sheet. When you publish a sheet, other users with access to the app can only view the sheet and its contents.

Follow these steps to publish the Salesperson Analysis sheet:

1. Find and open the **Salesperson Analysis** sheet.
2. Click on the sheet navigator button to view the sheets that were created in the app:

3. Find the **Salesperson Analysis** under the **My sheets** section.

4. Right-click on the sheet and select **Publish** from the pop-up menu:

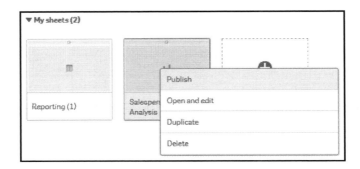

5. The **Publish sheet** dialog appears. Click the **Publish** button to confirm.
6. The sheet is published, and is moved from **My sheets** to **Published by me**, as you can see in the following screenshot:

7. Other users with access to the same app will find the published sheet in their
   Community section, as you can see in the following screenshot:

In this section, you learned how to publish a sheet and share the new analysis that we have
created with other users of the application.

Approving sheets to add them to a baseline

In this section, you will learn how to approve published sheets to add them to the baseline.
These are the base sheets of the app. Unlike published sheets, base sheets are included in
the app when it is duplicated or exported. Adding sheets to your base sheets enables you to
develop the base sheets of your app with more than one developer in the same app, unlike
developing an app in the personal workspace with just one developer at a time.

Follow these steps to approve the **Salesperson Analysis** sheet:

1. Find the **Salesperson Analysis** in the **Sheets** navigation panel, under the **Published by me** section:

2. Right-click on the sheet and select **Publish** from the pop-up menu:

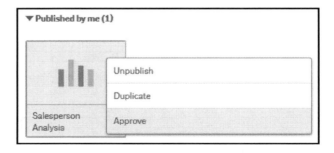

3. The sheet is approved, and is moved from **Published by me** to **Base sheets**, as you can see in the following screenshot:

Co-creating applications in Qlik Sense Cloud Business

Qlik Sense Cloud Business is a subscription that provides a group workspace where we can develop and share Qlik Sense apps with other users. It provides complete control over who can work on the apps and who can see the apps.

As a requirement for this example, you will need a subscription. If you don't have one, you can log in to `qlikcloud.com` with your Qlik ID and upgrade your account for a trial period of 30 days. No credit card details are needed. After you have purchased a business subscription, a new group will be added to your Qlik Sense Cloud.

For the sake of clarity, we have created a group with the name **Qlik sense Hands-on**. This group can be selected from the drop-down list in the menu, on the left:

The personal group contains the applications and data from the Qlik Sense Cloud basic account. It's not possible to move apps and data between groups. We need to export from one group and import into the other.

Follow these steps:

1. Click on the **Qlik Sense Hands-on** group to open the workspace.
2. Click on the **New** app button to import the Sales Analysis app that you have already downloaded from this book's repository.
3. Select **Upload an app** and click on the choose file button to select the file from the local disk.
4. Click on **Done** to close the dialog window. You will see the app in the workspace:

With the app in the workspace, we can start to invite other users to collaborate.

Managing members

The Qlik Sense Cloud allows us to invite up to 50 members per group workspace. To add members to your group workspace, do the following:

1. Click on **Manage members** on the right-hand side of the screen.
2. Click on **Invite members** in the **Members** tab.
3. In the **Invite** dialog, type in the email of the person who you want to invite and click on **Send invites**.

For the sake of clarity, we sent an email to **User1 Hands-on Qlik Sense**, so you can see this name in the table of members, as shown in the following screenshot:

The user that was sent the invite will receive a notification by email. If they have a Qlik Sense Cloud account, they will also be notified the next time that they log in. If they do not have an account, they will have to create one.

To allow for the co-creation of apps, we need to give workspace editor permission to the new user. This permission grants the user read and edit access to the apps in the workspace. Click on the checkbox to grant workspace editor permission:

Click on **Done** to confirm. Now, **User1** has access to the group and can edit the apps stored in the workspace. In the following screenshot, we can see the group that's available to the user in the drop-down list on the left-hand side of the screen. We can also see the app in the content area:

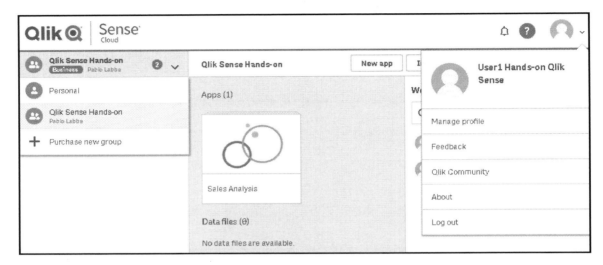

Editing the application with multiple users

When we add a user to the workspace, we grant them access to editing apps in the workspace. When a user with edit rights opens an app, it is locked to all other users. In the following screenshot, which shows the **User1** workspace, we can see a label on top of the app icon, with the name of the user editing the app:

Only one user can edit the app at a time in the workspace. The app is unlocked when the user editing the app closes the web browser tab that's used to edit it.

Sharing the app with users

To allow multiple users access to the app at the same time, we need to publish the app to a stream. The apps in a stream are read-only for all users.

First, you need to create a stream (if you do not have one already). Follow these steps to create a stream:

1. Click on **Manage members** on the right-hand side of the screen.
2. Click on **Create stream** in the **Members** tab.
3. In the stream dialog, type `Sales` and click on **Save**.
4. Click on the checkbox to grant view access to the new stream for a user. The member list will look as follows:

5. Click on **Done** to confirm the changes.

After you have created the stream, it will be displayed in the menu, on the left-hand side:

To publish the **Sales Analysis** app to the **Sales** stream, follow these steps:

1. Right-click on the **Sales** app icon.
2. Select **Publish** from the pop-up menu.
3. In the publish app dialog, select the **Sales** stream and click on **Publish**.

4. A label will be displayed at the top of the app icon, showing where the app is published:

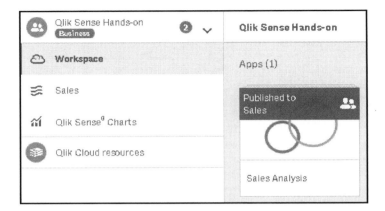

5. We can select the **Sales** stream and the app that's been published, as follows:

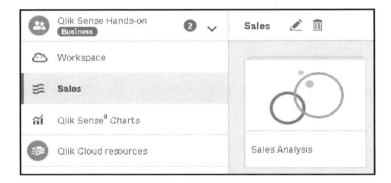

Publishing changes to a published application

When an app is published to a stream, a copy of the app is created in the stream, so changes made in the app stored in the workspace are not immediately reflected in the published copy.

To update the published app with changes made in the workspace copy, follow these steps:

1. Select the workspace from the menu on the left
2. Right-click on **Sales Analysis**

3. Select **Publish changes** from the pop-up menu
4. In the dialog, click on **Publish changes**

When the publishing process is finished, the following message will be displayed at the bottom of the screen:

The changes to app 'Sales Analysis' were successfully published.

The app in the stream is now updated with the changes.

Summary

In this chapter, you learned about the self-service analytics features provided by Qlik Sense Enterprise and Qlik Sense Cloud Business. You learned how to build new sheets and create new visualizations by using the Master items library. You also learned how to publish sheets to share insights with other users, and how to approve a published sheet as a base sheet for developers to use. Finally, you learned how to use Qlik Sense Cloud Business for the co-creation of apps with other developers, and how to publish an app to the stream so that it can be viewed.

In the next chapter, you will learn how to create data forecasting by using the advanced analytics features of Qlik Sense.

Further reading

To learn more about the functions that were used in this chapter, access the Qlik Sense online help, as follows:

- *Publishing workflow* on Qlik Help, `https://help.qlik.com/en-US/sense/November2018/Subsystems/Hub/Content/Sense_Hub/Publishing/publishing-workflow.htm`
- *Managing Qlik Cloud Business* on Qlik Help: `https://help.qlik.com/en-US/sense-cloud/Subsystems/CloudHub/Content/Sense_Hub/Cloud/groups-workspaces-streams-cloud.htm`

11
Data Forecasting Using Advanced Analytics

The importance of data forecasting needs to be highlighted—its use cases, why we feel the need to dedicate a whole chapter to it, why it's essential in the field of business. Then we will slowly move into using Qlik for data forecasting and lastly, jot down all the activities we shall be carrying out through the course of this chapter.

Organizations must adapt to a constantly changing world. To make those adjustments, its management needs to predict what may happen in the future. Being assertive about making forecasts can mean the difference between being ready to adapt to a new market or new situations.

In the past couple of years, advanced analytics using data science tools has become increasingly important to all organizations because it uses mathematics and statistics to enable more accurate results in data analysis. Now, we are going to see how we can leverage our Qlik Sense analysis, helping our users (or ourselves) to prepare data forecasts.

In this chapter, we will work together to enable the Qlik Sense applications to predict how our business **Key Performance Indicator (KPI)** will perform in the future. This is not about using technology to predict business behavior, but instead, a matter of using technologies from data science such as **machine learning (ML)** or forecasting, in order to predict business behavior.

The following topics will be covered in this chapter:

- How to install R and Python onto your computer or server
- How to load the required libraries
- How to configure your Qlik Sense environment to connect to R and Python platforms
- How to use the R and Python modules in your Qlik applications

Technical requirements

The technologies that are used in this chapter are as follows:

- Qlik Sense Enterprise or Qlik Sense Desktop
- R (https://www.r-project.org/)
- Python (https://www.python.org/)
- Windows command line

 You can find the code for this chapter on GitHub at the following link: https://github.com/PacktPublishing/Hands-On-Business-Intelligence-with-Qlik-Sense/tree/master/Chapter11.

Qlik Sense Engine and Server Side Extensions

Qlik Sense Engine can be extended to use analytic connections, usually called **Advanced Analytics Integration (AAI)**, that integrates external analysis. An analytic connection extends engine capacity, adding expressions that can be used in charts or scripts. When Qlik Sense needs to use these analytics connections, Qlik Sense Engine calls that external calculation engine, executing functions that are usually named **Server Side Extensions (SSE)**. For example, you could create an analytic connection to R and use statistical expressions thorough a SSE when you load the data from your script.

In this section, we will discuss how Qlik technology implements those connections and extensions to connect to platforms like R and Python.

Qlik approach to data science platforms

Qlik's approach to handling data science is through integration with third-party platforms using APIs. We can enable Qlik Sense (Desktop or Enterprise) to connect to Python, R, Spark, Java, C#, or other programming languages, leveraging the user's ability to analyze data. We can also use forecasting, clustering, correlations, or whatever we need to analyze data. As an example, we are going to use Python sklearn and R for data forecast modeling.

Using the related terms, Qlik enables AAI through SSE, extending the regular **Qlik Indexing Engine (QIX)** behavior by transferring data chunks from the Qlik Engine to other server(s) that implement a function that performs the calculation and returns the result to Qlik Engine.

Before we take a closer look at the next section, you have to be familiar with the difference between the following screenshots. Here's the first one:

Here is the second one:

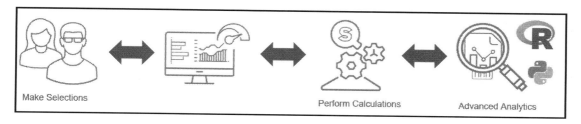

As you can see, there is another software component (which can be executed anywhere, from the same machine that Qlik Sense is running on, or even on another machine) that handles all calculations that could not be made by the Qlik Engine.

How SSE works

SSE is usually based around **Remote Procedure Call (gRPC)**. This is a multilanguage and cross platform library that is based on defining a service, its methods, and return types.

Using gRPC, a client (software part) can connect to another machine (server) and run a method or function as if it were a local component. This enables the idea of *services*, so we can create distributed applications that have connections between clients and servers, and messages (data) can be distributed between them:

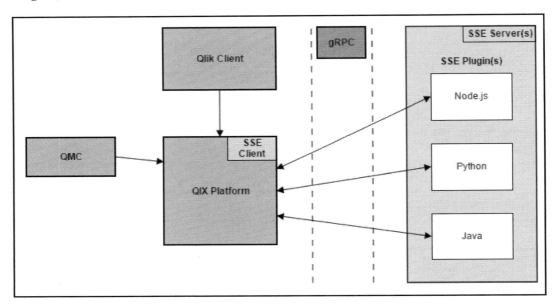

SSE functions

When implementing SSE functions, there are two approaches:

- Implementing a function that receives a string that contains code and values. Here, the SSE parses the string, evaluates the code, and calculates the answer. An example of this is as follows; we are passing a very simple script that counts customers (count(CustomerID)) and passes this value to R, which will print the value multiplied by 2:

```
R.ScriptEval('print(q$value*2)',count(CustomerID) as value)
```

- Implementing a function that is precompiled and accepts only parameters for a calculation. In the following example, we are aggregating SalesAmmount by Week and using these as parameters, so the function will create a simple linear regression based on those values:

```
Linear.simple([OrderDate.autoCalendar.Week],sum(SalesAmmount))
```

Both approaches (using a script from the Qlik side or encapsulating all the code into functions from the server side) have pros and cons, as outlined in the following table. You can decide later which is best suited to your needs:

Script from Qlik side	Encapsulated functions
More flexibility	You can work with two teams: one programming in Qlik and data scientists implementing the models using R, Python, and many others.
All code stays on the same repository	More governance because you can control what models can be exposed to Qlik.

Preparing your R environment

From the R Wikipedia page at `https://en.wikipedia.org/wiki/R_(programming_language)`:

> *"R is a programming language and free software environment for statistical computing and graphics supported by the R Foundation for Statistical Computing. The R language is widely used among statisticians and data miners for developing statistical software and data analysis."*

This language is well-known with data scientists that have implemented a lot of modules that can be located in websites. This makes it easy to understand and learn how to implement data forecasting.

In this section, we are going to work together to configure the R environment. We're going to install the R software and install the libraries that shall be used in the examples throughout this chapter.

Installing R

We are now going to install an R environment into a Windows machine and use it on a Qlik Sense Desktop. As the whole package is free, you don't have to worry about licensed software.

While this chapter is being written, we kept in mind the latest version of R, that is, 3.5.2, in mind, which can be downloaded from `https://cloud.r-project.org/bin/windows/base/R-3.5.2-win.exe`. Please check whether or not there is a new version of this when you try to install it yourself.

When you access the link we mentioned earlier, here is what you see:

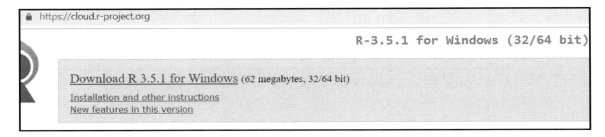

After you download it and run the installer, we are going to see a screen like this. Let's use the **English** version in this chapter:

Now, we will see the license agreement. By clicking **Next**, we are accepting the **GNU GENERAL PUBLIC LICENSE**:

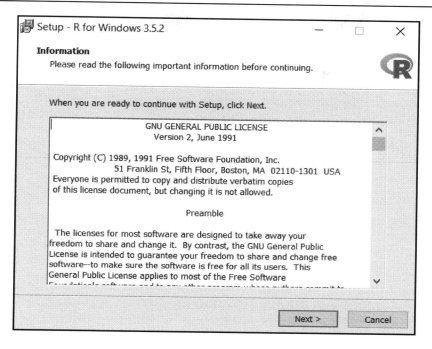

At this screen, please choose a path outside of \Program Files so that we don't need any special administrative rights on the computer:

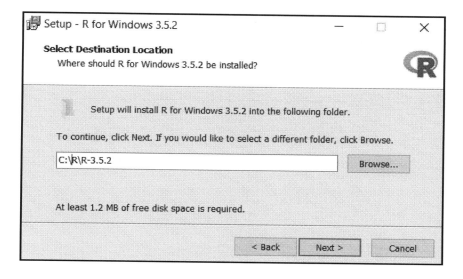

After doing this, choose all the packages and accept all the default values by pressing **Next** on every screen. The installation process will take no more than a few minutes:

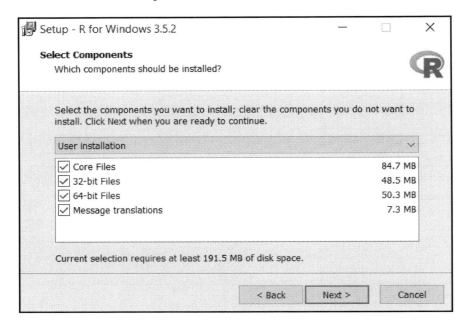

The installation will begin:

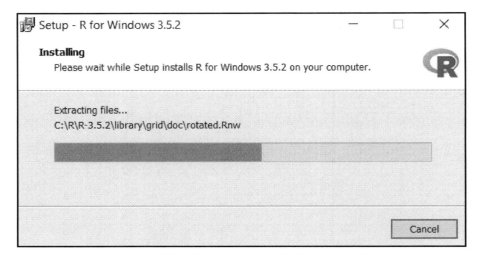

After the installation is complete, click on **Finish** to exit the setup:

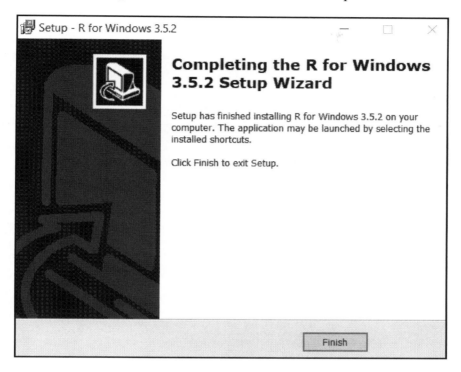

We can run R by running Windows Explorer and going to where we have chosen to install it:

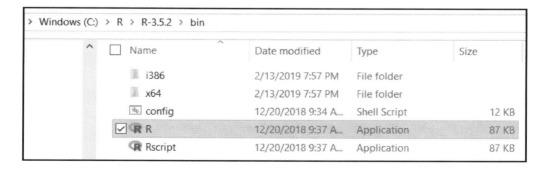

We will be prompted with a screen, just like the one that's shown in the following screenshot:

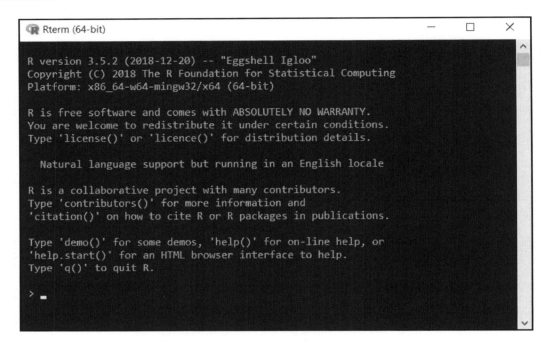

Type version and hit *Enter*. You should then see a screen similar to the one that's shown in the following screenshot (this may vary, depending on your configuration). Don't worry about different versions—just check if R is responding to our commands:

```
R Rterm (64-bit)                                              —    □    ×

You are welcome to redistribute it under certain conditions.
Type 'license()' or 'licence()' for distribution details.

  Natural language support but running in an English locale

R is a collaborative project with many contributors.
Type 'contributors()' for more information and
'citation()' on how to cite R or R packages in publications.

Type 'demo()' for some demos, 'help()' for on-line help, or
'help.start()' for an HTML browser interface to help.
Type 'q()' to quit R.

> version
               _
platform       x86_64-w64-mingw32
arch           x86_64
os             mingw32
system         x86_64, mingw32
status
major          3
minor          5.2
year           2018
month          12
day            20
svn rev        75870
language       R
version.string R version 3.5.2 (2018-12-20)
nickname       Eggshell Igloo
> _
```

Installing Rserve()

We need some additional packages to enable R to process our scripts and accept requests from Qlik Sense; let's install these packages now.

First of all, we need to install `Rserve`, the package that enables a TCP/IP server, which provides connections, making it possible to integrate R as a server. R is interactive; we type commands at the prompt and see the results. We need to transform R into a server so that it can act as a backend for Qlik Sense. To install `Rserve`, please access your console and type the following:

```
install.packages("Rserve", lib = "C:\\R\\R-3.5.2\\library")
```

Please adjust this path to where we have installed R from our *Installing R* section (probably `C:\\R\\R-3.5.2\\library`) and hit *Enter*. A screen will be displayed so that you can see the CRAN mirror (the server where the software can be downloaded). The default should be enough for our needs:

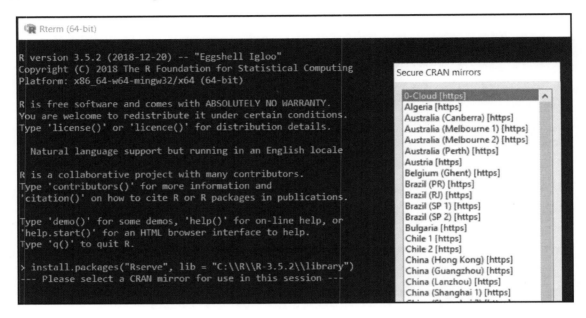

You should then see a screen like the following. Please search for the **'Rserve' successfully unpacked** message, as follows:

```
> install.packages("Rserve", lib = "C:\\R\\R-3.5.1\\library")
--- Please select a CRAN mirror for use in this session ---
tentando a URL 'https://cloud.r-project.org/bin/windows/contrib/3.5/Rserve_1.7-$
Content type 'application/zip' length 638177 bytes (623 KB)
downloaded 623 KB

package 'Rserve' successfully unpacked and MD5 sums checked

The downloaded binary packages are in
        C:\Users\cuv\AppData\Local\Temp\Rtmp6H6klP\downloaded_packages
> |
```

Let's test to see if everything is okay here, as follows:

```
> library(Rserve)
> Rserve()
```

You should see a message like the following, attesting that everything is okay and that Rserve is running:

```
Starting Rserve...
 "C:\R\R-35~1.2\library\Rserve\libs\x64\Rserve.exe"
> Rserve: Ok, ready to answer queries.
```

Installing more packages

R is highly modularized, which implies that, depending on what you want to run, you have to preload the correct packages. For this chapter, let's download several packages that will enable our R installation with modules that are ready to process the scripts that we need to use into Qlik Sense.

Type in the following commands and check if all of them run correctly. Depending on your network connection, this can take a few minutes, so grab some coffee while you wait:

```
install.packages("jsonlite", lib = "C:\\R\\R-3.5.2\\library")
install.packages("ChainLadder", lib = "C:\\R\\R-3.5.2\\library")
install.packages("forecast", lib = "C:\\R\\R-3.5.2\\library")
install.packages("rpart", lib = "C:\\R\\R-3.5.2\\library")
install.packages("partykit", lib = "C:\\R\\R-3.5.2\\library")
install.packages("tseries", lib = "C:\\R\\R-3.5.2\\library")
q()
```

The packages that we have installed in the preceding steps are described as follows:

- The jsonlite parses and generates JSON optimized objects (https://cran.r-project.org/web/packages/jsonlite/index.html)
- The ChainLadder provides statistical methods and models (https://cran.r-project.org/web/packages/ChainLadder/index.html)
- The forecast methods for forecast (https://cran.r-project.org/web/packages/forecast/index.html)
- The rpart classification and regression modules (https://cran.r-project.org/web/packages/rpart/rpart.pdf)
- The partykit models for regression (https://cran.r-project.org/web/packages/partykit/index.html)
- The tseries time series and financial analysis (https://cran.r-project.org/web/packages/tseries/index.html)

Installing the SSE plugin

Qlik provides a plugin to enable the communication between Rserve and Qlik Sense (Desktop or Enterprise). Qlik shares this plugin in its GitHub repository. You should check which one is the latest version at https://github.com/qlik-oss/sse-r-plugin/releases. While I was writing this chapter, the current version was 1.2.1. Please download and unzip this anywhere you want.

Configuring Qlik Sense

We have finally reached the stage where we will configure the Qlik Sense box to use the R environment. According to the Qlik Sense edition at hand (Desktop or Enterprise), we have to make different configurations to enable the Qlik environment to use the analytics connections (we described them previously in this chapter).

Qlik Sense Desktop

To configure Qlik Sense Desktop, carry out the following steps:

1. Locate your Settings.ini (usually located in C:\Users\[your user]\Documents\Qlik\Sense). If it is not there, you can create an empty one using Notepad (or another text editor).
2. Add a line with the following content:

   SSEPlugin=R,localhost:50051

 Make sure that there is a blank line at the end of the file. This is necessary because, if the file does not have this empty line, the last line can be skipped.

What does each parameter mean? Let's explain these, as follows:

- SSEPlugin: This command instructs us to use Qlik Sense to load a plugin.
- R: Shortcut name for your connection. This should be **unique** to your configuration. Any time you type R into your chart expressions, Qlik will know that your plugin will handle the calculation, referring to your script functions (for example, R.ScriptEval()).
- The localhost: The hostname or IP of where your version of R is installed.
- The 50051: The TCP/IP port.

Qlik Sense Enterprise

To enable analytic connections in Qlik Sense Enterprise, you must have admin rights and access to the **Qlik Management Console (QMC)**. The steps to configure Qlik Sense Enterprise are as follows:

1. Open the QMC and click on **Analytic connections**.
2. Press **Create New** and fill in the form with the following values (please refer to the last section for the meaning of the values), leaving another field with the default value:
   - **Name**: R
   - **Host**: localhost
   - **Port**: 50051

These are shown in the following screenshot:

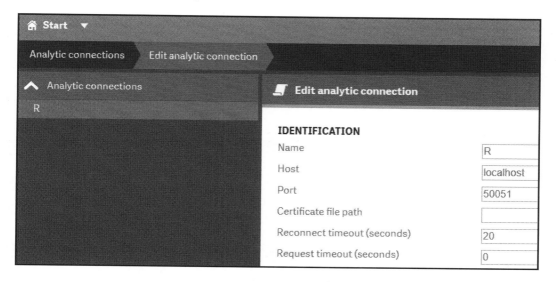

Starting all services

Now, let's start the R environment, `Rserve()`, and the plugin, preparing our Qlik Sense Desktop to connect to the R environment:

1. Begin by running `Rserve`. Please locate where you have installed R and search for `Rserve`. Usually, it resides under
   `C:\R\R-3.5.2\library\Rserve\libs\x64`:

Windows (C:) › R › R-3.5.1 › library › Rserve › libs › x64			
☐ Nome	Data de modific...	Tipo	Tamanho
📄 Rserve.dll	29/10/2018 10:03	Extensão de aplica...	80 KB
📋 Rserve	29/10/2018 10:03	Aplicativo	144 KB
📋 Rserve_d	29/10/2018 10:03	Aplicativo	160 KB

2. Copy and paste `Rserve.dll`, `Rserve.exe`, and `Rserve_d.exe` into the `C:\R\R-3.5.2\bin\x64` folder and then double-click on `Rserve.exe`. A command-line application will open and look something like this:

   ```
   C:\R\R-3.5.1\bin\x64\Rserve.exe
   Rserve: Ok, ready to answer queries.
   ```

3. We are going to run the SSE plugin, locate where it has been downloaded, and unzip the file you have downloaded before running the `SSEtoRserve.exe` program. You should see a message like the following one:

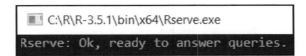

```
2018-10-29 11:12:26.7205|INFO|SSEtoRserve.Program|No certificates defined. Opening insecure channel.
2018-10-29 11:12:26.7205|INFO|SSEtoRserve.RServeEvaluator|Capabilities created: identifier (Qlik SSEtoRserve plugin),
rsion (v1.2.1), allowScript (True), defined functions (No functions defined)
2018-10-29 11:12:26.7489|INFO|SSEtoRserve.RserveConnection|Connected to RServe 127.0.0.1:6311 with user (empty user)
Press any key to stop SSEtoRserve...
2018-10-29 11:12:27.3783|INFO|SSEtoRserve.Program|gRPC listening on port 50051
```

Now, you have an R installation with the proper packages running and one server with **port 50051** opened to connections, so Qlik Sense can connect to the advanced analytics platform, exchange data, and perform calculations.

Using the R extension in a Qlik Sense application

After our preparation in the previous section, the Qlik Sense box is ready to use R as SSE. Let's carry out a simple test to check if the R installation is running properly:

1. Open Qlik Sense Desktop (or Enterprise) and create a new application, or open an existing one.
2. Add a KPI with this simple expression that prints a math result **(1+2)**: `R.ScriptEvalStr('print(1+2)')`.
3. Verify that the Qlik Sense KPI has an output that looks like this:

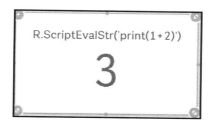

If it does not print exactly **3**, we have to check the logs so that we have an idea about what went wrong. Close Qlik Sense and check the logs, particularly `[yourmachine]_SSE_Engine_[date].log`, where there will be useful troubleshooting information.

Let's use a more complex test to check if our scripts are accepting aggregations as parameters. Using the application that we created in `Chapter 2`, *Loading Data in Qlik Sense*, please add a **Key Performance Indicator** (**KPI**) object with the expression **Count(OrderDate)**, which should show **830** as a value:

Let's use this value as a parameter for R and make a simple calculation. Please add another KPI and use the following as an expression:

```
R.ScriptEval('print(q$value*2)' ,count(CustomerID) as value)
```

Let's try to understand every part of this expression:

- `R.ScriptEval`: We are asking R to process a function that receives a number and returns a number (check the following table for the four functions that the plugin can process)
- `print(q$value*2)`: An R script that receives a parameter, multiplies it by 2, and then prints the result
- `count(CustomerID) as value`: Qlik code that calculates an aggregation (count) and then renames it as a parameter to R

The following table contains functions:

Function name	Function type	Argument type	Return type
ScriptEval	Scalar, Tensor	Numeric	Numeric
ScriptEvalStr	Scalar, Tensor	String	String
ScriptAggr	Aggregation	Numeric	Numeric
ScriptAggrStr	Aggregation	String	String

As you can see, you can now pass any R script as a parameter, provide any value as a parameter, and ask R to calculate the result.

Just out of curiosity, check the `SSEtoRserve` screen and look at the logs for every interaction. The logs should look like this:

```
2018-10-29 21:10:09.3160|INFO|SSEtoRserve.RServeEvaluator|EvaluateScript
call with hashid(54802698) got Param names: value
2018-10-29 21:10:09.3160|DEBUG|SSEtoRserve.RServeEvaluator|Evaluating R
script, hashid (54802698): print(q$value*2)
2018-10-29 21:10:09.3160|INFO|SSEtoRserve.RServeEvaluator|Rserve result: 1
rows, hashid (54802698)
2018-10-29 21:10:09.3160|DEBUG|SSEtoRserve.RServeEvaluator|Took 3 ms,
hashid (54802698)
```

Now, let's look at some more complex use cases of the R integration. Of course, as a user, they can write their own R scripts, but there's an extension that implements a lot of the hard jobs for us. This extension was released on GitHub at `https://github.com/mhamano/advanced-analytics-toolbox`. Download and install this.

If you have trouble installing Qlik Sense Extensions, please check the documentation at `https://help.qlik.com/en-US/sense-developer/September2018/Subsystems/Extensions/Content/Sense_Extensions/Howtos/deploy-extensions.htm`.

After installing the extension, we can drag and drop it from the **Custom objects**, as follows:

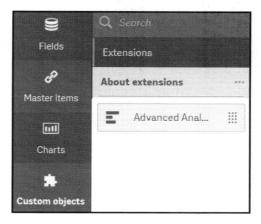

Now, we're presented with a set of scripts of data science that are ready to be used with the R environment:

There is a very useful algorithm for a forecast called **Autoregressive Integrated Moving Average (ARIMA)**. Deeper knowledge about this is beyond the scope of the book, but you can learn more about it here at `https://datascienceplus.com/forecasting-with-arima-part-i/`. Locate this under **Time series analysis**, as shown in the following screenshot:

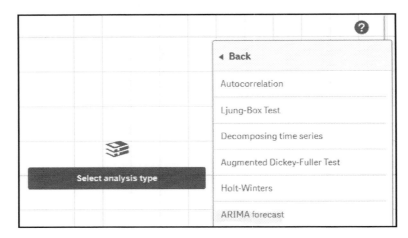

We have to provide which dimension we want to analyze (time series) and the variable (measure). As an example, we can use `OrderDate.autoCalendar.Week` as the dimension and `Sum(SalesAmmount)` as the measure.

After we have filled in these parameters, we will see a graph like the following:

The blue line (light gray) is the observed value for the measure (the actual values of that week), and we can see the following other three values:

- **Fit**: The forecast value
- **Upper**: Upper limit according to confidence interval
- **Lower**: Lower limit according to confidence interval

We can set a lot of parameters (including **Confidence level**) at the **Analysis Settings** sections of our object settings, as depicted in the following screenshot:

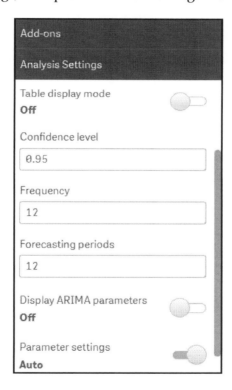

Preparing your Python environment

In this section, we will be preparing an environment to connect Qlik Sense to Python SSEs. Python SSEs are similar to R extensions.

When you use Python, you have two approaches that you can follow:

- Installing Python on the machine from scratch, configuring all libraries, installing, or developing the code, and testing all the pieces
- Using a container that includes Python, the libraries, and the necessary code

In this book, we are going to follow the first approach and in the *Further reading* section, there are links that enable us to use the second approach.

Installing Python

When installing Python, we recommend using version 3.6.7. This can be downloaded at `https://www.python.org/ftp/python/3.6.7/python-3.6.7-amd64.exe`:

1. Save the file that we downloaded from the link we mentioned earlier and run it. A popup will appear, choose the **Customize installation** option, as shown in the following screenshot:

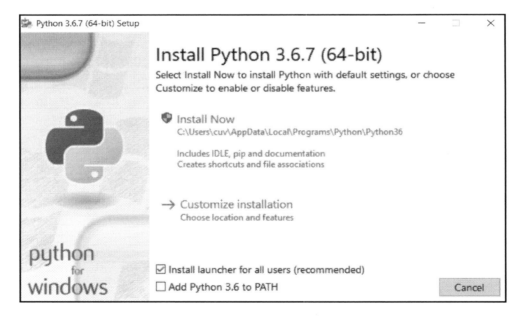

2. Check all the options and click **Next**, as shown here:

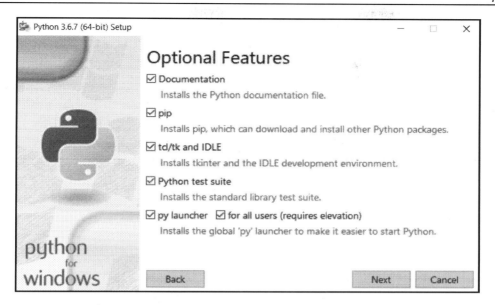

3. Choose a less nested folder, as follows:

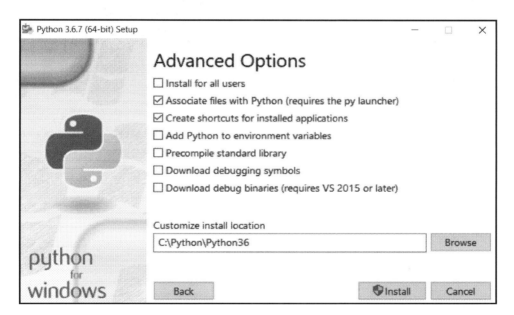

4. Hit **Install** and wait for the installation to complete (this should take no more than a few minutes).

Updating Python pip

Python `pip` is a module that installs, removes, and updates other modules. It is essential that `pip` is updated, as this enables us to install other modules. To do that, open a command line on your computer and type in the following command:

```
cd C:\Python\Python36\Scripts (or the folder where Python is installed)
python —m pip install ——upgrade pip
```

We are going to see a screen like the following, confirming that `pip` was updated:

Installing TensorFlow

For this example, we are going to need TensorFlow. The TensorFlow framework is defined in the original documentation at `https://www.tensorflow.org/tutorials/`:

> *"TensorFlow is an open-source machine learning library for research and production."*

To install TensorFlow, open a command line on your computer and type in the following command:

```
cd C:\Python\Python36\Scripts (or the folder where Python is installed)
pip install tensorflow
```

We are going to have to wait a few minutes since this framework has a lot of sub components and dependencies.

Using a Python extension

Within the scope of this chapter, we've prepared a Python module (simple and unprepared to use in production) that implemented three different models for linear regression. Even though linear regression is often inappropriate for time-series analysis, this method is well-known and easy to understand, so it serves as the following:

- **Simple**: Runs the linear regression expression $y=Wx + b$
- **Estimator**: Uses TensorFlow's built-in estimator to help automate training, testing, and predicting
- **Polynomial**: Uses TensorFlow (this time without an Estimator) to run training and predict a polynomial linear regression expression

We can find it on the GitHub repository at `https://github.com/cleveranjos/SSE-LinearRegression` and download it as a ZIP file to your computer using the green **Clone or download** button.

Unzip the package at any location on the computer and open up the Command Prompt, where you unzip it and run the extension, as follows:

```
c:\Python\Python36\python.exe ExtensionService_LinearRegression.py
```

The following is what we see:

Configuring Qlik Sense

Now, we're going to configure our Qlik Sense box so that it can use our Python Extension. According to the Qlik Sense offering at hand (Desktop or Enterprise), we have to make different configurations to enable the Qlik environment to connect so that we can data science platforms.

Qlik Sense Desktop

To configure Qlik Sense Desktop, carry out the following steps:

1. Locate `Settings.ini` (this is usually located at `C:\Users\[your user]\Documents\Qlik\Sense`). If it is not there, you can create an empty one using Notepad (or another text editor).
2. Add a line with the following content:

   `SSEPlugin=Linear,localhost:50054`

Make sure there is a blank line at the end of the file.

The following outlines what each parameter means:

- `SSEPlugin`: This command instructs Qlik Sense to load a SSE plugin.
- `Linear`: Shortcut name for your connection. This should be unique to your configuration. Any time you type `Linear` into your chart expressions, Qlik will know that your plugin will handle the calculation, referring to your script's functions.
- `localhost`: The hostname or IP of where your Python extension is installed.
- `50054`: The TCP/IP port.

Qlik Sense Enterprise

To configure SSE usage onto your Qlik Sense Enterprise installation, follow these steps:

1. Open QMC and click on **Analytic connections**.
2. Press **Create New** and fill the form with those values (please refer to the last section for the meaning of them), leaving other fields with default values:
   - **Name**: `Linear`
   - **Host**: `localhost`
   - **Port**: `50054`

These are shown in the following screenshot:

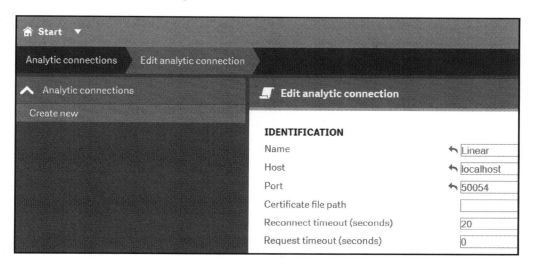

Using the Python SSE in your apps

Now that the Python environment is all set, we can use the functions we've enabled to allow linear regressions to analyze the data on the default data model.

Start by adding a line graph to your app. Use the **Order Week** as a dimension and add `Sum(SalesAmmount)` as a measure; check if you get an output.

Post this and add a linear regression line. Please add another measure with `Linear.simple ([OrderDate.autoCalendar.Week],sum(SalesAmmount))` as an expression.

The red line is calculated using our Python module, returning the values for our simple method.

When we've downloaded the GitHub package, there's a file named `DataTrends.qvf`. Please import this into Qlik Sense and check the examples for the other two methods. In this screen, you can compare linear regression using native Qlik functions and the three methods (**Simple Linear, Linear Regression with Estimator**, and **Polynomial Linear Regression**):

Summary

In this chapter, we were able to learn that Qlik is capable of exchanging data with external platforms, enabling some calculations to be made for modern data science tools. We've also learned how to install the necessary software and make adjustments to the Qlik Sense box to connect to various platforms.

In addition to this, we've created some analysis for our Qlik Sense applications that can use R and/or Python, leveraging the user's experience with time-series analysis.

In the next chapter, we are going to see how to deploy Qlik Sense apps for mobile devices.

Questions

1. Why do we need to connect Qlik to data science tools?
2. How does Qlik connect to data science tools like R or Python?
3. What are SSEs?
4. Which Qlik Sense offers are capable of using SSEs?
5. How can I add an extension to Qlik Sense to use an SSE?
6. What kind of analysis can we do using the Advanced Analytics Toolbox?

Further reading

You can find a lot of information on what we have covered in this chapter at the following links:

- SSE (https://community.qlik.com/community/value-added-products/server-side-extensions-sse)
- Qlik OSS (https://github.com/qlik-oss/server-side-extension)
- *The R Project for Statistical Computing* (https://www.r-project.org/)
- Learning Python (https://www.learnpython.org/)
- *What is a Container?* (https://www.docker.com/resources/what-container)
- Installing Docker (https://www.docker.com/get-started)
- Some data science containers (https://hub.docker.com/r/cleveranjos)

Deploying Qlik Sense Apps for Mobile/Tablets

In this chapter, we will show you how to deploy the Sales Analysis application we already built for usage in mobile devices and tablets. This enables us to freely access information wherever we are, even if we don't have a network connection. You will learn how to craft your dashboard so that it can be visualized in a small screen. We will discuss what we need in order to enable an application to be downloaded to a device and used offline. These activities are important to create a great experience for users when they interact with the application from a small device.

The following topics will be covered in this chapter:

- Setting up the Sales Analysis app for mobile usage
- Choosing the right client (web browser or mobile app)
- Preparing the Sales Analysis app for offline usage

Technical requirements

For this chapter, download the `.qvf` file for this application, which is called `Sales Analysis Mobile`, from GitHub at the following link: `https://github.com/PacktPublishing/Hands-On-Business-Intelligence-with-Qlik-Sense/tree/master/Chapter12`.

After downloading the application, carry out these steps as appropriate:

- If you are using Qlik Sense Desktop, place the application in the `Qlik\Sense\Apps` folder, which is located in the `Documents` folder.
- If you are using Qlik Sense Enterprise, open the **Qlik Management Console (QMC)** and use the **Import** button in the *Apps Management* section to import the sample app.
- If you are using Qlik Sense Cloud, upload the application to your personal workspace.

Setting up the Sales Analysis app for mobile usage

Qlik Sense provides a responsive layout that adapts navigation and user interface elements, such as menus and charts, to work nicely regardless of the device and screen size you are using when working with it.

In this section, we will learn how the responsive layouts work to create applications with sheets that will look good on small screens.

Responsive layouts

The responsive layout reorganizes the objects by scanning the screen using a z-path. I call this the z-path because the responsive interface reads all objects following a *z pattern*, and each object found in the path is placed with one following the other when the dashboard is displayed in a small screen. The following screenshot depicts the the z-path of a sample dashboard in the **Desktop view**. On the right side of the image, we see a sample of a **Mobile view** with the charts placed one after the other according to the z-path:

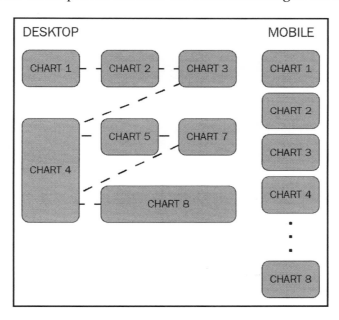

The **Mobile view** presented in the sample preceding screenshot is a simulation to better understand how the objects are placed. The following screenshot shows how it really looks on a mobile device:

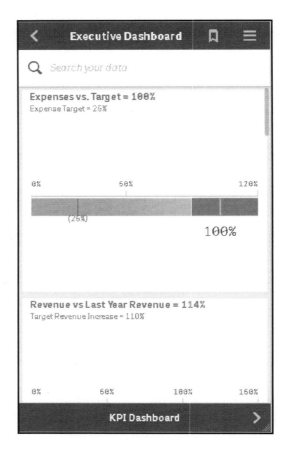

We need to scroll down to review all the objects on the sheet.

Responsive object design

The charts have a responsive design, adapting their layout to show detailed or summarized information based on the available space in the screen.

In the following example, the size of the line chart is so small that it only shows a trend line:

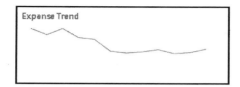

Here is the same chart in full screen in the Desktop view:

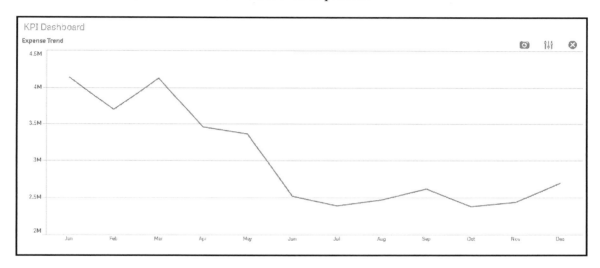

Here is an example of the same chart in a Mobile view:

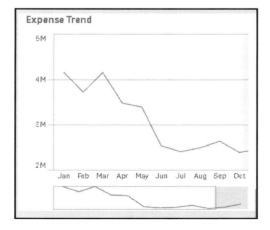

We don't have control over what can be seen or hidden when the chart is small. Qlik Sense automatically adjusts each object to give us the best visualizations. Switching the view of an object to full screen will show its hidden details, including axis labels, titles, grid lines, legends, and so on.

Reviewing the responsive design of the Sales Analysis application

In this section, we will test how our Sales Analysis will look in a small device. To do this task, you don't need a mobile device. You can use the responsive design mode tool from your web browser to simulate a small screen. For the sake of clarity, we will use Firefox as our web browser to show this feature.

Before we begin, open the Sales Analysis application on your desktop by using one of the following environments.

If you are using Qlik Sense Desktop, perform the following steps:

1. First, ensure that Qlik Sense Desktop is running
2. Open Firefox and type `http://localhost:4848/hub` in the address box to open the Qlik Sense Desktop hub through the browser
3. Open the Sales Analysis app
4. Open the Dashboard sheet

If you are using Qlik Sense Enterprise, perform the following steps:

1. Open Firefox and type `https://<servername>/hub` in the address box to open Qlik Sense Enterprise
2. Type your credentials
3. Open the Sales Analysis application from your personal workspace
4. Open the Dashboard sheet

If you are using Qlik Sense Cloud, perform the following steps:

1. Open Firefox and type `https://qlikcloud.com` in the address box to open Qlik Sense Cloud.
2. Type your credentials.
3. Open the Sales Analysis application from your personal workspace.
4. Open the Dashboard sheet.

Go through the following steps to enter the responsive design mode on the web browser:

1. Open Firefox and press *F12* to open the developer tool. The screen may look like the following screenshot:

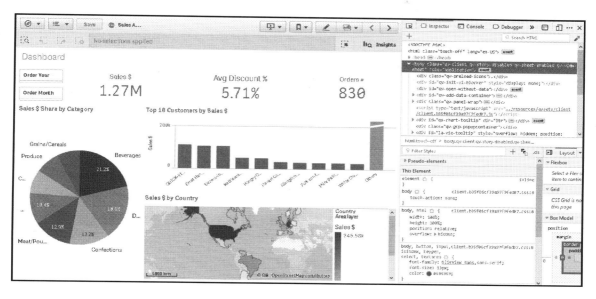

2. To enter the responsive mode, click on the icon indicated as follows in the top-right corner of the screen:

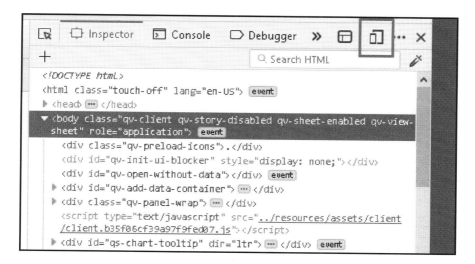

3. Firefox will switch the visualization of the web page to the responsive layout, as follows:

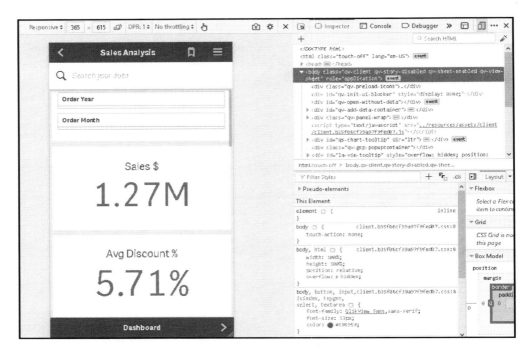

This is exactly the layout we will see in our mobile device.

4. Click on the **Responsive** button to switch the screen size between the devices that are already pre-defined, or edit the list and add more screen size options to test:

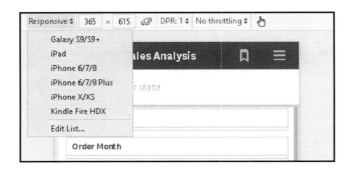

5. Select **iPhone 6/7/8 Plus** to see how it will look on these devices:

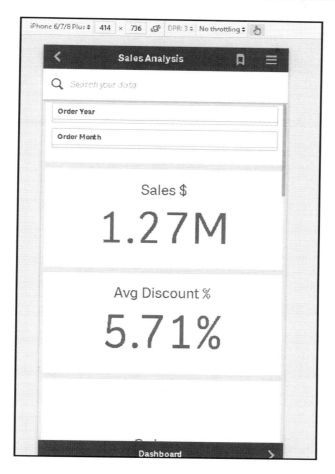

6. Click on the **X** button at the top-right corner to close the responsive mode:

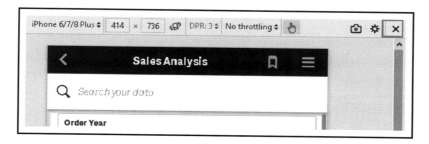

To enter the responsive design mode again, use the *Ctrl+ Shift + M* shortcut at any time on the web browser.

Let's go to the responsive mode design and scroll down to the Mobile view. We will see the charts of the sheet in the following order:

- **Filter panel**
- **KPI Sales $**
- **KPI Avg Discount %**
- **KPI Orders #**
- **Pie Chart Sales $ Share by Category**
- **Bar Chart Top 10 Customers by Sales $**
- **Map Sales $ by Country**

The **Key Performance Indicator (KPI)** visualizations come in first place, followed by the pie, bar, and map charts that give more details about the data. This is recommended because the KPI visualizations get the attention of users looking for summarized information in the first place and provide more detailed information when the user scrolls down the screen.

The Quick view sheet

The Sales application already has a sheet called **Quick view**. This sheet was created to allow the mobile user to see all necessary information in a single page without scrolling. It contains just a text box and a bar chart.

You can see an example in the following screenshot:

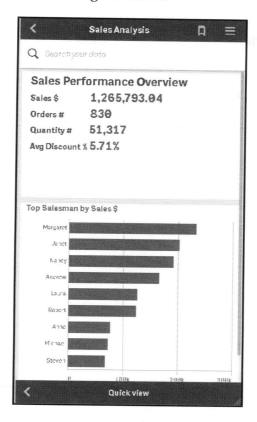

You can select the **Quick view** sheet from the application overview or the sheet selector, as seen in the following screenshot:

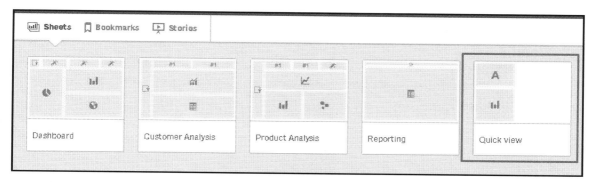

The Quick view sheet has two objects:

- **Text and Image**: The **Text and Image** object displays summary information for the following metrics: **Sales $**, **Orders #**, **Quantity #**, and **Avg Discount %**:

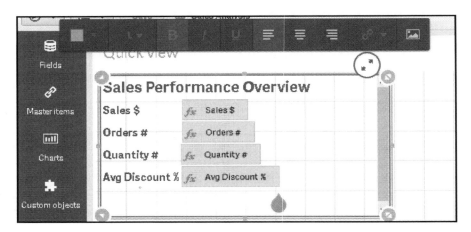

The Text and Image visualization does not provide a column alignment by default, so we used a trick here. We added several periods in white until the expression box was aligned with the expressions of each row, as depicted in the next screenshot. This isn't a perfect alignment, but it is better than nothing. In the following screenshot, we can see the hidden characters:

- **Bar chart**: This contains alternative dimensions and measures, enabling the user to dynamically switch between them.

When the user taps on the chart, it opens in a full screen. In the full screen, you have access to the visual exploration menu at the top of screen:

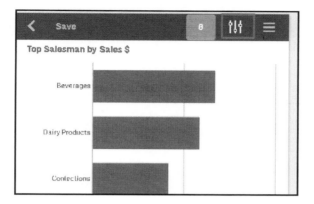

In the visual exploration menu, you can switch between the dimensions and measures that were already added as alternatives. In the following example, **Category** was selected as the dimension and **Orders** # was selected as the measure:

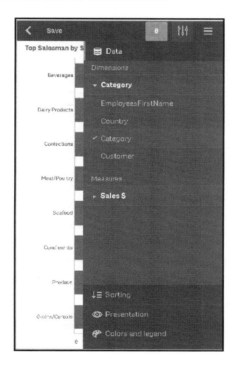

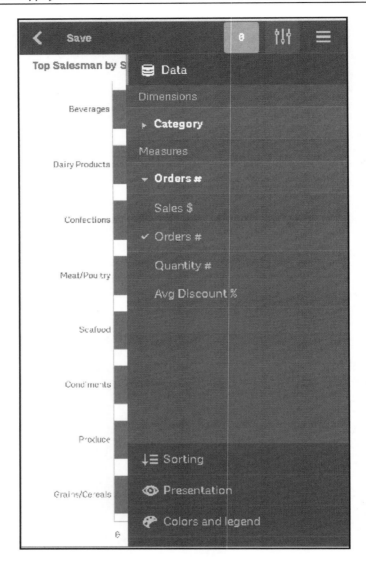

The final result is the bar chart showing the top categories by the number of orders:

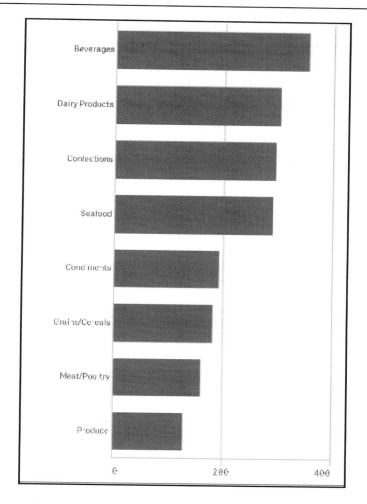

Users can be instructed to go directly to the **Quick view** sheet prepared specially to be used in mobile devices. They can play with the alternative measures and dimensions in the bar chart to freely explore the data.

Choosing the right client

Qlik Sense provides access to applications from the web browser or mobile applications. Each client provides at least a few of the features we will see in the following list:

- **Desktop or tablet browser**:
    - Can create content (applications, sheets, objects, bookmarks, and stories) and also navigate and visualize content
    - Can publish and manage published applications that you own

- **Mobile browser**:
    - Can only navigate and visualize content (applications, sheets, and visualizations)
    - Can play stories but not edit them or create new stories
    - Can create bookmarks and use existing bookmarks

    The mobile browser is the best choice for online use. We can create bookmarks that can be used to reduce the data usage of an app that we need to download as a mobile app.

- **Mobile application**:
    - Can only navigate through and visualize content (applications, sheets, and visualizations)
    - Can play stories but not edit them or create new stories
    - Can use existing bookmarks
    - Can download applications and access them offline (only iOS)

 The mobile app is available for iOS and Android, but only iOS provides offline access.

The mobile app is the appropriate choice when we need to access applications offline on an iPhone or iPad.

Preparing the Sales Analysis app for offline usage

When developing or adjusting an application for offline usage, consider the following points:

- **The complexity and size of the application**: Create simple and small applications of a few megabytes in size and fewer sheets and objects. The Qlik Sense Mobile application runs on an iOS device with much lower CPU performance and available memory compared to a computer that uses a web browser to connect to a Qlik Sense Enterprise server. You can perform tests on an iOS device with system specifications that match those of your application consumer. Download the application, open and make selections in the data, and observe the behavior. The apps need to be small. The download is aborted if the app is not ready for download in 90 seconds when requested from the server.
- **Extensions**: Extensions are allowed in the Qlik Sense app. They are downloaded to the mobile device together with the applications, but they need to use local resources if the app needs to work offline. Thus, it makes sense to keep our device specifications in mind.
- **Reduce the application size on download**: We can create bookmarks in the app to be used by users when downloading the app. The bookmarks will reduce the data and the size of the app when it is downloaded.

To download the app with reduced data, do the following in the Mobile app hub:

1. Tap on the ••• button under the Qlik Sense app box to open the app details window.
2. Tap on ▼ Reduce.
3. Select a bookmark and then tap **Download**. The app is downloaded only with the data associated with the bookmark.

Summary

In this chapter, we have learned how to prepare and deploy an app for mobile usage. We learned about how responsive layout works and how the objects are placed in a Mobile view. We learned about the functionalities available on each client to help us choose the ideal client for each use case. Finally, we learned how to set up an app for offline usage, and about the limitations and features to reduce the size of the app when downloading it to a device.

Qlik Sense is powerful, and provides so many features that it is impossible to cover in a single book. Here, we have covered the basics and the most important features you need to know about building compelling Qlik Sense applications. You should have learned the foundations that will allow you to proceed by yourself.

Thank you for reading. I hope you have enjoyed the book!

Other Books You May Enjoy

If you enjoyed this book, you may be interested in these other books by Packt:

Qlik Sense Cookbook - Second Edition
Pablo Labbe, Philip Hand, Neeraj Kharpate

ISBN: 9781788997058

- Source, preview, and distribute your data through interactive dashboards
- Explore and work with the latest visualization functions
- Learn how to write and use script subroutines
- Make your UI advanced and intuitive with custom objects and indicators
- Use visualization extensions for your Qlik Sense dashboard
- Work with Aggr and learn to use it within set analysis

Mastering Qlik Sense
Martin Mahler, Juan Ignacio Vitantonio

ISBN: 9781783554027

- Understand the importance of self-service analytics and the IKEA-effect
- Explore all the available data modeling techniques and create efficient and optimized data models
- Master security rules and translate permission requirements into security rule logic
- Familiarize yourself with different types of Master Key Item(MKI) and know how and when to use MKI.
- Script and write sophisticated ETL code within Qlik Sense to facilitate all data modeling and data loading techniques
- Get an extensive overview of which APIs are available in Qlik Sense and how to take advantage of a technology with an API
- Develop basic mashup HTML pages and deploy successful mashup projects

Leave a review - let other readers know what you think

Please share your thoughts on this book with others by leaving a review on the site that you bought it from. If you purchased the book from Amazon, please leave us an honest review on this book's Amazon page. This is vital so that other potential readers can see and use your unbiased opinion to make purchasing decisions, we can understand what our customers think about our products, and our authors can see your feedback on the title that they have worked with Packt to create. It will only take a few minutes of your time, but is valuable to other potential customers, our authors, and Packt. Thank you!

Index

testing 324, 326, 327

T

table associations 61, 64
TensorFlow framework
  URL 396
TensorFlow
  installing 396
TOTAL qualifier
  relative share, calculating over dimension 255, 258
  relative share, calculating over total amount 252, 255
  using, for aggregation scope 251
types, joins
  about 88

inner join 93
join 88
left join 90
outer join 88
right join 91

V

visualization objects
  creating 131, 133
visualization platform 14
visualizations
  creating, manually 152, 157
  creating, with chart suggestions 142, 146, 152
  generating, with Insights Advisor 134, 137
  generating, with Insights Advisor for selected
    fields 138, 141